VOCATIONAL PHILANTHROPY AND BRITISH WOMEN'S WRITING, 1790-1810

Vocational Philanthropy and British Women's Writing, 1790-1810

Wollstonecraft, More, Edgeworth, Wordsworth

PATRICIA COMITINI
Quinnipiac University, USA

ASHGATE

© Patricia Comitini 2005

Published by
Ashgate Publishing Limited
Gower House
Croft Road
Aldershot
Hants GU11 3HR
England

Ashgate Publishing Company
Suite 420
101 Cherry Street
Burlington, VT 05401-4405
USA

Ashgate website: http://www.ashgate.com

British Library Cataloguing in Publication Data
Comitini, Patricia
Vocational philanthropy and British women's writing, 1790–1810 : Wollstonecraft, More, Edgeworth, Wordsworth 1.Wollstonecraft, Mary, 1759–1797— Criticism and interpretation 2.More, Hannah, 1745–1833—Criticism and interpretation 3.Edgeworth, Maria, 1767–1849—Criticism and interpretation 4.Wordsworth, Dorothy, 1771–1855— Criticism and interpretation 5.English literature—18th century—History and criticism 6.English Literature—19th century—History and criticism 7.English literature—Women authors 8.Humanitarianism in literature 9.Charity in Literature
I.Title
820.9'355'9033

Library of Congress Cataloging-in-Publication Data
Comitini, Patricia.
 Vocational philanthropy and British women's writing, 1790–1810 : Wollstonecraft, More, Edgeworth, Wordsworth / Patricia Comitini.
    p. cm.
 Includes bibliographical references and index.
 ISBN 0-7546-5042-1 (alk. paper)
 1. English prose literature—Women authors—History and criticism. 2. Wollstonecraft, Mary, 1759–1797. Vindication of the rights of woman. 3. English prose literature—18th century—History and criticism. 4. English prose literature—19th century—History and criticism. 5. More, Hannah, 1745–1833—Criticism and interpretation. 6. Wordsworth, Dorothy, 1771–1855—Diaries. 7. Edgeworth, Maria, 1767–1849. Belinda. 8. Literature and society—Great Britain. 9. Women and literature—Great Britain. 10. Humanitarianism in literature. 11. Charities—Great Britain. I. Title

PR756.W65C66 2005
828'.608093556—dc22
                                                                                           2004016883
ISBN 0 7546 5042 1

Printed and bound in Great Britain by TJ International Ltd, Padstow, Cornwall

Contents

Acknowledgements

When I first began to work on my dissertation, which became the premise for this book, my director looked at me squarely and said, 'You're writing a thesis on Romanticism without being very Romantic about it.' He was right. I think it is important to remember that while Romanticism exists, it is not a natural occurrence and there are other possible ways to construct literary history that include women writers and do not follow the precepts of Romantic discourse. I offer this book as another way to understand the writing of this period, and the knowledge that it produces hopefully tells a different narrative of self-development and creativity.

It is my pleasure to be able to formally thank the many people and institutions that have in one way or another contributed to the production of this book. I would like to thank Quinnipiac University for giving me a succession of research grants which gave me time to research, think and write. I am grateful to the librarians and staff at the Beinecke Rare Book and Manuscript Library, The Sterling Memorial Library at Yale University and The Frank Melville Jr. Memorial Library at Stony Brook University for helping me find much of the material needed to complete this book. Special thanks must go to Norma Keegan at The Arnold Bernhard Library at Quinnipiac University for her patience with my requests. Thanks are also due to the members of English Department at Quinnipiac University, who have given me an academic home that is collegial and supportive.

Since this book is based upon my Ph.D. thesis, it seems fitting to give special thanks to my director, Clifford Siskin, who encouraged my interest in the unlikely connection between reading texts and philanthropy, and who has shaped my thinking about Romanticism in more ways than it is possible to state. I also need to thank the many people who have read versions of the manuscript in part or in total, especially Pearl Brown, Lucinda Cole, Maria Jerinic, Anne Mellor, Adrienne Munich, the late Michael Sprinker and the number of anonymous readers who have also given me extensive commentary. Each reader offered feedback and criticism that helped push me to refine my argument, rethink my assumptions, and clarify my interpretations.

Special thanks are due to Erika Gaffney and Ann Donahue, my editors at Ashgate, Ann Newell, the editorial manager, and Pete Coles, the desk editor. They have made the review and editorial processes almost enjoyable. A version of chapter 5 appeared previously as '"More Than Half a Poet": Vocational Philanthropy and Dorothy Wordsworth's *Grasmere Journals*' in *European Romantic Review* 14 (September 2003) 307-322. I am grateful to Routledge (www.tandf.co.uk) for their permission to use this material.

Finally, I would like to thank my family. First, thanks to my daughter Tess, who was born halfway through the writing of this book. She has brought an inexpressible joy into my life, and the pleasure of her company has balanced the many hours spent researching and writing. Second, thanks are due to my parents who really didn't understand what I was doing all this time, but who were proud of me just the same. Lastly, thanks to W. Thomas Pepper who has made all things possible for me. His unfailing encouragement and intellectual compatibility have supported me when I needed it most, and even when I didn't. For that, this book is dedicated to him.

Introduction

This Philanthropy (which we have not a proper word in English to express) is everywhere manifest in our Author.
Dryden, 1693

This book examines how writing was used as a form of philanthropy by upper- and middling-class women during the late eighteenth and early nineteenth centuries. Today, philanthropy connotes benevolence and altruism, usually taking the form of voluntarily giving money or time. However, in the eighteenth century, philanthropy often referred to a feeling of love for mankind and the desire to help improve mankind for the benefit of society as a whole. As the quote from Dryden indicates, this feeling of philanthropy—the love of mankind—is a relatively new term by the early eighteenth century. Often, this philanthropic feeling guided charitable action. Improvement was accomplished through the regulation of labor and domestic duties, medical practices, Sunday and Charity schools and 'Friendly Societies.' Towards the end of the eighteenth century, charity takes on a distinctive tone of 'self-help' and the philanthropic work of women's writing becomes disciplining readers into desiring self-improvement.[1] Benevolence was an act of writing.

My study focuses on late eighteenth-century women writers, and the philanthropic impulse that runs through much of their writing during this period. Though there is a vast amount of eighteenth-century literature written by men which defines the problem of poverty, its economic impact on the state and the state of English society, and various dissertations on solutions, it is women who heed the call to the 'vocation' of philanthropy and charity, and consequently this social practice, and the benevolent and altruistic qualities associated with it, becomes 'feminized' at this point in history.[2] Thus, the practice of what I have come to call 'vocational philanthropy' in this book is a principally feminine arena of endeavor, not because benevolence and sympathetic understanding were natural to women, but because the ideological association of women with these qualities increasingly provided agency for middling-class women to enter a field of public discourse about poverty and the state of English society. However, like many of their male counterparts, their response in this public debate was to see poverty and social devolution as individual moral problems—problems that were located, and thus could be solved, in the private sphere. Vocational philanthropy, at this particular historical moment, becomes a field of specialized feminine knowledge, particularly suited to women's rational benevolence, sympathy, and leisure time.

This project began by drawing and examining links between what has been called the 'self-help' movement of philanthropy in the late eighteenth century, the assumption of women as 'charitable Ladies' at the same historical moment (which continued well into the nineteenth century),[3] and the upsurge in the number of women writers and the volume of women's writing across genres from about

1780 onward.[4] My objective was to show that these phenomena were interrelated. I knew I was on to something when I came upon a long footnote while reading Hannah More's *Strictures on a Modern System of Female Education*, written in 1798:

> It would be a noble employment, and well becoming the tenderness of their sex, if ladies were to consider the superintendence of the poor as their immediate office. They are peculiarly fitted for it, for from their own habits of life they are more intimately acquainted with domestic wants than the other sex; and in certain instances of sickness and sufferings peculiar to themselves, they should be expected to have more sympathy; and they obviously have more leisure. (*Strictures* 332)

Middling-class women, Hannah More contends, simply make better philanthropists than men. Knowledge of domestic needs and routine, sympathetic bodily suffering, and time to devote to charitable activities are requirements which allow middling-class women to relate effectively to the poor. Proper leisure time and the abstraction of 'love' to include humanity as an extension of the family also enable women to possess the special ability to discern who is 'deserving' of help by evaluating the habits and values of the poor according to standards women devise because of their special moral sensitivity or, to use the language of the eighteenth century, women's sensibility.

Leisure, sympathetic understanding, and domesticity 'peculiarly' fit women for charitable work. And the Bluestocking Hannah More practiced what she preached to young women. During 1784-1801 when she lived at Cowslip Green, More organized charity schools in Cheddar, Shipham and Nailsea, as well as other Sunday schools scattered about the Mendips; she organized 'Female Friendly' Societies, and campaigned for the abolition of the slave trade. At the same time that she rose to be a prominent female philanthropist with the encouragement of William Wilberforce and Bishop of London, Beilby Porteus, More continued to be a prodigious author, designing *The Cheap Repository*, and writing tales for it, writing politically and socially relevant poems and essays, an educational treatise, and a 'didactic' novel. While reading, I wondered how these two realms of endeavor—authorship and philanthropy—could be compatible; how could each realm legitimate the other as a specifically feminine undertaking, as More's quote suggested. Just what kind of philanthropy was she practicing?

An answer was hinted at in More's advertisement to *The Cheap Repository Tracts*. Its stated aim was to '*improve* the habits, and raise the principles of the common people, at a time when dangers and temptations, moral and political, were multiplied beyond any former period [...]' (emphasis mine, 190). Thus, there was evidence that her discourse had been infused with a philanthropic function: producing discourses to 'improve the habits and raise principles' in 'times of moral and political danger' could function as kind of philanthropy, though a kind that we, as twenty-first-century readers, might not recognize. While it may seem thoroughly 'natural' for us, the possibility that reading material could function to improve readers, particularly women and the poor, was a fairly novel concept in the eighteenth century. Because reading for amelioration is such a natural, everyday part of our lives, we forget that literature (conceived in the broadest sense for our purposes) needed to be constructed as a medium through which readers desire to become better persons. Paul Keen argues in *The Crisis of Literature* that the production and proliferation of literature in the late eighteenth century stems from the Enlightenment assumption (or illusion) of a 'free' dissemination of ideas (27-28). The notions of individual improvement and societal progress are linked to the impetus to write discourses on how that 'improvement' and 'progress' is to be achieved. As Keen points out, while men perhaps can openly participate in the public sphere, women who do so come under intense scrutiny (135-141). Alternately, Anne Mellor in *Mothers of the Nation* rightly points out that women, despite the dangers to their femininity, 'participated fully in the public sphere' (2). How can both accounts of women's participation in the public sphere be true? My argument focuses on how that participation was enabled under the guise of benevolence to improve individuals and, ultimately, society. We may have overlooked the philanthropic impetus of late eighteenth-century women writers. The work of these women writers enabled the transition in poor relief from supplementing material needs to a new kind of charitable action that focused on individual improvement, a transition that, in its effect, would help to mediate social and political contestation between the privileged and poor.

And the 1790s were dangerous times, as More's advertisement points out. As will be discussed in more detail in chapter 1, the existing economic conditions which made philanthropy and charitable endeavor a viable social practice throughout the eighteenth century, were a response to the social and economic upheavals accompanying the transition from feudal/mercantilist to capitalist relations. Charity in the seventeenth century had been vested in a more or less direct system of parish doles and allotments for the relief of the destitute, infirm or elderly. But by the turn of the eighteenth century, philanthropic endeavors were commercial affairs, modeled on London's joint-stock companies; charity capital was accumulated from relatively anonymous donors by subscription, and buildings were built, such as hospitals for foundlings, the sick, the pregnant, as well as orphanages, charity and Sunday schools, churches, and workhouses. This kind of 'associated' philanthropy, as historian David Owen calls it, played an important role at mid-century in the movement to provide for the material needs of the poor. But despite these efforts, few of the poor had achieved what Patrick Colquhoun, an eighteenth-century observer, called a level of 'independent' poverty: that is, the ability to survive on an independent income from farming, wage-labor and cottage industry, rather than relying on alms, charity or other forms of assistance. Poverty had become a problem that had social and economic consequences for landowners who supported parish relief and those of the monied classes who needed laborers. The source of the dilemma comes from the need to regulate both the behavior of the poor and the benevolence of the privileged. Frederic Eden, an eighteenth-century political economist, states that the class divide was defined '*not* [by] the possession of land or money, but the *command* of labor that distinguishes the opulent from the laboring part of the community' (1).

By the late eighteenth century, a different form of philanthropy emerged that sought to superintend the poor, but was not necessarily charity in the common forms of giving time and money that we understand today. At this time, there was an increasing emphasis on the individual amelioration of the poor by supervisory and voluntary means: the surplus in the labor market had not produced the kind of citizens and workers necessary to suit the needs of incipient agricultural and industrial capitalism, and the task that most kinds of philanthropy would undertake was to unite social 'usefulness' with the privileged sense of moral behavior. The philanthropist becomes a mediator who will give the poor the ideological tools to achieve this unification. Historian Donna Andrew has defined this change as the philanthropy of 'self help' in the last two decades of the eighteenth century.[5]

However, if the poor's problems were conceived as 'moral' and therefore 'personal,' which could be ameliorated by raising their principles, then the privileged mediators who care for the poor must have a heightened 'moral instinct,' as a passage from Robert Eden's *The Harmony of Benevolence* (1755) points out:

> There is unquestionably a moral instinct which instantly discerns in certain Cases, what is right and what is wrong, by a kind of Sensation and Taste independent of Reason and Reflection; for who that claims a Title to Humanity, in its strictest Acceptation, does not immediately, without debating about it feel a sense of Compassion which prompts him to relieve any one Misery or Pain? (12)[6]

The charitable act in the latter half of the eighteenth century is increasingly dependent on aesthetic perception and benevolent sensibility. Philanthropy as a medium of demonstrating benevolence is dependent upon cultivating proper levels of aesthetic sensibility. Both parties, whether privileged or poor, could be 'improved' by this individualized participation in philanthropy. And while it had been difficult for women to participate in the 'associated' philanthropy of the earlier eighteenth century because it depended on the subscription of capital, during the latter half, women became more visible in the public arena of charitable endeavor because philanthropy relied on feeling and judicious discrimination. As Janet Todd has observed, women in the late eighteenth century, whether spinsters or married, could participate in 'one clear growth area of economic involvement: charity and philanthropy' (Todd *Sign* 205). The establishment of Sunday and charity schools for the poor, the anti-slavery movement and the British war effort gave middling-class women agency to act and a vocation that suited their position in society. In contrast to 'associated' philanthropy which proposed to alleviate immediate material suffering though monetary expenditure, vocational philanthropy fosters the love of mankind, and converted, in Linda Colley's words, women's '*desire* to act into an overwhelming *duty* to do so' (277).

Thus, philanthropy's function to ameliorate individuals' material needs at mid-century is succeeded by what I call 'vocational philanthropy' in the late eighteenth century. Vocational philanthropy is a social practice which produces literary discourses designed to 'teach' individuals how to improve their 'habits and behaviors,' to use Hannah More's phrase, displacing the public problems of social and economic inequities onto a problematic of individual improvement which would not reduce those inequities, but rationalize them, and contribute to the recreation of 'social harmony through the reunification of interclass bonds and interests' (Andrew 169). By helping to define middling-class ideologies of equal opportunity, the virtue of labor, and most importantly, the constant improvement of self and land, women writers participated in the reformation of society by laying out the pattern for the continued development of capitalist social relations. Prose narrative, and other forms of writing, becomes a medium in which these ideologies are used to educate the desires of the upper class and the emergent middling classes for their social and economic responsibilities towards the poor. Concomitantly, if these values could be taught to and desired by the laboring classes and the upper and middling classes alike, then the 'public good' and sympathetic harmony would be achieved.

My use of the concept of ideology, and my account of its production through the material practices of reading and writing, might need some explanation since ideology is a term that is used in various ways and misused frequently. First, I will propose a concept of ideology in its broadest sense: it allows a subject to 'imagine' him/herself in a *relationship* to his or her real conditions of existence.[7] This broad definition of ideology adheres closely to the Althusserian usage, which, in its strict sense, necessarily exists in a practice (such as writing or reading) which seeks to 'represent in its imaginary distortion not the existing relations of production (and all the other relations that derive form them), but above all the (imaginary) relationship of individuals to the relations of production [...]' (Althusser 165). 'Imaginary,' is used in the Lacanian sense here and is most easily, though perhaps a little reductively, understood as an individual's automatic perceptions (preconceptions) of reality. Ideology, then, structures those perceptions, organizing one's ability to make sense of those perceptions in relationship to reality. Thus, ideology is not necessarily 'false' or 'fictional,' though it may refract or distort reality.[8]

However, I am also using a more narrow definition of ideology as a 'dominant' social force. This usage does not, however, entail a stable, univocal set of meanings that is conspiratorially projected onto the 'blank' space (or minds) of the upper and lower classes. A dominant ideology must always negotiate with other 'subordinate' ideologies, which prevents it from being consistent, coherent and complete. According to Terry Eagleton, its 'open-endedness' is exactly what makes a dominant ideology so fallible: 'a successful ruling ideology must engage significantly with genuine wants, needs and desires; but this is also its Achilles heel, forcing it to recognize an "other" to itself and inscribing this otherness as a potentially disruptive force within its own forms' (*Ideology* 45). Ideology is permanently incomplete and often has an inherent contradiction; therefore, it must perpetually reproduce itself in its specific practices to maintain its power. But ideology in its dominant bourgeois form must make those wants, needs and desires seem freely chosen in order to transform individuals into subjects. This is the enabling condition of ideology. Ideology, therefore, has the power to 'interpellate' individuals as 'free' subjects 'in order that [they] shall (freely) accept [their] subjection' (Althusser 181-182).

To illustrate this effect, let us turn to an overriding assumption observed in traditional scholarship on philanthropy by Betsy Rogers, David Owen and J.K.

Jordan: that benevolence, on the part of those privileged enough to display it, is somehow natural or inborn. Certainly, benevolence as a personal attribute is entirely possible and even desirable. But the positive valorization of benevolence is precisely a sign that those who are or wish to be benevolent have been successfully interpellated by this ideology—a way to understand how one lives his or her relations to reality. On this level, I would suggest that benevolence, with its implications for how one lives in a society, is a particular ideology that structures the individual subject and the relations between many subjects. Rather than conceiving of benevolence as a 'natural' attribute, we can see it as a mechanism (or an ideological practice, if you will) for disciplining the middling classes as well as cultivating a new relationship to the poor; no doubt the privileged intended to change the behaviors and values of the poor, in varying degrees, in order to enable them to 'improve' themselves at least to the degree that they accept their place in the hierarchical structure of social relations. However, by positioning the poor in this way, the middling class must be similarly placed in a position of desire: their good deeds must project something about their deserved place in the social hierarchy. Ideology, in this productive sense of dominant social relations, is not something that is necessarily true or false; rather, it exists for the purposes of structuring social relations of power, which regulate how individuals understand their social totality.

On another level, ideology can generate ideas, desires, and actions which can be thought objectionable because they motivate oppressive forms of power relations. Therefore, when subjects are interpellated, the ideologies which enable them to 'feel, perceive and act' in social reality may, in effect, place them in a disadvantaged position and make them culpable in their own oppression or exploitation. Benevolence as an ideology distorts the social problems in a way that unifies the middling and upper classes, rationalizes a solution to an economic problem, legitimates and naturalizes power relations.[9]

But there is another component to the transmission of ideology. Let us continue with our discussion of the ideology of benevolence, taking, as an example, Robert Eden's *The Harmony of Benevolence* mentioned above. I have already stated that philanthropy is dependent on cultivating an aesthetic sensibility—that 'true' misery must be discerned and felt by the privileged. In this sense, according to eighteenth-century moral philosophers like the Earl of Shaftsbury and Adam Smith, the aesthetic enables a particular ethical ideology—'what is right and what is wrong'—to relay itself through the feelings and senses producing a 'spontaneous' social action under the guise of a natural 'moral instinct,' or what is called 'sympathy.'[10] Adam Smith stresses in *The Theory of Moral Sentiments* that imagination is the source of sympathetic understanding: 'By the imagination we place ourselves in his situation, we conceive ourselves enduring all the same torments, we enter as it were into his body, and become in some measure the same person with him, and thence from some idea of his sensations, and even feel something which [...] is not altogether unlike them' (12). If imagination enables individuals to see themselves in a sympathetic relation to others, it also enables individuals to internalize the external spectator. This internalized spectator assumes the position of moral guide—a disinterested mediator between feeling and judgment that restrains sentiment and elevates sensibility (26-28). Benevolence, as a dominant ideology, takes material form through the social act of this formulation of sympathy.[11] Aesthetic perception is what joins feeling and action in that it allows the privileged to sacrifice their 'selfish' materiality for a moment and elevate themselves to participate in the universal manifestation of social good that is *pleasurable*.[12] For as Adam Smith states, 'to feel much for others and little for ourselves, that to restrain our selfish passions, and to indulge our benevolent affections, constitutes the perfection of human nature' (30). Benevolence operates as a moral medium through which virtue, privilege and power are recognized and displayed. But to have this sensibility is not always to act upon it. If virtue is conditioned by an aesthetic response, philanthropy is the medium through which that response is manifested judiciously. Cultivating proper discrimination, as well as self-regulation of the giver's pleasure, is the middling classes' duty to the poor.[13] It is not then, that the poor become aesthetic objects—a conclusion that one could draw from Robert Eden's *A Harmony of Benevolence*—but that morality is itself 'aestheticized.'[14] The truly moral subject perceives it as pleasurable to choose to relieve the misery and pain of those who truly deserve it. Otherwise, benevolence may be seen as aristocratic self-indulgence and vanity, something that Hannah More is quick to reject as 'sentimental' charity:

> When feeling stimulates only to self-indulgence; when the more exquisite affections of sympathy and pity evaporate in sentiment, instead of flowing out in active charity, and affording assistance, protection, or consolation to every species of distress within its reach, it is an evidence that the feeling is of a spurious kind; and instead of being nourished as an amiable tenderness, it should be subdued as a fond and base self-love. (*Strictures* 383)

This demonstration of moral virtue is the manifestation of an aesthetic response which separates those who are to be categorized among the 'better ranks' from those who are to be categorized among the lower ranks. As Robert Markley, in his observations about *A Sentimental Journey*, has noted, money becomes a 'palpable, materialist manifestation of good nature as a commodity' (210). Of course, if this is true then anyone who demonstrates the proper and judicious benevolence is admitted to these 'better' ranks. Class lines—aristocrat or middling class—are no longer operable in matters of moral virtue. Markley, describing the aesthetic response of sentiment, claims that it 'thus represents the bourgeois usurpation of and accommodation to what formerly had been considered aristocratic prerogatives' (217). This kind of aesthetic response manifests the problem of changing class relations, which 'tries to assert "traditional" values and to accommodate as "gentlemen" increasing numbers of economically [...] aggressive merchants, professionals, small landowners, and moneymen' (Markley 217).

This is why philanthropy must operate under a 'cloak': it must appear to function in terms of the personal as opposed to the political, and the moral as opposed to the economic.[15] This effectively shifts the field of debate from the realm of the material to the realm of the 'universal'; the negotiation of these two realms is properly an ideological problem of aesthetics. Morality and aesthetics are tied together in a precarious class-conditioned relationship. Philanthropy as a medium of demonstration becomes an aesthetic 'solution' to the historical problem of poverty. Cultivating aesthetic sensibility becomes increasingly important in terms of guarding the social totality and providing for its improvement.

The key to accomplishing the cultivation of moral sensibility is reading. While morality is 'aestheticized,' levels of literacy and, concurrently, levels of aesthetic sensitivity are entrees to proper 'moral virtue.'[16] It is not a coincidence that Adam Smith invites the judgment of 'productions of all the arts' based upon how they will stimulate the 'perfection' of human nature (32). 'Good judgment and taste' will proceed from an acute sensibility and self-command that is above the 'rude vulgar of mankind' (30). Levels of literacy ideologically define the already economically-determined difference between the classes, and explain that difference in the levels of morality that the privileged and the poor can attain. Literacy rates overall in the eighteenth century were rising, but late in the century educating the poor to read, but not necessarily to write, became important as the mission of educational reformers. However, as Jacqueline Pearson has pointed out, the ability to read is not exactly the same as the habit of reading (11). It is the habit of reading that concerns middling-class women writers, and the proliferation of discourse and heuristic reading practices become central to the notions of charity and philanthropy.

Issues of literacy in the eighteenth century, and even today, are complicated by definitions.[17] What defines literacy, or even a habit of reading, and how can they be measured accurately or effectively? While the ability to read and the ability to make aesthetic judgments are certainly important to the argument I am making, what is also important is literacy's role in social transformation. To examine this role, a new concept of literacy is needed, one that is less dependent upon empirical studies (though they do tell us something of importance) and one that instead focuses on the social nature of literacy (reading and writing) and literacy practices in their historical contexts. Brian Street contends that particular practices and concepts of reading and writing are 'already embedded in an ideology and cannot be isolated or treated as "neutral" or merely "technical"' (1). Street's overall claim is that even though literacy may be associated with such notions as 'progress,' 'civilization,' 'individual liberty' and 'social mobility,' all concepts which were significantly debated in the late eighteenth century, these notions in themselves are ideologies that inform and construct the very definition and practices of literacy (2). To divorce a study of literacy from its historical context, and to see it as an isolated variable that has as its natural effect 'progress,' 'civilization,' 'liberty' and 'social mobility,' is to misinterpret as the effect the ideological practice in which reading and writing is located. It is possible that these 'effects' of literacy are a part of literacy's own rhetoric at this particular historical moment. The privileging of reading over oral forms of communication may suggest that what is really at stake is social control and stability. Because England is a highly stratified society, literacy worked to reify class distinctions based on cultural hegemony—the ability to read, leisure time to read, and the level of 'enjoyment' of reading. As Harvey Graff's research has shown, 'Literacy and its uses were becoming one sign of the emerging transformation of the social structure and the development of modern social classes' (*Legacies* 246). Central to a discussion about literacy is what literacy symbolically means to those who have it as well as those who do not.

For the middling classes, particular moral and aesthetic responses, cultivated through reading, help form sympathetic bonds; literacy becomes one basis for social harmony.[18] In personal terms, benevolence and philanthropy are self-gratifying; but in societal terms, they are ideological practices which enable social and economic problems to be re-imagined and a society to be transformed. Good judgment and taste of the privileged justify their own class position. Possessing a greater ability to respond aesthetically, the upper classes are better able to use literacy to discern and articulate who is deserving of improvement in the lower classes, and how that improvement will be measured. Perhaps this is one reason why the uses of literacy are a focus of much philanthropic effort in the late eighteenth century, as well as a source of debate. Viewing literacy in this way helps us understand considerations of social order. Collective goals for the development of literacy—decrease in crime, vice and political protest, for instance—outweighed personal achievement and intellectual growth, especially for the lower classes; literacy, at least in theory, was a means toward social stability (Kaestle 'Scylla' 178).

The women writers I study, Hannah More, Mary Wollstonecraft, Maria Edgeworth and Dorothy Wordsworth, share an interest in philanthropy and philanthropic practice—fostering the love of mankind—and an interest in the social nature of literacy. While these women writers have become somewhat 'canonical' to studies of late eighteenth- and early nineteenth-century writing, this conjuncture of literacy and philanthropy has not been adequately explored even while their political, religious or aesthetic concerns have been. By linking philanthropy and the 'vocation' of women's writing to improve the 'human condition,' vocational philanthropy emerges, joining the private notions of morality, family, and love to the public needs of good citizens, industrious laborers and class consolidation. It enables a particular kind of feminine benevolence, one that provides an impetus for women's discursive endeavors: to 'teach' man- and woman-kind, to 'teach' the middling and laboring classes their changing relations to one another. Vocational philanthropy does not give people money to improve their social and economic conditions; it gives people texts to read in order to 'imagine' improvement.

This study of the relationship between philanthropy and discourse has not been a subject of much critical or scholarly work. Two exceptions are the recent work by Beth Fowkes Tobin and Dorice Williams Elliott.[19] Tobin focuses on how the middle classes represent themselves in eighteenth- and nineteenth-century novels as the appropriate moral and economic authorities over the poor in order to discredit the paternalistic notions of the gentry and the aristocracy. While Tobin does not make an argument linked to the notion of philanthropy, she does begin an investigation into how charity, in the narrower sense of dispensing money, is used by both middle-class men and women as a strategy of surveillance in order to regulate the behaviors of the poor. Likewise, Elliott focuses on representations of feminine philanthropy in novels, but she does so as a vehicle to examine women's changing subjectivity and their social roles from the mid-eighteenth century to the Victorian era. While Elliott's work has invaluable insights on how philanthropy redefined the way nineteenth-century society conceived of women's nature and their sphere of influence, and Tobin's book convincingly describes the battle for who will 'superintend' the poor, neither study highlights how forms of writing and reading various discourses can function as philanthropic acts, disciplining readers into understanding their appropriate roles by cultivating the proper moral sensibilities, regardless of class. Therefore, my argument is not that there are representations of women's charitable endeavors in texts—there have been these images at least since Samuel Richardson's *Pamela*—but that literature in the late eighteenth century enabled writing to function as a form of benevolence and as an act of philanthropy.

In this sense, I am returning to the broader eighteenth-century definition of philanthropy, first brought into the language in the seventeenth century and which persisted in common usage until the nineteenth. Philanthropy encompasses a general sense of the 'love to mankind' and a particular sense that includes the practical effort to 'promote the happiness and well-being of one's fellow-men' (*OED* 774).[20] But how and what kind of 'effort' is attempted is historically contingent on how the problem of poverty is defined by those able to give relief.

This necessary historical argument will be discussed in chapter 1. The chapters which follow will discuss specific examples to illustrate that it is a combination of writing across genres which repeatedly 'teaches' the reader how to read and how to read 'correctly,' often directing readers to other discourses, thereby reenvisioning the combined acts of reading and writing as an act of charity: instead of giving money, linen or food, one gives texts. Therefore, this book does not offer a universal definition of specific genres or search for a discourse of philanthropy. Nor does it seek to claim religious or political conviction as the primary impetus for the interest in philanthropy, though religious and political affiliations are important for certain writers and will be discussed in that context. What it does expose, I think, is that philanthropic concerns—ameliorating the condition of mankind—is a historical concern which provides a function for 'didactic,' 'educational' or 'domestic' literature in this period, for a variety of different audiences, or perhaps in the case of Dorothy Wordsworth a private audience. If reading practices are important to the cultivation of certain types of moral and aesthetic sensibility among the various classes, then it is important that what follows in each chapter is a sustained reading of the texts in order to explore the relationship between form (the heuristic method) and content (ideological representation).

If middling-class women are to be the linch-pin of vocational philanthropy, then they must be positioned as the moral center around which a new society revolves. Women are legitimized as the subjects who can foster social change and sympathetic love for mankind because they are rewritten in the late eighteenth century as 'most natural,' to use Wollstonecraft's phrase. *A Vindication of the Rights of Woman* is the example of vocational philanthropy discussed in chapter 2 because the educational treatise is premised upon a 'rewriting' of feminine morality based upon a 'rereading' of masculine discourse. Being able to 'read' men's writing critically, recognizing its 'artificiality' and dislodging its legitimacy, created a space for women's writing which presented the 'truth' of social relationships—a powerful truth which is defined by Wollstonecraft—that women have been morally, as well as politically, subordinated to men. This observation is not new to Wollstonecraft scholarship, but one of the primary features overlooked in the criticism of *VRW* is its pedagogical function, especially interesting seen the context of its companion treatise *A Vindication of the Rights of Man*. It is not only an educational and political treatise, but its rhetorical strategy attempted to teach women how to read rationally in order that they may be able to 'consider the moral and civil interests of mankind' (4). Wollstonecraft's primary argument is that women who read rationally and women who produce a 'truthful' representation of women in the content of their social realities, must precede the improvement of society in general, and will, as a consequence, increase the rationality and morality of all citizens. This endeavor characterizes an important feature of vocational philanthropy: women, particularly, must read and ultimately write discourses that critically expose imaginary relations in order to teach themselves and others for the sake of the 'progression' of humankind.

The next chapter examines how Hannah More's *The Cheap Repository for Moral and Religious Tracts* and Maria Edgeworth's *Popular Tales* take the notion of rational reading and discursive production one step farther than Wollstonecraft by producing 'moral tales' for the lower orders. By teaching what and how to read, literacy is extended to those who had not previously had the need for 'moral guidance': the lower middling class and the poor. Growing out of the eighteenth-century charity school movement, these tales disseminated ideologies necessary for the poor's literal survival in a changed economy, but also justified the capitalist system of relations as natural, and derided the older, aristocratic system of paternalism as corrupted. More's and Edgeworth's wide-scale discursive projects strove to guarantee a degree of moral uniformity among all the classes, making their content—the benevolence of the middling classes, the value of both intellectual and manual labor, respect for private property, and domestic affection—seem universal to both classes. Thus, charity, as it is depicted in these tales, is not the circulation of money to aid the poor, but the circulation of sympathetic understanding through discourses that rewrite the relationship between the middling classes and the laboring poor.

However, reinterpellating the lower orders into a sympathetic and productive relationship with the middling classes would be ineffectual if the middling classes were not similarly reinterpellated. Therefore, Maria Edgeworth continued illustrating her and her father's, Richard Lovell Edgeworth, educational theories in her novels or, more accurately, her moral tales for the literate middling classes. *Belinda* is Edgeworth's first fictional attempt to illustrate how a woman's inherent sympathy and benevolence can change others positively. Through its structure, Edgeworth's fiction teaches the middling-class woman that domestic pleasure comes from sympathetic benevolence, which is indicated by the pleasure one gains from improving others. This endeavor echoes Wollstonecraft's call to women readers in *VRW*. Thus, Wollstonecraft's productive terms—family and discourse—reappear.

The final chapter reads Dorothy Wordsworth's *Grasmere Journal* as a record of the benevolent and productive woman, both in terms of the domestic sphere and in terms of the improvement of the poor. Her discourse ties together: women's rational capability to be self-regulating subjects, as Mary Wollstonecraft's *VRW* discusses; women's supervisory skill over others' manners and morals, which Maria Edgeworth's and Hannah More's moral tales detailed; and women as the productive center of domestic desire as depicted in Edgeworth's novel *Belinda*. Dorothy Wordsworth's text demonstrates through what we now think of as a private genre—the journal—the 'internalization' of benevolent, middling-class, feminine identity. Thus, the *Grasmere Journal* straddles the line between private and public modes of discourse because it accommodates this different 'internalized' feminine model that is both highly literate and rational—as proposed by both More and Wollstonecraft. And, the model produces writing for both private use and public consumption.

Vocational philanthropy is productive of a feminine community that is similarly interested and invested in constructing pedagogical literature which will benefit 'mankind in general'; it creates a kind of feminine discourse that is productive of texts, knowledge and sensibility. This notion of feminine production has been absent from even recent criticism of late eighteenth- and early nineteenth-century women writers. Using vocational philanthropy as a lens, we can see how women writers form a communal identity by producing discourses that first categorize gender and then categorize class identities. Within the structures of these discourses, a model of moral and benevolent womanhood is produced as well as narratives of moral degrees of subjective improvement which attempt to transform all class identities: reading becomes a means of reconstructing the subject as one who desires improvement. Writing is pursued as a vocation of women's gender (a special duty which 'peculiarly' suits women) that has philanthropy as its aim: to increase the well-being of mankind. Thus, vocational philanthropy is an endeavor which builds various communities through identifying constituencies which share the ideologies of benevolence, work, and improvement, but naturally live them differently. Despite the writers' different political and religious backgrounds, they all shared the belief that the 1790s was a time of social, economic and moral transition. And middling-class women expressed their particular stake in the outcome of that transition.

The success of these women writers is proven by their invisibility—their absorption—into our ideas about femininity, literacy and literary history. The 'naturalness' within which feminine benevolence become enacted in daily lives—as Dorothy Wordsworth's *Grasmere Journal* attests to—participates in the 'forgetting' of these texts' philanthropic function, and these women writers as a productive social force.[21] The important work had been done: women have been acculturated to read, write, and reform the underprivileged, and through these acts, they interpellate other individuals into subjects who desire improvement. With this desire established, 'individual development,' as it comes to be called in the discourse of Romanticism, can occur. But improvement is primary to the bourgeois subject and it is a feature that we, as literary historians, assume has always already been present. Since this ideology of improvement is seen as continuous with the historical development of the benevolent middling-class woman—the moral guardian of nineteenth-century society—it is important to understand the writings of these, and other, women writers of the late eighteenth and early nineteenth centuries if we are to understand how a new system of social relations becomes 'naturally' accepted by women, men, and the middling and lower classes.

Notes

1 See Donna Andrew, *Philanthropy and Police: London Charity in the Eighteenth Century* (Princeton: Princeton UP, 1989) 163-196.

2 Dorice Williams Elliott discusses this process in *The Angel out of the House: Philanthropy and Gender in Nineteenth Century England* (Charlottesville: U of Virginia P, 2002).

3 See Jessica Girard, 'Lady Bountiful: Women of the Landed Classes and Rural Philanthropy,' *Victorian Studies* 30 (1987): 183-210.

4 Cheryl Turner, *Living By the Pen: Women Writers in the Eighteenth Century* (NewYork: Routledge, 1992) 36-8.

5 See Andrew 163.

6 Robert Eden's *Harmony of Benevolence, A Sermon Preached in the Cathedral-Church of Worcester, September 10, 1755* (London: W. Sandby, no date) is a very interesting sermon intended to inspire the privileged to fulfill their duties as stewards of the poor. The way in which he constructs the sermon reveals the aesthetic connection between benevolence and charitable acts. He begins with a discussion of sacred music, a part of which is poetry, which should inspire by 'merit and beauty' the act of worship. But worship would be in vain unless followed by worthy acts which would cultivate 'Divine Harmony.' And, in a striking analogy, he draws an aesthetic connection between music, benevolence and charity: 'To give us an opportunity of imitating him, and performing his Will in this Respect, he has ordained the various Mixtures of Riches and Poverty, Happiness and Distress, to answer very wise and valuable Purposes; for the Diversity of Ranks and Circumstances of life contribute towards a regular and general scheme of Providence as the Mixture of different musical Notes, by their mutual Application and Correspondence, produce Beauty an Regularity of Composition: As long, indeed, as they continue in separate and distinct State they can never produce harmony; but by being properly blended, and by receiving mutual Assistance from each other, they delight the ear and warm the heart,' 14-15.

7 See Louis Althusser's much debated thesis on ideology in 'Ideology and ideological State Apparatuses (Notes towards an Investigation),' *Lenin and Philosophy* (New York: Monthly Review, 1971) 127-186. For alternative understandings of the term and uses of ideology, see Terry Eagleton, *Ideology: an introduction* (New York: Verso, 1992) and David Hawkes, *Ideology* (New York: Routlege, 1995).

8 While this might seem a unique way to understand the term 'imaginary' in Althusser's work, the basis for Althusser's thesis on ideology is Jacques Lacan's relationship between the imaginary and symbolic realms: 'The imaginary economy has meaning, we gain some purchase on it, only in so far as it is transcribed in to the symbolic order, where a ternary relation is imposed [...]. From the start, his experience is organized in the symbolic order. The legal order into which he is inducted almost from the beginning gives signification to these imaginary relations, as a function of what I call the unconscious discourse of the subject [...]. The images will take on their meaning in a

wider discourse, in which the entire history of the subject is integrated.' See Jacques Lacan, *The Seminar of Jacques Lacan, Book II: The Ego in Freud's Theory and in the Technique of Psychoanalysis 1954-1955*, ed. Jacques-Alain Miller, trans. Sylvana Tomaselli (New York: Norton, 1988; 1991) 255. I am indebted to W. Thomas Pepper for his insight into the use of the term 'imaginary' and its application to the theory of ideology.

9   This definition of ideology is influenced by Eagleton's discussion in *Ideology* 43-45.

10 See Terry Eagleton, *The Ideology of the Aesthetic* (Cambridge: Basil Blackwell, 1990) 31-69, for a more detailed formulation of the function of aesthetic in the eighteenth century.

11 In traditional Marxist theory of literature, the literary function is distinct from the ideological function of discourse and both are removed from a scientific function of discourse—one that produces knowledge. While I would keep the category of science separate from the category of ideology, I would argue that 'aesthetic,' as a historical concept, is necessary in the functioning of both literary and non-literary texts. I would agree with Tony Bennett's assessment in *Formalism and Marxism* (New York: Metheun, 1979) in that what is needed is not a 'theory of literature as such but a historically concrete analysis of the different relationships which may exist between different forms of fictional writing and the ideologies to which they allude,' 133. This opens up the category of ideological texts substantially and creates possibilities for evaluating them and the historical processes in which they are implicated.

12 See Andrew 21.

13 See Andrew 200-201.

14 For the alternative interpretation of the poor as aesthetic objects, see Robert Markley, 'Sentimentality as Performance: Shaftesbury, Sterne, and the Theatrics of Virtue,' *The New Eighteenth Century*, eds. Felicity Nussbaum and Laura Brown (New York: Methuen, 1987) 210-230; and John Barrell, 'Sportive labour: the farmworker in eighteenth-century poetry and painting,' *The English Rural Community*, ed. Brian Short (New York: Cambridge UP, 1992) 105-132.

15 I am purposely misrepresenting Betsy Rogers' title *The Cloak of Charity, Studies in Eighteenth-Century Philanthropy* (London: Metheun, 1949).

16 Adam Smith, *The Theory of Moral Sentiments* (New York: Cambridge, 2002) 30.

17 For a discussion of the problems of definition and empirical study of literacy, see Carl F. Kaestle, 'The History of Literacy and the History of Readers' *Perspectives on Literacy*, eds. Eugene R. Kintgen, Barry M. Kroll and Mike Rose (Carbondale: Southern Illinois UP, 1988) 96-98.

18 For a perspective on the formation of sympathetic social bonds in discourses in the latter half of the eighteenth century see Lucinda Cole, '(Anti)Feminist Sympathies: The Politics of Relationship in Smith, Wollstonecraft and More,' *ELH* 58 (1991): 107-140.

19 See Beth Fowkes Tobin, *Superintending the Poor: Charitable Ladies & Paternal Landlords in British Fiction, 1770-1860* (New Haven: Yale UP, 1993) and Dorice Elliott, *Angel Out of the House*.

20 'Philanthropy' was sometimes used interchangeably with charity in the eighteenth century, though the term 'charity' has a much longer history. Charity has a specifically Christian connotation of 'god's love to man' and 'man's love of God,' and it is connected closely with almsgiving since the twelveth century. See "Charity" and "Philanthropy," *The Oxford English Dictionary* 1989 ed.

21 See Clifford Siskin, 'Eighteenth-Century Periodicals and the Romantic Rise of the Novel,' *Studies in the Novel*, 26 (1994): 26-42. This idea is also based on Michel

Foucault's notion of 'subjugated knowledges.' See *Power/Knowledge: Selected Interviews and Other Writings 1972-1977* (New York: Pantheon, 1980) 82.

Chapter 1

History, Philanthropy and Benevolent Femininity

There is a legend that Charity was born of the marriage of Poverty with Abundance, and certainly it cannot come into existence without the presence of these two side by side [...]. Charity, called into action by the privations of the poor, even if it cannot yield any solution for the problem of poverty, does reveal the views of society on this problem. The history of charity is the history of the changes which have occurred in the attitude of the rich towards the poor.
Betsy Rogers, *Cloak of Charity,* 1949

Instead of providing employment for increasing population charitable opinion turned to the improvement of public morale [...]. What was needed was further discrimination: charity must be given, even to the deserving, only in the manner most conducive to the improvement of manners and morals.
Donna Andrew, *Philanthropy and Police,* 1989

Charity as a social practice, and its broader philosophical dimension, philanthropy, are gauges with which to measure the changes of 'attitude' between two levels of societies, the 'rich' and the 'poor,' as the first epigram points out. The study of the 'attitude' of the privileged towards the poor cannot simply, or unproblematically, be reflected in the history of particular philanthropists or in the societal 'movements' of philanthropy. In general, philanthropy throughout the eighteenth century had been looked upon as a solution to England's social ills—depopulation, economic privation, disease, criminality. The term 'solution' is problematic; philanthropy intervened in poverty as if it were one, but actually had little power to change the social and economic conditions which create the need for its existence. However, increasingly towards the end of the eighteenth century, as Donna Andrew points out, philanthropy became less a material solution to the problems of economic deprivation and more of an ideological one which is predicated on 'private' notions of morality, family and benevolence rather than on public structures such as economic support from the parish system, charitable institutions, or stable employment. In effect, philanthropy functions to engender new and different kinds of relations of power between the privileged and the poor by the end of the eighteenth century. The belief was that philanthropy could improve the human condition by linking these private notions of morality, family and benevolence to the public needs of good citizens, industrious laborers and inter-class harmony. What are the conditions that make this connection possible?

History and Philanthropy

Poverty and privation had always existed, but the discrepancy between the privileged and poor became a particular late eighteenth-century concern. As Gertrude Himmelfarb points out in *The Idea of Poverty*, poverty was redefined as a problem for which a solution needed to be found during the eighteenth century, rather than a naturally occurring phenomenon within society (7-8). Twentieth-century scholars of philanthropy have tended to view the eighteenth century as an age of benevolence. Betsy Rogers' *Cloak of Charity* and David Owen's compendium *English Philanthropy 1660-1960* describe some of the societal transformations that charitable actions engendered. Charity and philanthropy, as they are commonly understood by these studies, exist exclusively for the betterment of poor people and the legitimation of the benevolence of the middling classes. *Cloak of Charity* focuses on eminent eighteenth-century philanthropists, from Jonas Hanway to William Wilberforce, and describes their achievements from the founding of charitable Societies to building hospitals for various segments of the population to establishing schools. *English Philanthropy* details various 'movements' within the branches of philanthropy from the charity school movement in the eighteenth century to the welfare movement in the twentieth. These texts sever charity and philanthropy from historical determinants that make these 'movements' or benevolent human acts possible. Both of these studies cite the eighteenth century as the 'golden age' of societal improvement, but do not specify the social and economic conditions which make philanthropy necessary to this segment of history. To counterbalance both these histories, in this abbreviated version of the history of eighteenth-century philanthropy, I will sketch out some of the conditions of possibility for the concern for the laboring classes and the poor (terms often used interchangeably) and some of the reasons for the emergence of philanthropy in the eighteenth century.

It is true that charitable organizations mitigated some of the social and economic problems caused by a societal structure in transition from aristocratic paternalism to incipient agricultural and industrial capitalism. In the seventeenth century, when peasant agriculture dominated rural society, the more or less economically independent peasantry, regardless of the size of the landholding, was able to subsist on the cultivation of its own crops (Hobsbawm 33). Except for a minority of commercial farmers who sold a permanent surplus crop to the urban market, and of peasants whose holdings were so small that they were obliged to take wage work in agriculture or industry, the agrarian system was largely, though certainly not absolutely, self-sufficient in its ability to support its population (Hobsbawm 32-33).

But during the course of the eighteenth century, several legal and economic changes dramatically stratified social and economic relations. The first was that land was turned into a commodity that was purchasable and saleable (Hobsbawm 181). To this end the Enclosure Acts, particularly of 1760 and 1770, effectively swept away the 'ancient collective economy of the village' (Hobsbawm 49). Even though enclosures had been occurring since the sixteenth century, amounting to twenty-four percent of England's total land area, eighteen percent of it was enclosed by Parliament in two short phases of activity in the 1760s and 1770s (Turner 25). In addition, the lands enclosed during these years were located in the south and east Midlands area; these lands consisted of densely arable soils which were converted after enclosures to grassland farming, and lighter soils found in the commons extended the arable land into marginal areas used for pastoral farming (Turner 26). Because of enclosure, 'use rights' to common land, which provided pastureland, firewood, game-hunting and gleaning after harvest, as had been the custom for centuries, were criminalized (Valenze 30-31). M.E. Turner points out some of the effects of this twenty-year span of enclosure: the conversion of arable land to pasture (26); the concurrent relationship between enclosure and population growth (28); the loss of local rights to commons for general village use to depasture animals, gather wood for fuel, and for recreation (32); the transformation of land into 'real' property and its consolidation by a minority of landowners who could afford the costs of enclosure, crop production and taxes (Turner 32-33; Wells 'Development' 31).

The agricultural depression of 1730-1750, as Roger Wells suggests, resulted in many bankruptcies, especially among less substantial tenant farmers ('Development' 31). This depression may have stimulated the consolidation of lands into larger farms and signaled a new pattern in tenantry which reduced the number of farmers. Rising prices for their crops in the latter half of the eighteenth century accelerated the accumulation of capital in the agricultural sector, which was invested in further enclosure, drainage, farm buildings, etc. (Wells 'Development' 31; Valenze 33). The capital thus required to compete in agricultural production prohibited the survival of small landed proprietors (Wells 'Development' 32). In turn, landowners sold food for 'profit,' forcing the poor to buy food they previously could have grown, hunted or gleaned (Valenze 33, 41). Coupled with the failure of industries to develop in the south and east of England, partially because of the consolidation of enclosure lands, few alternatives to agricultural employment existed.

As a result, the effects of enclosure on the standard of living and the level of employment for a previously 'self-sufficient' agricultural laborer were enormous. Standards of living in the countryside were higher before 1750 than after (Wells 'Development' 32). Wells points out that this may have been partially responsible for triggering the population upsurge through the latter half of the eighteenth century ('Development' 32).[1] But whatever the case, since population outstripped the demand for labor, there was a growing supply of unemployed and underemployed laborers. A study by N.F.R. Crafts shows that throughout the second half of the eighteenth century employment was slow in all sectors, and in agriculture it had become increasingly seasonal and part time (71-72). Women in particular had benefited from the 'open village system' and customary 'use rights'; after 1750, though, women's employment narrowed even more than men's (Valenze 32-33, 40-43). Because of the large amount of surplus labor available, independent farmers responded by reducing their permanent workforce (Wells 'Development' 33). Crafts suggests this signaled a change in the structure of employment; the proportion of the labor force employed in agriculture decreased rapidly while the proportion employed in industry increased, even though much of the employment in industry continued to be in small-scale, handicraft activities (Crafts 71).[2] The consequence was greater dependence on large landholders for occasional agricultural work and on industry for wage-labor. Crafts suggests that the low productivity growth in both agricultural and industrial sectors inflated prices toward the last quarter of the eighteenth century and had the effect of producing a slow growth of real wages for workers (74). Therefore, by the late eighteenth century the standard of living for workers decreased as employment became casual and prices inflated.

These economic conditions exacerbated the strain on the existing system of statutory poor relief, which had existed since the sixteenth century. In the south and east especially, periodic and permanent unemployment assumed serious proportions in the late 1760s and 1770s (Wells 'Development' 33). The rising cost to the parish in order to maintain—in or out of workhouses—all those who were unable to maintain themselves under the old Poor Law was a serious point of concern to ratepayers (Wells 'Development' 32-33). To complicate matters, the Settlement Laws, which stated that the parish had to relieve only those who could prove residency and unemployment in their own parish, militated against migration to other regions where employment might be possible. As Wells states, 'relief was certain for an individual in his home parish; he was less likely to receive assistance elsewhere' ('Development' 32). Various systems were enforced to handle the problem of increasing claimants, such as the Roundsman System, Gilbert's Act and the Speenhamland System.[3] All of these were inadequate to handle the numbers of people now reliant on the parish or other means of private charity.

By the 1790s, economic conditions had worsened for the growing population of the laboring class. The scarcity of food (particularly grains—the 'bread and butter' of the laboring class) together with inflated food prices, which served to reduce the real wages of workers to the lowest level in three centuries, produced 'famine' conditions throughout the nation (Wells *Wretched* 1). Roger Wells argues that the use of the term 'famine' to describe the periods of 1794-1796 and 1799-1801 was avoided by both eighteenth-century political economists and contemporary agrarian and social historians (*Wretched* 2-11). Nonetheless, Wells argues that the conditions of famine existed, exacerbated by war, and analyzes the responses to them, such as food riots and rural arson by laborers and the growth of trade unions (*Wretched* 161-174); profit making by millers, prosperous farmers, and dealers (*Wretched* 22-32); the growth of the 'shopocracy' in urban centers hoping to capitalize on sale of their wares in the time of scarcity (*Wretched* 31); and government funding and stocking of imported grain (*Wretched* 184-195). For the poor living during this period, the lack of food and the decline of wages, if employed at all, created a particularly pitiable existence. Wells describes the conditions of the typical worker:

> All bar a tiny elite of workers were forced to economise, and ecomomise drastically whatever aid derived from self-help organisations, the poor law and charities [...]. Many were forced with varying rapidity, to reserve all funds for

food alone; replacement clothes and footwear, adequate heating and light, were also fairly immediate objects of economy for many too. Rents were partly or unpaid; arrears mounted. Market prices dictated dietary economies, though options varied with individuals' circumstances, regionally, and from time to time. (*Wretched* 318)

Even though the 'famine' conditions of 1794-6 and 1799-1801, escalating political tension in the forms of crime and food riots, and the subsequent strain on the Poor Law, merited concern on the part of the employing and affluent classes, little was done on an economic level to improve the situation. Roger Wells advances two reasons for this. First, the crises were expected to be temporary, so any strain on the relief fund in the short term was preferable to increased wage costs in the long run.[4] This view seems to be confirmed by the late eighteenth-century political economist Frederic Eden's belief that wages were adequate.[5] Second, the Poor Law placed the burden of relief on the community and the parish and not on the employer (Wells 'Development' 36). In other words, the paternalistic responsibility for the poor which was prevalent in a more or less feudal system properly belonged to entities outside the direct labor/capital split in an increasingly capitalist agricultural and industrial society:

> Employer reticence was at its most pronounced in agrarian communities, but many industrial and urban workers also experienced the direct relationship between their master's attitude and the degree of dependency on poor-law and charitable agencies. Many workers received limited charitable donations from their employers who used this manoeuver to stave-off permanent wage rises and derive kudos from their commonly much-publicised benevolence. (Wells *Wretched* 332)

Supplemental relief, in the form of charities and philanthropic endeavors, came to play a significant role in the alleviation of material suffering and the improvement of the individual. By making the social conditions necessary for laborers to be dependent on capital, laborers and the poor were also made more dependent on the parish system of poor relief and more private forms of philanthropy. Philanthropy and individual 'benevolence' began to play an important role in the maintenance of the social order.

Philanthropic Feeling and the Solution of Charity

The role that poor relief and charity played changed dramatically from the seventeenth to the eighteenth century, and changed again during the course of the eighteenth into the nineteenth century. This changing role parallels the altered pattern of economic and social relations. The stakes—in terms of supplying a labor force, mitigating starvation, and producing a new, viable rationale for mass-scale material inequity—became much higher given the economic and social changes taking place. Despite debates surrounding the efficacy of poor relief, Roger Wells claims that no one disputed 'its role as the fundamental progenitor of order'

(*Wretched* 288). Philanthropy and charity became united and increasingly important as the 'solution' to the problem of poverty as the eighteenth century progressed.

As W.K. Jordan's *Philanthropy in England, 1480-1660* makes clear, during the sixteenth and seventeenth centuries charity primarily took the form of monetary donations by private benefactors for direct poor relief, which were then transferred to the poor by the use of charitable trusts (40-41). The income from these trusts, whether the funds were constituted as doles or more regulated stipends, was dedicated to four areas of charity (Jordan 41-42). The first consisted of 'outright' relief: 'the relief of existing poverty, to the prevention of vagabondage and social ruin, and to maintaining poor families at least at the level of subsistence in their own homes' (Jordan 41). The second is the endowment of Almshouses to encourage 'competence' in the laborer. The third is 'charity general' to be given for broad uses at the discretion of the feoffees, parishes and municipal officers. The fourth is charity specifically given to the aged poor who are unable to work. Legitimacy and institutionalization were given to the charitable trust through Tudor legislation of the Poor Laws of 1597-1601, but only if private donations failed to bring the poor to subsistence level (Owen 1). The conception of charity during this period is still vested in the medieval system of parish allotments and doles in order to transfer funds to the poor for the more or less direct alleviation of poverty.

By the turn into the eighteenth century, 'philanthropy' comes into the vocabulary as a broader, more ambitious charitable attitude which benefits the public good through 'love to mankind; practical benevolence towards men in general.'[6] Throughout the eighteenth century and well into the nineteenth, philanthropy is a term that is generally used to define a feeling—a particular moral sensibility. However, this new ethical definition accompanies a new moral philosophy: relief should benefit the nation. While charity in the terms of the feudal system of doles, allotments, and endowments mentioned above still existed, private charity was transformed in the early eighteenth century—a time David Owen calls 'the age of benevolence.' Grafted onto a system of monetary donations was the emergence of what Owen calls 'associated philanthropy,' which accumulated charity 'capital' by relatively anonymous donors (3).[7] The enactment of a charitable endeavor was now based on the success of the early capitalist commercial joint-stock boom of the 1690s (Owen 12). The principal investors were not only aristocratic landowners, but also great overseas merchants and tradesmen; those with wealth were united in their attempts to help foster relief to the poor.[8] The rationale posited by these charitable companies was that the money invested would bring 'a dividend in the improved happiness and morality of the poor' (Clarke 23). The use of the word 'improved' here illustrates the overlapping eighteenth-century definitions of 'making something better' and 'making a profit out of something' (Williams 161-2). The use of the word 'happiness' is similar, meaning 'the state of pleasurable content of mind, which results from success or the attainment of what is considered good' as well as financial success and prosperity (*OED* 79-80). Both definitions continued in use until the mid-nineteenth century. Morality and economics are discursively intertwined.

The benevolent achievements of what David Owen calls 'associated philanthropy' amounted to conspicuous monuments: a system of charity and Sunday schools; a variety of hospitals for the sick, infirm, pregnant, as well as for foundlings and prostitutes; workhouses and legislative acts for the relief of debtors; the building of churches and prisons; and the rise of charitable Societies. It was hoped that private charity would constitute a powerful weapon against crime and poverty in the intermittent periods of crisis for what was, in the early eighteenth century, a relatively stable economic and political situation. And it was hoped that these monuments of philanthropy would mitigate some of the social and economic problems caused by incipient agricultural and industrial capitalism (Owen 4).

Whatever religious, political and economic motives there might have been which influenced the single benefactor in the seventeenth century or the 'associated' philanthropists in the eighteenth, charitable work never breached the notion of a god-given, paternalistic social hierarchy. Alongside the upper class fears of depopulation, crime, and political discontent of the lower orders, there was also a fear of social and economic transgression by the poor which took form in common methods of revolt in the later eighteenth century such as arson and rioting.[9] Poor women and children also resisted collectively by continuing to exercise the now illegal customary use rights of gleaning and wood-gathering (Valenze 40). It was hoped that associated philanthropy was at once a way to cope with the economic problems gradually eroding a traditional peasant culture and a preemptive strike at political discontent. It was meant to root out apathy and division, redeeming and reuniting the society (Colley 92). The improvements attempted were meant to stabilize and support the existing patterns of economic stratification, viewed by the upper and middling classes as natural and inevitable. The obligation of the privileged (loosely defined as both the aristocracy and the middling classes for our purposes right now) to deal with the problems caused by a changing economic system holds over from the idealist paternalism of an earlier social system, but is also invested with newer sentimental meanings: to support the poor enables the privileged to display their moral virtue, social power and 'natural' benevolence by the giving of money.[10] This visible manifestation of moral virtue defines social relationships by subordinating others according to their monetary dependence, further consolidating the upper ranks of land and trade.

Therefore, in the early to mid-eighteenth century the movement of improvement had consisted of building buildings (prisons, hospitals, schools, and churches), teaching literacy and basic arithmetic to the poor, relieving destitution through the giving of alms, and the establishment of societies to debate the origins of and solutions to poverty. But despite these achievements, the effects of poverty worsened. As Patrick Colquhoun lamented in *A Treatise on Indigence* (1806): 'the indigent have been clothed and fed; but few, very few, have recovered their former useful station of *independent poverty*' (62). Independent poverty for the poor meant surviving on a combination of subsistence farming, wage-earning and cottage industry; whereas dependent poverty meant surviving on the allowance given by the parish or other kinds of charity. Colquhoun calls this a state of 'indigence' the only real social 'evil.' Notwithstanding Colquhoun's judgment about poverty being a positive force for the production of 'civil' society, he seems to be historically correct in his observation, because, as we have seen, the level of independent poverty had been eroding to the level of dependent poverty by legislative and economic measures in the mid- to late eighteenth century. The social conditions that were necessary for laborers to become dependent on capital also created the conditions in which laborers were made more dependent on the parishes and private philanthropy.

Colquhoun's statement reveals an interesting recategorization of the laboring classes. The term 'poor,' which was used relatively loosely throughout the seventeenth and early eighteenth centuries to refer to most of the laboring population, underwent significant redefinition in various discourses, categorizing the poor into different classes: the worthy poor, the indigent, the independent poor, the dependent poor, the pauper, etc.[11] This redefinition of the poor depended on value judgments based on economic productivity which are inextricably tied to their perceived frugality, moral restraint, and diligence. As Frederic Eden comments in *The State of the Poor*, written in 1797 at the height of grain shortages:

> The prosperity of a country depends on the welfare of its labouring Poor, and no estimate can be formed of its population, industry, strength, virtue, and happiness without considering their condition. (2)

The first challenge for Eden, as well as other late eighteenth-century commentators on poverty, is to decide who the 'problematic' poor were: who did not contribute to the industry, strength, virtue and happiness of the nation. How some segments of the poor became 'problematic' is largely what Eden's dissertation focuses on. In a detailed review of the literature on poverty, from the creation of the original Poor Laws to his contemporaries' debate, Eden describes the arguments for and against the compulsory maintenance of poor and charity. Eden arrives at the conclusion, however, that the Poor Law 'may be said to offer an encouragement to debauchery' (94) and:

> the sum of good to be expected from the establishment of a compulsory maintenance for the Poor, will be far out-balanced by the sum of evil which it will inevitably create; that the certainty of a legal provision weakens the principles of natural affection, and destroys one of the strongest ties of society by rendering the exercise of domestic and social duties less necessary. (96-7)

Though Eden does not advocate repealing the Poor Laws in totality, he does want to see restriction to certain segments of the poor: the sick, infirm or old, or rather, the less-productive laborers.[12] To foster the 'natural affection' among the poor, and presumably between the poor and the privileged, Eden suggests that 'philanthropists' (used in a pejorative way that seems equivalent to our contemporary meaning of 'bleeding heart') would 'better serve the cause of the industrious peasant and manufacturer by pointing out the best means of reducing [the Poor's] expenses' because the 'miseries of the labouring Poor arose, less from the scantiness of their income (however much the philanthropist might wish it to be increased) than from their own improvidence and unthriftiness' (100). The rest of Eden's work is devoted to his observations of the poor in both northern and southern counties in England using their parochial reports. His descriptions detail the ways in which the laboring poor are improvident and unthrifty in terms of dress, beer, clothing and, not surprisingly, food, with the apparent intention of proving the burden of charity is to help the poor discipline themselves.[13]

This kind of advice is especially significant at mid-century, as historian Deborah Valenze has explained, when the image of the poor as 'a social threat' to the wealthy had been constructed 'as much from the fear of the rich as the activities of the poor' (27). By the late eighteenth century, there is an increasing focus on the individual amelioration of the poor: the impoverished must *deserve* improvement. The emphasis on individual virtues and appropriate attitudes highlights a conceptual maneuver away from depicting the poor as an already consolidated class with established rituals, attitudes and social expectations, and towards a conception of laborers as compartmentalized groups, that need to be judged, categorized and morally 'improved' by their social betters. If scholars have foregrounded the monumental improvements philanthropy and charity have encouraged in this age, they have not been as scrupulous in their investigation of the changes in the 'attitude' of the wealthy towards the poor, and how the Poor's own communities changed. Historian David Owen states that during these latter years,

> [...] the more wary approach to human distress, in part the consequence of fears induced by the Revolution, was sanctified by the prevailing social philosophy. If charity was a response to human need, it was also an instrument for inculcating approved social attitudes. The new philanthropist frowned on almsgiving, without careful investigation, and tended to judge charitable efforts by their success in encouraging recipients to stand on their own feet. Properly conceived, charity should be limited to the 'deserving,' that vaguely defined class of unfortunates which figures so heavily in nineteenth-century writing on the subject. (98)

Having the economic and social power to discern exactly who deserved help was the domain of the privileged upper- and middling-class philanthropist, as was the inculcation of the values that would make the poor deserving of help. This surplus in the labor market had not produced the 'right' kind of workers necessary to suit the needs of incipient agricultural and industrial capitalism.

Thus, the 'attitude' of the poor needed to be changed because the attitude of the privileged toward the poor had changed. Philanthropy, understood in the context of the prevailing social theory of the time, attempted to provide an ideological resolution to the problem of poverty: once the values that demonstrated one deserved help were inculcated—industry, religion, domestic affection, financial independence—then one's personal diligence would be rewarded and economic intervention no longer needed. The 'improved happiness' of the individual would be provided for without long-term financial investment on the part of the privileged. The impoverished who did not subscribe to these 'moral' values had only themselves to blame for their troubles and should not be dependent on the state or the benevolence of the privileged classes. As Eden's study points out, the upper class's concerns about poverty, crimes, increasing population, etc., among the poor were reconstructed as moral problems. Landowners, like Jethro Tull, complained that the poor were not industrious, and characterized the poor as an 'objectionable and alien race' (Valenze 44). Laboring-class women in particular, who had lost their ability to be economically productive, began to be characterized by undesirable impulses—disregard for morality and law—and consequently in need of reform (Valenze 25-6). Dorice Williams Elliott has pointed out that many philanthropic endeavors at mid-century focused on the reformation of women's sexuality: some examples are The Foundling Hospital provided for bastard children of women's (possibly illicit) sexual relations; the Magdalen Asylum for prostitutes, the Lock hospital which treated women for venereal diseases (38-9). Patrick Colquhoun in 1808 argues that:

> The morals of the inferior classes of society have been neglected [...]. Vicious habits, idleness, improvidence, and sottishness prevail in so great a degree, that until a right bias shall have been given to the minds of the Vulgar, joined to the greater portion of intelligence and respect to the economy of the Poor, one million of indigent will be added to another, requiring permanent or partial relief, producing ultimately such a gangrene in the body politic as to threaten its total dissolution. (63)

These moral problems—'vicious habits, idleness, improvidence, and sottishness'— could be alleviated by a 'voluntary' transformation in personal behavior on the part of the poor. In this respect, the only 'real' charity that should be practiced is moral inculcation. The philanthropist becomes a superintendent, one who will give the poor the ideological tools to achieve the transformation from a member of the undeserving poor to a worthy laborer. As Donna Andrew observes, by the end of the eighteenth and the beginning of the nineteenth century, 'true charity involved the improvement of the nation's morals and manners, as this came to be seen as not only the nation's prime need, but the only sphere in which charity had not been replaced by the operation of the market' (196), though one could reasonably conclude that this kind of improvement supported the operations of a strengthening market economy.

The shift in focus to individual amelioration is an interesting attempt to produce a solution to the problem of poverty posed by an expanding capitalist system. If industrial and landowning capitalists were reluctant to raise labor costs, straining the system of poor relief and leaving institutional and private forms of philanthropy burdened with the overflow, then individual amelioration represents an attractive solution to poverty. The effect of an institutional to individual shift is constituent of the formation of a new set of social relations. With a new emphasis on personal morality, a system of beliefs and values useful to and invested in the new capitalist system are inculcated to the poor by the privileged in order to serve the public arena of economic production; in other words, their moral 'improvement' is linked to their industry in the economic sphere. Once social power is deployed, the improvement in the more private arena of subject formation affects the public arena of economic production. How to accomplish this task?

One way to accomplish this is by producing discourses which will improve the habits, values and behaviors of the poor in relation to the privileged habits, values and behaviors—if the new system is to work properly. In other words, this new social formation must produce its productive forces and reproduce its relations of production. If the terrain of philanthropy shifts from 'monuments' to 'discourse,' then discourse can be seen as one site in which these new relations are 'imagined' and sustained by particular ideological practices. In essence, the working of the new 'self-help philanthropy,' espoused by people like Frederic Eden and Patrick Colquhoun, took two tacks. First, it was tied to traditional institutional monetary relief: in order to achieve the short-term goal of deterring undesirable laboring-class behavior, repressive and coercive tactics were used to dissuade the poor from getting monetary allowances. The overseers were to meticulously examine all claimants for poor relief. These authorities calculated the level of relief based on what the 'best' worker could earn, not what the average worker actually received (Wells 'Development' 37). The 'best' was defined by the vestry of the Church who, it was assumed, would have a greater collective knowledge of the workers. Whoever was deemed 'idle' and therefore ineligible for relief, was separated from those who were industrious and merited relief. Also, many minor regulations were mandated to govern the behavior of the poor, such as compulsory church attendance, the elimination of household dogs, and regulations prohibiting the time-honored right of gleaning (Wells 'Development' 38). A variety of laws were passed to deter criminality: prisons and workhouses were built and legislative reforms for debtors were enacted. In the short term, these more or less repressive measures enforced 'moral' behavior by the threat of starvation and displacement.

The second tack, however, was ideological: a compact of useful, ethical ideologies that would inculcate self-discipline and self-restraint, respect for social order, and domestic affection among the poor and laborers in order to secure social peace. Only such ideologies could combat the 'idleness and pauperism' which threatened to impede the economic progress and erode the social fabric of England. As concerns this study, the 'overseers' in this case were writers who intervened between the privileged and the lower classes in order to 'teach' this compact. This set of moral values and behaviors served the hegemonic interests of the middling class by creating a representation of morality for all classes that exists as a defensible explanation for the new social system's economic consequences.

This second project called for a broader, national method of instilling laboring-class morality as well as for the education of the upper class and the emergent middling classes in their new social and economic responsibilities towards the poor, which encompassed the abstract ideal of benevolence. Basic education—reading, writing and arithmetic—for the underprivileged was, at this historical point, one important, branch of philanthropy to which the middling classes were committed. Concomitantly, if these values could be taught to and *desired* by the laboring classes and the upper and middling classes alike, then the 'public good' and sympathetic harmony would be achieved. The shared values that 'self-help' philanthropy trumpeted were, of course, defined by the needs of the upper and middling classes, as well as their mode of dissemination: texts. After all, what is more solitary and personal than reading? Yet, reading has a collective goal of sharing and maintaining those values. Thus, literacy, and who controls the production of texts, becomes a primary means of social control and ideological dissemination.[14] Though attempted and accomplished with the utmost benevolent sincerity, what I have come to call vocational philanthropy is a contradictory form of 'self-help.'

The Goals of Literacy

Reading as a form of 'self-help' had the goal of inculcating 'appropriate' values across class lines, universalizing the habit of reading as something that was a desirable and, most importantly, a productive act that individuals could engage in that would lead them toward the progressive humanism touted by Enlightenment ideals: the values of reason, individual liberty and social mobility. Greater literacy would be a sign of social and economic progress. The uses of literacy would ameliorate the individual, both morally and spiritually, salvaging him from the 'death of religion' and the 'ravages of progress' (Graff *Literacy* 2-3, Street 2). These ideas were often espoused to varying degrees by many eighteenth-century educational reformers, including the women writers, Hannah More, Mary Wollstonecraft and Maria Edgeworth, that we shall study in the later chapters.

Recent scholarship on literacy, however, has questioned the association, or conflation, of literacy with progress. The 'uses' of literacy were not simple, straightforward complements of social and economic 'progress' (that is, growing British democracy and capitalism) ensuring free thought and liberalism. The notion of a concurrence between literacy and social progress is undercut by the raw literacy data of the eighteenth century, which suggests that the 'progress' of early industrialization hindered the growth of mass literacy for the vast majority of the population: the laborers saw little change in their rates of illiteracy while the upper classes were still universally literate. The group that benefited most from the educational push of literacy was the skilled artisans in the lower classes who experienced a sharp increase.[15] While it is true that for some professional, retail and trade occupations, functional literacy was required for the new cash nexus involved in commercialized agriculture and new industries, many if not most rural occupations and manufacturing trades did not require literacy. For Harvey J. Graff 'access to literacy, and its use, separated the experiences of different persons and groups within the population' (*Legacies* 236). Therefore, even within the laboring classes, the spread of literacy was uneven, and fairly random; and since the laboring classes were already situated within a literate culture the distinction between illiterate and literate had less meaning for functional purposes. Oral readings of printed matter in homes and taverns, for instance, bridged the gap between literate and illiterate. For the middle, professional and upper classes, literacy was a more even and universal cultural value and habit. It was these classes that developed a print culture in which reading daily became a part of life—from reading the bible, to newspapers, periodicals, novels, political material—because leisure time, circulating libraries and the lowered cost of books permitted it.[16]

Reading as a cultural value and habit signified a practice among the middling and upper classes that was already thought to provide self and societal improvement. The value and practice of reading could be accommodated to the self-help strategy of philanthropy, and provide the moral amelioration of the poor and laboring classes. In this context, debates about the 'dangers' of mass literacy emerged in the eighteenth century. Bernard Mandeville was one of the most prominent critics of charity schools, who argued in 'Essay on Charity and Charity-Schools' that the masses needed to be ignorant to be content in that lot as laborers. Given the dire economic conditions for the poor at the end of the eighteenth century, fears of political radicalism in the aftermath of the French and American Revolutions and the internal strife caused by urban growth and industrialization, literacy education was associated with social mobility and disorder for the opponents of mass literacy. First, it would make the lower classes unfit for their 'god-given' occupational role; second, it would subvert proper authority by 'disseminating seditious and atheistic ideas' (Kaestle 'Elite' 179). 'Untempered' literacy was viewed as a threat to social order and stability, a threat to the Church and State's authority, and morally questionable. Those reformers in favor of spreading literacy, such as Scottish reformer John MacFarlan, viewed it as the best way to ensure social order, instill morality and train 'citizens' (Graff *Literacy* 8; Graff *Legacies* 247, 262-3; Kaestle 'Elite' 180). Reformers prevailed by arguing that literacy would achieve the goals of the conservatives: that social and political stability would be maintained, the laborers and poor would be more disciplined and dutiful workers and citizens, and deference to authority would prevail (Graff *Legacies* 315). Illiteracy, from the point of view of the middling class, came to signify 'that the training required for civilization and progress remained incomplete [...] when reformers wrote of idleness, drunkenness, pauperism, vice, improvidence, crime and especially ignorance, they spoke to the social "problem" of those untrained and uncontrolled by the instillation of discipline and morality through controlled socialization aided and speeded by literacy' (Graff *Legacies* 323). Literacy becomes especially important to the moral inculcation of those 'habits and values,' as Hannah More stated, important to creating a stable English nation in a transforming economy (190). Reading was thought to be a necessary social practice that could shape the ways in which individuals 'imagine' themselves and their position within the social structure.

Assumptions about the power of reading were widespread, not only among the middling classes, but among the laboring classes as well. Thomas Laqueur's study of English elementary education in the late eighteenth and early nineteenth centuries states that laboring-class parents patronized private, venture schools by sending their children to school to learn reading voluntarily and at their own expense. He suggests that this is a primary reason for the increase in the literacy rate during that period, particularly among the upper echelons of the laboring class ('Growth' 196). Though it is clear that very often the learning in these schools was uneven and often interrupted given the demands of laboring-class life, and the literacy skills taught were usually functional, it does signify a laboring-class interest in reading. The demand among the laborers to learn to read follows Kaestle's suggestion that even though the reformers' arguments clearly attempted to limit the effects of literacy, the notion of social mobility was present in the possibilities of literacy ('Elite' 181). This too, however, could be seen as a social asset, or an investment in the moral economy of the social hierarchy. Meritocracy rewards those who comport themselves to the system; while some would 'rise,' those few would be 'especially loyal because ambition attaches one to the system,' and the overall goal would be the collective aim of social stability and a productive citizenry (Kaestle 'Elite' 181). Literacy for both the lower and middling classes meant a kind of cultural status, and both classes shared in a developing literary culture that valued reading as a potent social force, if for very different reasons.

Thus, Harvey J. Graff suggests that the uses of literacy were more important than the numbers of people reading:

> The inculcation of values, habits, norms, and attitudes to transform the masses, rather than skills alone or per se, was the developing task of schooling and its legitimating theme. Literacy properly was to serve as an instrument for training in a close and mutually reinforcing relationship with morality; that was to be, at least in theory, the source of cohesion and order [...]. (*Legacies* 12)

Literacy refashioned all classes, so that what and how literature was read becomes an important marker for class distinctions that emerged because of the growing middling-class print culture in the eighteenth century. Literacy is appropriated by the middling-class reformer and philanthropist as a means of moral inculcation and social control which maintained social stratification: 'Literacy and its uses were becoming one sign of the emerging transformation of the social structure and the development of modern social classes' (Graff *Legacies* 246). It is this transformation through literacy, as one branch of philanthropic activity, which provided women with the moral impetus and social imperative to enter a public debate about the reformation of English society; women's writing provided a means by which that reformation and transformation would not only be discussed, but also provided a means by which it could be accomplished—how society, and individuals within it, could be improved through reading.

The Intervention of Women

This interventionist strategy for organizing a new set of relations among the classes is part of the history of class struggle as well as of the history of disciplinary power: 'the work of directing, superintending and adjusting becomes one of the functions of capital, from the moment that the labor under capital's control becomes co-operative. As a specific function of capital, the directing function acquires its own special characteristics' (Marx 449). Cooperative control of labor is achieved through an intermediary kind of work which organizes the processes which 'direct,' 'superintend' and 'adjust' subjects, even outside the direct relations of production. In other words, one of the special characteristics of this disciplining function was to enable discourses to be written under the aegis of benevolence, which engenders and encourages certain 'imaginary relations' between the privileged and the poor.

For if ideology is to be effective and efficient, 'it must be pleasurable, intuitive, self-ratifying: in a word, aesthetic' (Eagleton *Aesthetic* 41). This 'imaginary relationship' occurs through the production of certain discourses designed to teach this relationship to both the poor and the middling classes. Writing texts becomes an act of benevolence; reading texts becomes a proper object of charity.

The function to 'improve' people materially through self-help philanthropy relies on the internalization of particular ideologies defined and disseminated through texts. The mechanism by which that 'help' is transformed into a discipinizing function of discourse is what I have come to call vocational philanthropy in this study. The philanthropic impetus of benevolence and the feelings of love for mankind are bracketed by the focus on the function of their discourses; that is, to foster the 'habit' of reading and appropriate kinds of reading practices that are regulated by gender and class status. These discourses are not tools by which desires are repressed, but exactly the opposite; they are forms that produce desires (although desires that are coded as desirable by middling-class women writers), and engage those desires on the level of form. These discourses thus give readers a kind of social empowerment, perhaps hitherto unimagined, enabled by the link between content and form; these discourses give the writers a social control over their material and audience. By producing ideologies of benevolence and personal improvement and attempting, through ideological interpellation, subjective transformation, vocational philanthropy legitimates the middling-class's concept of a self-contained and self-sustaining society, one that is produced and maintained by women writers and their texts. As a consequence, by using discourses to teach individuals how to 'improve,' the problems of real social inequities are displaced onto a problematic of individual improvement which would not dissipate those inequities, but aestheticize them.[17]

This notion of aesthetics is important because, as mentioned in the introduction, vocational philanthropy must operate under a cloak—benevolence appears as 'natural,' non-political, and economically disinterested. It is important that this kind of mediatory and supervisory work of writing is accomplished from outside the direct relations of labor and outside the dominance of the state in order to elide class considerations and to stem the tide of political upheaval which certainly worried various sectors of the middling and upper classes. Women's association with the private, domestic sphere provided the opportunity for women to engage in this kind of philanthropy, and their ready participation in a variety of other forms of philanthropy made them legitimate authorities. Dorice Williams Elliott has outlined three historical precedents for women's philanthropic activities in the eighteenth century. The first was the Lady Bountiful tradition in which aristocratic ladies were expected to perform charitable duties to the poor, providing some money, food, and medicine (23). The second precedent was religious, particularly in the legacy of the Catholic 'Sisters of Charity' which might have given impetus to the Anglican models of sisterhoods that appeared in the seventeenth, eighteenth and nineteenth centuries (24). The third precedent is the traditional association of sympathy with women; sympathy was seen as a natural attribute of women because of women's potential as mothers (25). The consolidation of these precedents enabled the formation of benevolent femininity as it had come to be culturally understood in the late eighteenth and early nineteenth centuries.

But this is not to say that because women's benevolent impetus appears to be constructed from within their association with the private sphere they did not engage in the public sphere of discourse. The vocational philanthropy practiced by women writers serves as a transversive space between public and private. As opposed to Elliott, who claims a professional status for women's philanthropy especially in the later nineteenth century (though Elliott's is a study of representations of charity and therefore different in function from the kind of philanthropy I am specifying in this study), as well as Paul Keen and Clifford Siskin who both see women's writing in this period as 'professional' work, I view the jointure of philanthropy and women's writing as 'a special calling'–a vocation—that proceeds from an emerging, and I would add transitional, feminine subjectivity that links discursive work with benevolent agency.[18] Magali Larson has indicated that the notion of vocation prior to the nineteenth century provided for a kind of 'work' or occupation that was relatively freely chosen, that entailed a 'sense of duty' and an 'ideal of service' (61-2). The work itself has some intrinsic value that cannot be quantified by wages or profit. This vocational space allows us to see a way out of the public/private debate about women's writing, but also allows room to explore the complex ideological problems connected with women writers as public figures and women as domestic subjects. My argument, then, is that women do not merely engage in philanthropic endeavors, one of which is writing texts, in greater numbers from this point onwards, but that this transversive space is at least one enabling condition of women's subjective transformation, women's literary production, and the reconception of the relationship between the polite and the poor through the effects of literacy. While the form of philanthropy is accessed by middling-class women (a virtuous, morally scrupulous impetus for action), the content (personal amelioration) is changed by their discursive participation in it. This occurrence is neither a natural nor revolutionary one; it is a historical one which joins the functions of philanthropy, literacy, and a new model of femininity at this particular moment. But again, it is a transitional moment when the market possibilities for women's writing coincides with broader political and economic crises.

Therefore, while it is rare to identify women as contributors to subscriptions for hospitals, schools, etc., or to claim they were engaged in the work of the many relief societies that sprang up throughout the early to mid-eighteenth century, the movement towards the more 'personal' and 'judicious' forms of philanthropy and charity is concomitant with the entrance of women into the feminine 'vocation' of philanthropy in the latter two decades of the century.[19] At the same time, a dramatic upsurge in the volume of women's writing begins in the 1780s (Turner 36-8). Women entered the writer's market in greater numbers, producing a variety of kinds of writing at an accelerated rate of production. Cheryl Turner's study of women writers in the eighteenth century suggests that 'certain literary and extra-literary factors were particularly influential of specific moments or watersheds in the development[al] [patterns]' (39). I suggest that one of those extra-literary factors was the changing form of philanthropy, which gave middling-class women moral agency and legitimacy for their discursive endeavors; by producing literature, they were able to participate in wide-scale philanthropy without the accumulation of capital and without sequestering themselves in 'sisterhoods,' as Sarah Scott's novel *Millennium Hall* seems to suggest at mid-century is desirable and appropriate for middling-class and aristocratic women, but only those women without domestic ties.[20] The appropriate moral values could be inculcated through discourse written primarily by women, not because benevolence and sympathy were women's natural attributes, but because these qualities were increasingly associated with femininity. This association provided agency for middling-class women writers to enter the field of public discourse to respond to a social problem in moral terms. Their inclusion in this public arena was concomitant with the cultivation of their aesthetic sensibilities and with the construction of morality founded upon a certain level of literacy.

The development of sentimental literature was a precursor to women's writing and women's perceived sympathetic understanding of the plight of others. Sentimental literature written by both men and women of the mid-eighteenth century was thought to inculcate the improvement of manners, while acting on literature's emotional response and affective power (Todd *Sensibility* 29). The point was to develop in the reader a special susceptibility to feelings and sensations, but that susceptibility must be internally regulated by the virtue of sympathy, a detached moral virtue that Adam Smith described in *A Theory of Moral Sentiments*. Though works like *A Sentimental Journey* and *The Man of Feeling* are often read as episodes in the developing novel form, the purpose of the texts in the literary culture of the period was to inculcate moral instruction and benevolence towards society, particularly shown through a male protagonist.[21] As Janet Todd states in *Sensibility*: 'precise response is taught to both character and reader' through an affecting episode in which 'true' sympathy, which includes discerning whether or not to give help to the poor and not merely a good deed on the part of a 'middling materialist,' is valorized (91). Having 'true' sympathy, as defined by this literature, was dependent on a shared class of readership, based in economic stature, education, and moral principle. Through reading a certain kind of discourse, the aesthetic effect received by a middling-class reader cultivates a sympathetic response, resulting in the belief that misery and material want can be alleviated by judicious charitable discernment, rather than by economic change.

But perhaps because of the failure of associated philanthropy to stem the tide of economic deprivation and the deterioration of economic conditions in the countryside of England discussed earlier in this chapter, the concept of masculine sentimental virtue lost its attraction towards the end of the century (Todd *Sensibility* 7). The later sentimental works of the 1760s and 1770s are more generally concerned with the outflowing of emotion, rather than moral reflection based on an emotional response (Todd *Sensibility* 92). Todd states in her evaluation of the novels which represent the 'man of feeling' that the 'cult of sensibility stressed qualities considered feminine in the sexual psychology of the time: intuitive sympathy, susceptibility, emotionalism and passivity' (*Sensibility*

110), pointing to an episode in the feminization of sensibility. At the same time, there was more emphasis in print on the need to exclude women from the public sphere, privatizing these sentiments again. Both sexes were deluged with conduct books, sermons, homilies, novels, and magazine articles insisting that good order and political stability depended on the maintenance of separate spheres for separate genders (Colley 253).[22] This tension was created by women's visibility in both spheres of influence. G.J. Barker-Benfield notes the increasing heterosocial contact in the eighteenth century, and attributes this to the 'culture of sensibility' which enabled a shared sensitivity to feelings and general benevolence (141). The inborn virtue of the sentimental man, as portrayed in novels by Mackenzie, Sterne and Goldsmith, is gradually shared, then transmuted into the 'woman of feeling.'

The 'new' benevolent woman of the late eighteenth century is constructed from a variety of pedagogical literature throughout the century, from conduct literature to the educational treatises of Catherine Macauley, Priscilla Wakefield, Hannah More, Mary Wollstonecraft and others, all of whom locate benevolence as a primary foundation for women's rationality and broad sympathy. Wakefield and More particularly discuss philanthropy as a duty of upper- and middling-class women.[23] Recently, Nancy Armstrong has discussed the impact of conduct literature in terms of the formation of middling-class feminine subjectivity, and though it is not necessary to rehearse her, and others', arguments here, we should remind ourselves that one crucial piece of Armstrong's argument is that the 'notion of charity was inexorably linked to the female role of household overseer' (93). As Dorice Williams Elliott's recent work has illustrated, middling-class women, for more or less the first time, are constructed by philanthropic discourse; they position themselves as the moral guardians of the citizenry and as a bridge between the domestic and public spheres at the turn into the nineteenth century. This model of femininity was constructed by tying together the early eighteenth-century focus on the rational equality of women's minds with an increasing interest later in the century in their biological connection to motherhood.[24] Together, feminine rationality and sympathy are the basis of social harmony. As is so clearly demonstrated in Wollstonecraft's *A Vindication of the Rights of Woman*, what ties together the generality of mind and the specificity of a woman's body is the power of her virtuous heart: 'make the heart clean, let it expand and feel for all that is human, instead of being narrowed by selfish passions; and let the mind frequently contemplate subjects that exercise understanding [...]' (124). As Wollstonecraft believed, the necessity of constructing feminine subjects was linked with the purpose of making better persons. Politics was indistinguishable from morality, so women as guardians of morality had some stakes in politics (Colley 274). This does not mean, however, that women wielded political power. Women powerfully influenced social relations, but did so under paradoxical conditions. In discourses advocating the education of women, such as we will see in chapter 2, philanthropy—ameliorating humanity—is linked to education because of women's 'special' human understanding and unique social position as (potential) mothers. Women's participation in the general improvement of the society is thus conceived as a 'natural' occurrence, though a public and political one. Understanding this alignment through the paradigm of vocational philanthropy helps us to understand women's contributions to both literature and societal transformation, without making the assertions of 'essentialism' that pervade Wollstonecraft's text and without positing an anachronistic 'feminist' political stance, that is problematic for other writers like Hannah More and Maria Edgeworth.

As far as viewing the purpose or 'value' of the literature women writers write, traditional scholarship has not treated the many texts produced during the period 1780-1820 kindly, and has relegated them to the confines of 'didactic' literature. Recently, however, a variety of scholars have begun to explore the ways in which these texts, particularly novels, operate in response to or in tandem with notions of Romanticism, the construction of femininity, and social reform.[25] One example of this latter category is Christine Krueger's reading of nineteenth-century novels by women writers within the tradition of preaching, which was a means of simultaneously constructing themselves as authors (and authorities) and empowering them to discursively participate in the field of social reform.[26] But even here, the emphasis is laid on the 'religious and political propaganda' of the 1790s (112). I would suggest, however, that in much of women's writing during this period, the dominant ideology produced is recognized as ideology: that is, a discourse that recognizes the gap between the 'real' (the material conditions of existence), and the 'imaginary' (the image which represents the relation of the individual to the real in order to legitimate the imaginary). The function of these discourses is to 'interpellate' subjects into a specific 'imaginary.' This distinct function for this kind of literature does not assume a reader who is already interpellated into 'imaginary' relations, or ideology, that the discourse produces; in other words, the reader does not share the values presented in the text.[27] The function for this kind of discourse is to interpellate individuals through ideology into a *different* 'imaginary' system of relations. This kind of literature aims to produce subjects, and not just ideologies which reinforce already-interpellated subjects. The social whole is thus consolidated by the 'effects' of this kind of ideological intervention, which helps subjects (whether the middling class or laborers) understand themselves and their 'proper' social positioning.

However, in an attempt to benefit the poor, vocational philanthropy benefits the middling-class woman. By producing texts, women writers inscribe not only the position of the poor in society and the position of middling class towards the poor, but also the position of women as the poor's moral guardians. This kind of writing represents a necessary social response to the problems of poverty, but one which positions women on the cusp of the public and private spheres, as I have been arguing, yet always maintains them within the dominant patriarchal system. As Linda Colley states, 'most women acquiesced to separate spheres in the sense that they accepted home and children, together with an amount of subordination to fathers and to husband, were their primary duties, though not the only ones' (262). The anxiety about keeping women within an active, fertile and contented domestic sphere deepened as more and more women appeared active and useful outside of it (Colley 241-242). But these visible public actions by women should not necessarily be equated with 'revolutionary' acts that defied the cultural prescription of a patriarchal system. The 'anxiety' mentioned in Colley's quote above is more or less constricted by appeals by writers, both male and female, to, in More's phrase, the 'profession of philanthropy' (332). Not only was engagement in philanthropy and charitable acts a way to structure appropriate class delineation, it kept women from other, less useful, pursuits, such as reading too much or not reading the right kind of material.[28] Consequently, attention to women's philanthropic purposefulness is enacted on two levels: the first, women writers shifted the focus from 'improper' literature to proper literature for women and for the poor. Thus, for example, when Hannah More describes Lucilla Stanley in her 'didactic' novel, *Coelebs in Search of a Wife*, her audience of women will be taught to reimagine what it means to be a virtuous woman and that, as Dorice Williams Elliot has shown, is invested in charity and benevolence, in modesty and rationality.[29] Women writers, in effect, produce literature that impels social reform, but not necessarily reform that will upset the delicate balance between genders, or classes for that matter, that British society had based itself upon. The 'revolution' in female manners that Mitzi Myers attributes to More, from whichever side of the political spectrum one is on, is a revolution that quells the anxieties that a growing female readership had produced. Hannah More produces literature that is 'proper' for women readers, and does not invest them with the libidinal desires that other, more pernicious, forms of literature like romances do. This is one reason why we no longer read More's novel or if we do we find it lacking in literary prowess; it is no longer prescriptive or descriptive of a modern construction of femininity.

The second enactment of women's philanthropic purposefulness is that in promoting the notion of female benevolence, these women writers produce an image of womanhood that is historically perspicuous to the problems caused by incipient capitalism and its needs. Looked at through the lens of vocational philanthropy, this transitional moment of women's writing is one that not only quells the anxieties of a growing female readership, but quells the anxieties of a growing lower-class readership from each end of the political spectrum from conservative to radical.[30] As the poor could not be trusted to judge what were appropriate reading materials, as More's discursive intervention called the *Cheap Repository* indicates, women writers intervened by producing literature that will transform laborers into subjects who imagine themselves within patriarchal structures as well as quell the unrest set in motion by 'reforms' both political and economic, as I have enumerated at the beginning of this chapter.

We have, thus, come full circle. In their contradictory status, women play a private *and* public role with respect to the valuation of gender and class identities. It is women's special sympathy, constructed upon a level of aesthetic sensibility in the late eighteenth and early nineteenth centuries, which enables the moral improvement of middling-class women, and their ability, in turn, to pass between the public and private spheres, enabling the moral improvement of the poor, the laboring classes and middling classes. Their discourses carve out a specific area in which women 'know best.' These discourses produced within the practice of vocational philanthropy point the way towards notions of progressive individualism, protestant ideology and humanitarian benevolence, signaling a new turn to the primacy of the individual 'subject.' They also signal the dissolution of traditional feudal bonds in favor of oppositions—between genders and classes—

which threaten to break down the bonds upon which eighteenth-century society had been built. It is not a coincidence that these were also the constituent ideologies in the discourses of Mary Wollstonecraft, Hannah More, Maria Edgeworth and Dorothy Wordsworth, as we shall see in the following chapters. Social disunity gives rise to the feminine as a guide to morality while, concurrently, it gives rise to the proliferation of discourses about the distinctions of genders and classes. Yet, these texts purport unity—of genders and classes—as their raison d'être. The intervention of women on a material level and women's writing on an ideological level mediates between classes and genders across political and religious barriers in order to harmonize the different parts of society into a cohesive whole. The paradigm of vocational philanthropy enables us as twentieth-century readers to glimpse how class, gender and discourse intersect during this crucial period of change in literary and social history.

Notes

1 For information on the rate of the population increase, see E.A. Wrigley 'Population Growth: England, 1680-1820,' *New Directions in Economic and Social History*, eds. Anne Digby and Charles Feinstein (London: Macmillan, 1989) 105-116.
2 Deborah Valenze discusses the 'invisibility' of the women's workforce and marginalization of the cottage industries in England during this period. See Valenze, *The First Industrial Woman* (New York: Oxford UP, 1995) 68-84.
3 For a detailed description of these parish systems, see Asa Briggs, *A Social History of England* (London: Weidenfeld & Nicolson, 1983) 172-176.
4 Roger Wells states, 'Many employers evoked a marked reluctance to shoulder the burdens of increased living costs by upping wages, even during the famines; this antagonized industrial relations.' See Wells, *Wretched Faces: Famine in Wartime England, 1793-1801* (New York: St. Martin's, 1988) 332. For additional details about rural reaction by the laboring classes to economic changes, see Wells, 'The Revolt of the South West, 1800-1: A Study in English Popular Protest,' *Crime, Protest and Popular Politics in Southern England, 1740-1850*, eds. John Rule and Roger Wells (London: Hambledon, 1997) 17-51.
5 See Sir Frederic Morton Eden, *The State of the Poor, A History of the Labouring Classes in England, with Parochial Reports*, ed. & abr. A.G.L. Rogers (1797; New York: Benjamin Blom, 1929, reissued 1971).
6 The actual citation from the *Oxford English Dictionary* reads 'love to mankind; practical benevolence towards men in general; the disposition or active effort to promote the happiness and well-being of one's fellow men' (774). The earliest citation noted which refers to this meaning only occurs in 1650.
7 See also Andrew for a useful discussion about what Owen calls 'associated philanthropy' 98-134.
8 Elliott discusses the example of Thomas Guy, a man who made his fortune in the South Sea Bubble, and who founded many charities including Guy's Hospital, *Angel Out of the House*, 13.
9 See Roger Wells, 'The Revolt' 17-51.
10 Linda Colley in *Britons: Forging a Nation, 1707-1837* (New Haven: Yale UP, 1992), states that philanthropy allowed merchants to mingle with people of rank and influence

(93). The consolidation of these two upper classes in the category of the 'privileged,' as I state here, is not just a shorthand term that lumps two distinct social classes together. In terms of philanthropy, these two classes functioned similarly, creating a mutually beneficial economy for themselves. I concur with Colley's assessment that this represents how 'patriotism' among the two classes 'worked together to demand wider citizenship and political change,' supporting her thesis that consolidation of the upper classes and unity between upper and lower classes were necessary to the making of the British nation. Colley concludes that before 1775, the relationship between trade and land 'was widely and correctly believed to be a mutually beneficial one' (100).

11 See Gertrude Himmelfarb, *The Idea of Poverty: England in the Early Industrial Age* (New York: Knopf, 1984) 8. See also Eden's *State of the Poor*, especially the first section in which he reviews seventeenth- and eighteenth-century literature on poverty and the poor laws. The shifting definitions of poverty, the poor, the dependent poor, the pauper, etc., can be readily seen in his survey. Patrick Colquhoun, likewise, makes a distinction between 'indigence' and 'poverty' leading to conclusion about who is 'productive' and who is not; see *A Treatise on Indigence* [...] (London: J. Hatchard, 1806) 7-8. Edmund Burke in *Thoughts and Details on Scarcity* (1795) denies a group called the poor existed, and instead calls them 'labourers,' and only then makes distinctions among them, like Colquhoun, based on their productivity or lack thereof; see *The Works of the Right Honorable Edmund Burke*, 6th ed., vol. 5 (Boston: Little, Brown, 1880) 134, 143-145.

12 See J.R. Poynter, *Society and Pauperism, English Ideas on Poor Relief, 1795-1834* (London: Routledge, 1969) for a more detailed discussion of the Poor Law debate in the eighteenth and early nineteenth centuries.

13 Eden, *State of the Poor* 100-128; Roger Wells also indicates that the government encouraged the curtailing of cereal consumption by laborers through both recommendation and legislation, but refused to endanger the profit-making associated with cereal production, milling, baking or selling. See *Wretched Faces*, 202-218.

14 Nancy Armstrong, *Desire and Domestic Fiction: A Political History of the Novel* (New York: Oxford UP, 1987) 91.

15 See Harvey J. Graff, *The Legacies of Literacy: Continuities and Contradictions in Western Culture and Society* (Bloomington: Indiana UP, 1987) 230-237.

16 There has been so much written about the rise of print culture in the eighteenth century that it is unnecessary for me to detail the rise here. For examples, see Alvin Kernan, *Samuel Johnson and the Impact of Print* (Princeton: Princeton UP, 1987) and Paul Keen, *The Crisis of Literature in the 1790s:Print Culture and the Public Sphere* (New York: Cambridge UP, 1999).

17 Ideologically, charity supports the economic structure it seeks to ameliorate, and thus perpetuates it, thus perpetuating the conditions, and problems, of poverty. Slavoj Zizek discusses the ideological form of the 'negation of the negation': thus, the very form of philanthropy is a criticism of burgeoning capitalism (that which creates philanthropy's conditions of existence), but it in the end, the solution secures it as a self-perpetuating problem. See Zizek, *For They Know Not What They Do: Enjoyment as a Political Factor* (New York: Verso, 1991) 186-187.

18 Keen, *Crisis of Literature*; Clifford Siskin, *The Work of Writing: Literature and Social Change in Britain, 1700-1830* (Baltimore: Johns Hopkins UP, 1998).

19 F.K. Prochaska in *Women and Philanthropy in Nineteenth-century England* (Oxford: Clarendon, 1980), notes that while philanthropy is widely associated with women in the nineteenth century, she is hard-pressed to find evidence of financial and personal

contributions to associated philanthropy in the eighteenth (38). This may be because subscriptions were put in their husbands' or fathers' names.

20 Sarah Scott's *A Description of Millennium Hall* [...], ed. Gary Kelly (1762; Orchard Park, NY: Broadview P, 1995) chronicles the 'associated' philanthropy of the fictional women founders of Millennium Hall.

21 Even in *Tristram Shandy*, Sterne endeavored to 'teach us to love the world and our fellow creature better than we do.' Quoted in James A. Work's introduction to the novel (Indianapolis: Odyssey P, 1940) lxvii.

22 This deluge of discourses would also seem to support Colley's thesis that 'at a time when women were being urged to look, feel, and behave in ways that were unambiguously womanly, many female Britons were in practice becoming more involved in the public sphere [...],' 254. I would add that the making of the British nation is contingent on harmonizing its class and gender disruptions. Women became involved in public activities such as philanthropy and discourse production because they were important ways that 'nationhood' is envisioned and achieved. See also Nancy Armstrong for her discussion of conduct book literature, 59-95 .

23 See Priscilla Wakefield, *Relections: On the Present Conditions of the Female Sex* (1798; New York: Garland, 1974); Hannah More, 'Strictures on a Modern System of Female Education' in *The Complete Works of Hannah More*, vol 1, (1798; New York: Harper and Bros, 1835).

24 Colley notes the 'cult of prolific maternity' in the second half of the eighteenth century, which encouraged women to breed, urged the benefits of maternal breast-feeding, and rescued foundlings, is an attempt to keep women busy and fertile in the domestic sphere, 240-241.

25 See, for examples, Paula R. Feldman and Theresa M. Kelley, eds., *Women Romantic Writers: Voices and Countervoices* (Hanover, NH: UP of New England, 1995); Carol Shiner Wilson and Joel Haefner, eds., *Re-visioning Romanticism: British Women Writers*, 1176-1837 (Philadelphia: U of Pennsylvania P, 1994); Paul Keen, *Crisis of Literature*; Anne K. Mellor, *Mothers of the Nation: Women's Political Writing in England, 1790-1830* (Bloomington: Indiana UP, 2000); Paula R. Backscheider, ed. *Revising Women: Eighteenth-Century 'Women's Fiction' and Social Engagement* (Baltimore: Johns Hopkins UP, 2000).

26 See Christine Krueger, *The Reader's Repentance: Women Preachers, Women Writers, and Nineteenth-Century Social Discourse* (Chicago: U of Chicago P, 1992).

27 For an example of traditional interpretations of 'didactic' texts, see J.M.S. Tompkins, *The Popular Novel in England* (Lincoln: U of Nebraska P, 1961).

28 See Jacqueline Pearson, *Women's Reading in Britain 1750-1835: A Dangerous Recreation* (New York: Cambridge UP 1999).

29 See Dorice Williams Elliott 54-80.

30 Keen discusses this anxiety admirably in *Crisis of Literature* 142-170. I will say, however, that he disconnects his discussions of British anxieties about a lower-class readership from anxieties about a female readership. I am suggesting they are connected in specific ways.

Chapter 2

The Benevolent Woman:
Rereading Mary Wollstonecraft's *A Vindication of the Rights of Woman*

It is time to effect a revolution in female manners[...]restore them their lost dignity—and make them, as a part of the human species, labour by reforming themselves to reform the world.
Mary Wollstonecraft, *A Vindication of the Rights of Woman,* 1792

In the advertisement to *A Vindication of the Rights of Woman*, Mary Wollstonecraft claims that the work was originally conceived as a single volume 'divided into three parts.' However, with 'fresh illustrations occurring' as she wrote, she decided to eventually add a second volume that would become a companion to the first. The first volume would focus on the general argument: women's rational equality with men, which she claimed arose from examining 'a few simple principles.' The second would focus on the particulars derived from the general argument: 'laws relating to women' and their 'peculiar duties.' She promised her readers that the second volume would be published in 'due time' and would 'complete' the sketches 'begun in the first' (Wollstonecraft *VRW* 6-7).[1]

In a footnote to *VRW*'s closing paragraphs, Wollstonecraft reminds her readers again of the forthcoming, but yet unwritten, second volume: 'I had further enlarged on the advantages which might reasonably be expected to result from an improvement in female manners, towards the general reformation of society' (194). But Wollstonecraft never wrote the second volume leaving *VRW*, published in 1792, an incomplete work.

Both the advertisement and the concluding note call attention to an important ideological function of *VRW*'s content and form: the creation of desire for reading and writing more texts. The advertisement creates a space in which more writing could be generated from writing already done; the note draws the readers' attention to the absence of the second volume constructing a desire to read more, and perhaps to write more, on the subject of women. Wollstonecraft's text produces a model of feminine desire that is generative, and that model is particularly important for women writers. On the level of content, it creates an ideological space in which her own text constructs a new version of 'true' femininity by meticulously critiquing other texts by (mostly) male writers. The space produced creates the condition for pre-desire: creating a desire for more and more writing on the subject of women. Pre-desire establishes the conditions for a future model of femininity with 'true' sensibility and proper desires. In this sense, Wollstonecraft presents herself as a critic, demonstrating that she can discriminate between what is true and what is imaginary.

On the level of form, she sets up new conceptual divisions to be modeled by the organization of *VRW*. She must distinguish between the universal elements of virtue ('simple principles') and the particulars of gendered subject formation (duties of parents and education); she must distinguish between what she perceives as the 'natural' capabilities of women and what she labels as the 'artificial' ideal of women illustrated in texts like Rousseau's *Emile* and Dr. Gregory's *A Father's Legacy to his Daughters*. Therefore, the complexity of her argument hinges not so much on its content—the rational education of middling-class women was generally accepted by the late eighteenth-century public—but on its form.[2] Her text thus conceived serves as a starting point for other writing which will have as its ideological purpose the reevaluation of femininity and 'moral virtue,' prescriptions for a new feminine model and its interpellation through parenthood and education. Most importantly, her text will serve as a manifesto for how this new woman can affect societal improvement. Through *VRW*'s rhetoric, a desire for a range of writing on the subject of women is developed, and, with 'fresh illustrations' always occurring, one discourse gives rise to another, critiquing, supporting, and refining ideas.

Wollstonecraft develops a discourse on the feminine and, within the pages of *VRW*, a new model of feminine subjectivity is envisioned. The production of this kind of feminine subjectivity depends on middling-class women's ability to read, understand, discriminate among and negotiate between texts. The developing discourse creates a desire for improvement as women become rational readers and writers of texts, a precursor to the notion of subjects who 'develop' in terms of their psychological state of mind which is not yet constructed and would be historically anachronistic. Instead, the desire for their and others' moral 'improvement' becomes the impetus for the middling-class acts of reading and writing.[3] This is the conjuncture which produces vocational philanthropy. Therefore, the ideological work of *VRW* is twofold: it makes aesthetic and categorical divisions between the universal and the particular, the ideal and the real, and sets the stage for the production of more writing that conceives of women as particular kinds of subjects who will desire improvement and who will, collaterally, desire more reading. These desires—for improvement and for reading—will stimulate not only women to act on proper moral and sympathetic principles, but lead to the progress of 'society in general.' In order for societal improvement to occur, however, Wollstonecraft claims that the improvement of women must precede the improvement of the general society. *VRW*, viewed in the context of *A Vindication of the Rights of Men* and *Letters Written During a Short Residence in Sweden, Norway and Denmark* clearly situates her emerging model of the feminine within a broader philosophical and Jacobin political agenda, with her ostensible goal to ameliorate mankind. Writing is necessary to reenvision both women and the state, the private and the public, because both have been corrupted by 'artificial' discourses that sustain the 'pestiferous purple,' commending the tyranny of the upper class over the middle class and the poor and men over women. *VRW* promises aesthetic and political gratification as a result of its incomplete form, but it also leaves a gap to be filled by other women writing, reading, and improving themselves and society.

Creating a Space for the Truly Feminine

Mary Wollstonecraft's *VRW* has produced a wide range of scholarship. Some of it focuses on its attempt to revise feminine manners and morals according to various paradigms: a masculine model of feminine desire which eventually 'fails'; the inculcation of self-control of both women's and men's desires; or the effort to 'revolutionize' feminine and domestic manners.[4] Others focus on its pre-feminist philosophy or politics: its intersection of 'radical' Jacobin and feminist politics; its function as a philosophical and political treatise aimed at men; or its purpose as a feminist educational treatise.[5] In all these readings, however, her text is viewed as a polemic on how women are falsely represented and, therefore, how they are trapped within the constraints of masculine discourse because the 'feminine' does not have an adequate mode of representation. While scholarship often positions Wollstonecraft and her writing within the debate of women's subjectivity and women's agency, the questions about the formal effect of reading and the function of reading within Wollstonecraft's vision of womanhood have not been addressed.

Wollstonecraft's text attempts to produce a discourse in which a new ideology of the feminine can be generated outside the late eighteenth-century 'system of semiotic discriminations' as one critic puts it.[6] In order to do this, however, Wollstonecraft positions her text within the current semiotic system in order to disrupt the established masculine concepts of beauty and desire, within which femininity is trapped. In this sense, Wollstonecraft uses her text as a piece of 'literary' criticism, rather than as an explicit feminist polemic or Jacobin political tract, so that she can enable a rhetorical space from which a woman can discriminate among texts. It is not just what she proposes, her content, that is so powerful, but how she dislodges other writers' content. Through *VRW*'s intertextual organization, critiques of other writers, a generic mixing of education and political treatises, she produces a 'desire' to read, to discriminate among texts, to be instructed by them (when possible), and to be 'improved' because of them. It also enables a space for women's writing to be produced once reading has become an integral part of women's behavior.

The structure of *VRW* is loosely divided into three parts: first, the statement of the problem: the degradation of women; second, its origins and causes: men's misunderstanding of the virtue of women; third, the possible correctives to this problem: educational programs at both the familial and national level. While *VRW*'s structure is relatively simple, the argument is complicated by its insistence on liberal democracy as a future corrective to women's debased moral condition. Although loosely written as an educational tract, the text is a conflation of various kinds of discourses: an educational tract for women, a republican manifesto, and a treatise on moral philosophy.[7] Its principal argument links the depreciation of women's 'natural' morality with the entrenched patriarchal structures of hereditary property ownership and legal privileges, a generic mixing of the discourses of moral and political economy. It would thus be difficult to separate Wollstonecraft's gender politics from her republicanism in both content and form. The text is informed by Bourgeois Radicalism, stressing the values of consistent moral improvement and equal opportunity—the very things she argues women are excluded from achieving in both *VRW* and *A Vindication of the Rights of Men*. In *VRM*, her reply to Edmund Burke's description of women as 'little, smooth, delicate, fair creatures' in *A Philosophical Enquiry into the Origins of our Ideas of the Sublime and the Beautiful* demonstrates that men and women must be made to understand that 'there is a beauty in virtue, a charm in order' (Wollstonecraft *VRM* 81) and that this change can only occur by liberty: 'Inequality of rank must ever impede the growth of virtue, by vitiating the mind that submits or domineers; that is ever employed to procure nourishment for the body, or amusement for the mind' (Wollstonecraft *VRM* 81).

What impedes women from desiring equality, and achieving true virtue, is the prevalent conceptions of womanhood prescribed in discourses like Burke's. In the first section of *VRW*, Wollstonecraft sets up her target: to expose the fallacy upon which women's education is based—to render women pleasing to men. She then embarks on an analysis of conduct literature which has a lesson for her readers: to distinguish between 'truth' and 'falsity' in discourse. She claims to speak in 'the simple language of truth' and would rather address 'the head than the heart.' Her discourse will have none of the features readers are used to in masculine conduct literature, which is designed to pique sentiment ('the heart') with false language and ideas. Wollstonecraft's sarcasm punctuates her illustration of what male conduct book writers perceive as natural for women:

> [Dr. Gregory] advises [women] to cultivate a fondness for dress, because a fondness for dress, he asserts, is natural to them. I am unable to comprehend what either he or Rousseau mean, when they frequently use this indefinite term. If they told us that in a preexistent state the soul was fond of dress, and brought this inclination with it into a new body, I should listen to them with a half smile, as I often do when I hear a rant about innate elegance [...]. It is not natural; but arises, like false ambition in men, from a love of power. (28)

By turning a 'natural' propensity into an 'indefinite' term, Wollstonecraft dislodges notions that she feels reflect not universal understanding but a particular instance of male dominance. She stresses a recategorization of the 'natural' and 'unnatural,' concluding that women's behavior is due to the 'artificial' definitions of what is 'natural' for women: dissimulation of feelings (28), the art of feigning a 'sickly delicacy' in order to secure affection (29), and withholding one's affection in order to suspend the love of one's husband (30). Masculine desire is thus construed mockingly by Wollstonecraft as love. In this section, Wollstonecraft defines love by what it is not: a transitory passion in which 'chance and sensation take the place of choice and reason' (30). Later on, she will attempt to construct a different definition of love.

Wollstonecraft's aim is to put the masculine definition of 'natural' into question by debunking thematic features of masculine discourse. Her argument about desire turns to the insertion of an abstract entity, Nature. Nature is representative of God, who 'has made all things right; but man has sought him out many inventions to mar the work' (Wollstonecraft 29-30). Nature and women are equated in the passage just as desire and men are equated in the former passage. To prove this, she cites the 'natural' and 'Godlike' qualities that women possess: 'gentleness of manners, forbearance and long-suffering.' However, these qualities have been perverted by the system of discourse created by men, perpetuating imperfection. Women now have 'narrow, uncultivated' minds:

> but what a different aspect it assumes when it is the submissive demeanor of
> dependence, the support of weakness that loves, because it wants protection; and
> is forbearing, because it must silently endure injuries [...]. Abject as this picture
> appears, it is the portrait of an accomplished woman, according to the received
> opinion of female excellence, separated by specious reasoners from human
> excellence. (Wollstonecraft 33)

The 'received opinion' and 'specious reasoners' highlight the artificial and irrational understanding of 'female excellence.' Within the discursive system, male desire is legitimated, legitimizing, in turn, women's 'imperfection': the unnatural is presented as natural. Men pervert women and misjudge their natural, God-given and 'God-like' capacities she assumes exist outside the discourse of man. Even worse, the truly natural woman is unrepresentable: 'what does history disclose but marks of inferiority, and how few women have emancipated themselves from the galling yoke of sovereign man? [...] I have been led to imagine that the few extraordinary women who have rushed in eccentrical directions out of the orbit prescribed to their sex, were male spirits, confined by mistake in female frames' (Wollstonecraft 35). Wollstonecraft's sardonic conclusion is that most women are not able to demonstrate their 'true' natures, and those women who have escaped male desire are 'imaginary' women who are not really women at all, but men in disguise. By turning the perceived concept of 'natural' womanhood into an 'indefinite' term, she can make the claim that the truly 'natural' woman has yet to be represented.

Therefore, delineating what is 'true' and 'false' knowledge, and constructing a new concept of femininity that is uncorrupted by the excesses of man are integral to her project. Because reading is the primary means of disseminating knowledge, changing female understanding and manners—what Wollstonecraft calls the revolution—must start with writing a body of criticism which will expose the perceived wisdom about 'female excellence' as false knowledge and as an imaginary construct of men. This implies that 'real' women exist in a space not yet representable. Wollstonecraft's primary purpose for this treatise is to create a space for other discourses by women and about women: 'Rousseau exerts himself to prove that all was right originally; a crowd of authors that all is now right; and I, that all will be right' (*VRW* 15). The future is a space, as Mary Poovey contends, 'which schools desire into another version of disinterested contemplation' (96). But while Poovey views this as a negative outcome, it can be seen as a positive one. Wollstonecraft's 'disinterested contemplation,' or rather critical distance, questions the discursive systems of understanding, disrupting the late eighteenth century's language of gender differentiation. In Wollstonecraft's causal analysis, virtue must be 'disinterested' in the sense that morality is defined by actions motivated not by one's own interests, but by a concern for others. Moral philosophers, like the Earl of Shaftesbury, based their concept of virtue on this 'disinterested' position.[8] It is also the basis of social sympathy exemplified by Adam Smith's notion of the internal spectator who can imagine not only sympathy for another's situation, but also maintain a critical distance by which to examine his/her own passionate responses to a situation. Both virtue and sympathy, then, naturally exist beyond discursive structures that imprison women. The revolution Wollstonecraft speaks of can only occur if a 'check' on masculine knowledge is accomplished by women who can read 'correctly.' Wollstonecraft positions herself and her text as the 'disinterested' spectator who possesses the correct sensibilities, and who is concerned with the inculcation of a kind of virtue.

Setting herself up as 'disinterested' spectator, who receives pleasure from contemplating the 'public good,' has a rhetorical purpose: to separate her text from what she perceives as affected 'sentimental' discourses that privilege feeling over reason, like Rousseau's *Emile*.[9] This disinterested stance also has one other implication for the future production of discourses on the feminine: Wollstonecraft sets herself up as the mediator between these discourses and the reading public. Presenting herself as unprejudiced by sentiment and thus 'natural,' as opposed to other 'unnatural' women whom she labels the 'Ladies,' she is able to perceive the truth behind the lies. She can therefore 'objectively' argue against the masculine truths of educational treatises and argue for bourgeois political ends. Her argument blends a kind of 'scientific' observation with the moral purpose of a rhetorician. One passage in particular demonstrates this rhetorical move:

> Let me now as from an eminence survey the world stripped of all its false delusive charms. The clear atmosphere enables me to see each object in its true point of view, while my heart is still [...]. I rub my eyes and think, perchance, that I am just awaking from a lively dream [...]. I see the sons and daughters of men pursuing shadows, and anxiously wasting their powers to feed passions which have no

adequate object[...]To see a mortal adorn an object with imaginary charms, and then fall down and worship the idol which he had himself set up—how ridiculous! (Wollstonecraft *VRW* 110-111)

When Wollstonecraft, as a character in her own treatise, descends from the eminence, and mixes with her 'fellow creatures,' she feels 'hurried along the common stream; ambition, love, hope, and fear, exert their wonted power' (112). But, 'the cold hand of circumspection,' or reason, allows her to distance herself from, and satirize, the imaginary trappings of female manners.

Another example of the way she is able to mediate between 'sentimental discourses' and her own is her ironic portrayal of the relative weakness of woman's body in comparison to the strength of the male body. Women's delicacy, their slightness of figure, their coquettish demeanor, their 'dependent' minds all serve to inspire men's passions. In Wollstonecraft's momentary acceptance of Burke's definition of the Beautiful, men are 'flattered into compliance' by women (Burke *Enquiry* 103). This kind of 'unnatural' power that women possess produces and sustains men's desire for them. Her portrayal affects male desire in an unexpected way: that is, women gain control over men because they play on male 'weakness.' The male becomes feminized and sentimental, weak and effeminate.[10] But Wollstonecraft interrupts her own argument by referring the reader to a supplemental note which quotes extensively from Rousseau's educational novel, *Emile*: '[...]Women have most wit, men have most genius; women observe, men reason: from the concurrence of both we derive the clearest light and the most perfect knowledge, which the human mind is, of itself, capable of attaining [...]. The world is the book of women' (*VRW* 39). Inserting a piece taken from Rousseau's text underscores the point of her own: that knowledge derived from masculine reason is inherently 'imperfect.' But by putting it into the context of her argument, its effect is delegitimized; women can read Rousseau, analyze and reason for themselves whether or not his ideas are true. By quoting from another writer's text, Wollstonecraft attempts to demonstrate control over the truth effect of those passages. She gives readers a lesson in how to associate ideas and read properly.

Consequently, she constructs a disinterested feminine position in order to make sense out of others' writings, categorizing them and critiquing them for women, primarily, whom she condescendingly considers incapable of discerning the difference between sense and sensibility (*VRW* 183). This, again, is a strategic rhetorical move: as a critic she is able to reiterate her point about checking the knowledge contained in other discourses:

the best method, I believe, that can be adopted to correct a fondness for novels is to ridicule them: not indiscriminately, for then it would have little effect; but, if a judicious person, with some turn for humour, would read several to a young girl, and point out both by tones, and apt comparisons with pathetic incidents and heroic characters in history, how foolishly and ridiculously they caricatured human nature, just opinions might be substituted instead of romantic sentiments. (Wollstonecraft *VRW* 185)

Regretfully, though, 'judicious' women are few and cannot readily perform this particular duty for younger women. The majority of women and 'particularly ladies of fashion' cannot be trusted to separate the 'truth' in discourse from the artifice of novels and other books. Because of their education, women are still susceptible to being duped into accepting the feminine ideals portrayed in these books. Wollstonecraft and her text must stand in for that judicious mentor. As an author, Wollstonecraft constructs herself as 'the judicious person'—an intermediary—who will critically read books for women, substituting 'just opinions' for 'romantic sentiments.' Her text will demonstrate just how that reading should be done. With femininity stripped of romantic illusion, the real femininity—or rather, Wollstonecraft's emerging vision of femininity—must be 'taught' to women. This is the first step towards constructing a space for women's reading and writing practices: to teach women their true nature.

The above passage also elaborates on the relationship between books, thinking and behavior. Because false notions about feminine beauty and delicacy are encouraged by a patriarchal discursive system, these notions smother women's 'natural' mental capacities for rational thought. Their impressions of the world are reinforced by their 'association of ideas, which everything conspires to twist into all their habits of thinking, or to speak with more precision, of feeling' (Wollstonecraft *VRW* 117). Contemporary books, written for the instruction of women, are merely artful displays of male desire, inculcating ideas that make women desirable to men, and giving, in Wollstonecraft's words, 'a sexual character to the mind' (117). Improvement of women's minds is unrealistic unless women learn to critique fictional discourses themselves, as she does in the second section of *VRW*, and, just as importantly, to create a new set of discourses which inculcate reason and a new order of 'taste' as well as a new model of femininity.[11] Wollstonecraft herself had already undertaken this task in her 1789 anthology *The Female Reader*. In this reader, aimed at young women readers, Wollstonecraft included various excerpts from contemporary and biblical sources, categorizing them into sections aimed at inculcating reason, sensibility and benevolence—the central principles on which a femininity should be based. She includes, for instance, excerpts from Sarah Trimmer's *The Oeconomy of Charity* under 'Didactic and Moral Pieces,' and 'Descriptive Pieces' by Hume, Cowper, and Goldsmith. Her aim was to 'imprint useful lessons on the mind, and cultivate the taste at the same time' (Wollstonecraft *FR* 55), with the acquisition of virtue as the primary goal of reading this material: 'As we are created accountable creatures, we must run the race ourselves, and by our own exertions acquire virtue: the utmost our friends can do is to point out the right road, and clear away some of the loose rubbish which might at first retard our progress' (Wollstonecraft *FR* 60).

While *The Female Reader* presents material that Wollstonecraft felt would inculcate the proper moral sentiments, *VRW* takes a different tack to clearing away the 'rubbish.' In an effort to control the effect of discourses she sees as pernicious, she intersperses her comments with quotations from the authors so that she can do for her readers what the older woman, described in the above passage, does for a 'young girl.' Her critique of Rousseau, for example, cites long passages from *Emile*, stopping only occasionally to satirically comment on them: 'Rousseau is not the only man who has indirectly said that merely the person of a young woman, without any mind, unless animal spirits come under that description, is very pleasing' (Wollstonecraft *VRW* 81). Similarly, she quotes Fordyce, then retaliates with her own rhetoric: 'Idle empty words! What can such delusive flattery lead to, but vanity and folly [...]. In sermons or novels, however, voluptuousness is always true to its text' (Wollstonecraft 95). Even women writers on the subject of education, like Hester Thrale Piozzi and Madame Genlis, are not exempt from Wollstonecraft's criticism. They too boast of the 'prerogative of man—the prerogative that may emphatically be called the iron sceptre of tyranny' (Wollstonecraft 101). Thus, she claims that these women adopt 'masculine sentiments' which foster the womanly art of pleasing because they are incapable of thinking (Wollstonecraft 103). Wollstonecraft rails against the artifice of these upper-class writers saying, 'I should not let a young person read her works, unless I would afterwards converse on the subjects, and point out the contradictions' (105).[12] Of all the authors she mentions in this chapter, she recommends Mrs. Hester Chapone and Mrs. Catherine Macaulay to her readers, because their educational programs for women coincide with her own (Wollstonecraft *VRW* 106). And it is important that she does not quote from them at all; rather, she encourages readers, again in her footnotes, to seek out these books and read them on their own. They are deemed 'truthful' and therefore do not need mediation between text and reader.

While quoting and commenting on these texts, she continually draws the reader's attention to one point: these texts primarily focus on the female body and the sensations it is supposed to produce in men. The existing ideas of feminine beauty and education are entrenched in the artifice of language and the imagination inspired by masculine discourses. For Wollstonecraft, social practice conforms to the understanding produced in discourse. Therefore, a different understanding of the feminine needs to be produced: one that will situate understanding (the mind) in relation to the gendered body. This is what Wollstonecraft calls the real woman who exists outside discourse. *VRW* is an attempt to produce that model from within the gaps of masculine discourse. Wollstonecraft, the writer, will:

> aim at being useful, and sincerity will render me unaffected; for, wishing rather to persuade by the force of my arguments, than dazzle by the elegance of my language, I shall not waste my time in rounding periods or in fabricating the turgid bombast of artificial feelings [...]. These pretty superlatives, dropping glibly from the tongue, vitiate the taste, and create a kind of sickly delicacy that turns away from simple unadorned truth [...]. (*VRW* 10)

Interestingly, Wollstonecraft sets herself up as the critic as well as the 'unpresentable' female in these passages. While most other women are passively duped into believing men's illusions, she demonstrates her ability to discern between the unnatural 'masculine' ideas about femininity and women's 'true' natures because of the reading and writing she does. Set up early on, this point of view in *VRW* is of one woman who has escaped 'the orbit prescribed to' her sex, but who is not a male spirit; rather, she is a woman representing herself, demonstrating her rational abilities in order to disrupt the imaginary gender relations secured by male desire. But because she is a 'natural' anomaly, God is her only recourse to prove that the perceived 'nature of women' is really unnatural: 'thanks to that Being who impressed [utopian dreams] on my soul, and gave me sufficient strength of mind to dare to exert my own reason, till becoming dependent only on him for the support of my virtue, I view, with indignation, the mistaken notions that enslave my sex' (Wollstonecraft *VRW* 37). God signifies the 'true' universal with which she, as a writer and critic, and her discourse are coextensive. Her argument about the system of discourse turns back to this abstract concept of God as 'the perfection of man' with herself and her gender as its representation. Her unpinning of the false but accepted concept of femininity found in male discourses and played out in gender relations is an attempt to legitimize a different 'truth'; one not prescribed in the 'artificial' desires of imperfect man, but one prescribed by women with the goal of the 'perfection of man' as its utopian dream. Wollstonecraft's feminist rhetoric is coextensive with the goals of philanthropy, and is part of the material practice of reading and writing that will enable those utopian dreams to become reality in the future.

If, for Wollstonecraft, 'it is time to effect a revolution in female manners [...] restore them their lost dignity—and make them, as a part of the human species, labour by reforming themselves to reform the world' (*VRW* 45), then that revolution is one that will enable gradual subjective change and lead to the progress of humankind by a kind of recursive exercising of textual power: 'till women are more rationally educated, the progress of human virtue and improvement in knowledge must receive continual checks' (Wollstonecraft *VRW* 40). Therefore, Wollstonecraft's call to arms, so to speak, is actually a call to arm women with texts: her solution to improve 'impeded' women and the nation, through reading, is an ideological endeavor. A revolution will be performed by women, like Wollstonecraft, who will rationally read discourses, as she does in *VRW*. Wollstonecraft uses *VRW*, an educational treatise, as the starting point of this revolutionary process.[13] As she states, it is important for women to do the work of 'reforming themselves' in order to aid the progress of knowledge and reformation of society that has been stunted and corrupted by men and their desire for sexual dominance over women. By making this connection, however, her text provides a justification for women to traverse the private into the public sphere.

Traversing the Public and the Private Spheres

In addition to questioning the 'truth' of educational literature, Wollstonecraft questions a set of political 'truths,' which had not been explicitly linked to the education of women. Women's faulted and corrupted power over men is akin to the power monarchs and their regents possess over the 'middling' classes and the poor. Women are figures for the corrupted monarchy:

> Women, as well as despots, have now, perhaps, more power than they would have if the world, divided and subdivided into kingdoms and families, were governed by laws deduced from the exercise of reason; but in obtaining it, to carry on the comparison, their character is degraded, and the licentiousness spread through the whole aggregate of society. (Wollstonecraft *VRW* 40)[14]

The interweaving of these seemingly disparate arguments—one on true femininity and the other on aristocratic privilege—suggests a connection between gender and the body politic. The mixture of educational/conduct literature with a republican political manifesto emphasizes this connection. The mixing of these two genres punctuates her points about the horrors of the sexuality of women (because they have more power than men) and the horrors of unmerited rank and privilege (primarily the upper classes over the middling), but it also creates an implicit link to public discourses of moral philosophy. When she discusses the position of men in society, she uses terms connoting 'property' and 'power': 'Birth, riches, and every extrinsic advantage that exalt a man above his fellows, without any mental exertion, sink him in reality below them' (Wollstonecraft *VRW* 45). Man (specifically the upper class) has power because of 'extrinsic advantage' rather than intrinsic merit. His power is sustained by a 'desire of present enjoyment and narrowness of understanding' (Wollstonecraft *VRW* 45). Women, on the other hand, are not just unwitting victims of men and monarchy in the hereditary system of property rights and privilege, but are active participants:

> Women it is true, obtaining power by unjust means, by practising or fostering vice, evidently lose the rank which reason would assign them, and they become either abject slaves or capricious tyrants. They lose all simplicity, all dignity of mind, in acquiring power, and act as men are observed to act when they have been exalted by the same means. (Wollstonecraft *VRW* 45)

For Wollstonecraft, the political rhetoric of women as 'slaves' or 'tyrants' is more than metaphorical; it is imprinted as a political assumption throughout *VRW*. Coming on the heels of her *A Vindication of the Rights of Men* (1790), the two *Vindications* can be seen as two parts to a whole philosophy that is informed by the notion of what Wollstonecraft's mentor, Dr. Richard Price, called 'universal benevolence.' While Wollstonecraft mentions and defends the principles of Dr. Price, universal benevolence seems to reverberate throughout Wollstonecraft's work.[15] Price's sermon 'A Discourse on the Love of Our Country,' which in part provoked Edmund Burke's *Reflections on the Revolution in France*, specifies that universal benevolence is the principle from which love of country springs: 'Nothing can be more friendly to the general rights of mankind; and were [benevolence] duly regarded and practiced every man would consider every other man as his brother [...]' (Price 358). To reach this goal, Price outlines three basic components that must be present: truth, virtue and liberty. Truth must be cultivated in order to 'enlighten' and 'elevate' mankind by instruction (Price 360); virtue must be cultivated in order to 'discourage vice in all its forms' which will effect a 'reformation in manners and virtuous practice' (Price 361); liberty must be cultivated so that an 'enlightened and virtuous country' will result in a 'free country' (363). Written to celebrate the anniversary of England's Glorious Revolution, the sermon claims that revolution was an 'imperfect' one which must be continued until equal constitutional representation is achieved (368). If the three principles of truth, virtue and liberty can be achieved, then universal benevolence will be the result. Wollstonecraft's emphasis on these principles in both *VRM* and *VRW* are informed by the general principles set forth by her mentor.

    VRM, however, focuses on class relations, rather than *VRW*'s focus on gender relations, and in doing so emphasizes men's political and economic practices rather than the more abstract issues of women's subjectivity and education. For Wollstonecraft, corrupt political practice, or rather the entrenched privileges of the aristocracy and upper gentry, is the cause of England's, and Europe's, 'imperfection': 'The civilization which has taken place in Europe has been very partial, and, like every custom that an arbitrary point of honour has established, refines manner at the expense of morals...And what has stopped its progress?—hereditary property—hereditary honours' (*VRM* 39). This statement is echoed in her *Letters Written During a Short Residence in Sweden, Norway and Denmark*: 'the chief use of property be power, in the shape of the respect it procures' leaving her to conclude that the 'adoration of property is the root of all evil' (Wollstonecraft *Letters* 325). In this letter, however, she is not referring to the aristocracy, but to the 'commercial frauds' of Norwegians' and Hamburg's 'mushroom fortunes' which come from war profiteering. Tasteless greed is not guided by principles of truth, virtue or liberty; liberty can exist where truth and virtue do not. Thus, Wollstonecraft observes that when a 'man ceases to love humanity, and then individuals, as he advances in the chase after wealth; as one clashes with his interest, the other with his pleasures: to business, as it is termed, every thing must give way; nay, is sacrificed; and all the endearing charities of citizen, husband, father, brother, become empty names' (Wollstonecraft *Letters* 342). Many men, if not most, have lost or perhaps vanquished the guiding principles of truth and virtue, and therefore have not achieved true liberty, but have 'sacrificed' their familial and civil duties to the goals of wealth and luxury.

    The poor are the figures for the oppressed in *VRM* for whom Wollstonecraft demonstrates great sympathy throughout the treatise; for her, the poor are a natural fact of society, but this does not mean they do not have to possess the fundamental values of truth, virtue and liberty. Just as the upper classes are corrupted by their 'immoral nature,' so too are the poor. She views them as 'tyrants,' like the artificial women in *VRW*, because they have used cunning to gain some measure of power over the privileged:

> If the poor are in distress, they [the rich] will make some benevolent exertions to assist them; they will confer obligations, but not do justice. Benevolence is a very amiable specious quality;[...]The poor consider the rich as their lawful prey; but we ought not too severely to animadvert on their ingratitude. When they receive an alms they are commonly grateful at the moment; but old habits quickly return, and cunning has ever been a substitute for force. (Wollstonecraft *VRM* 88)

The rich are no better. The wealthy's desire to correct this injustice is the consequence of short-sighted benevolence, as opposed to Price's concept of universal benevolence: 'Because the sight of distress, or an affecting narrative, made its blood flow with more velocity, and the heart, literally speaking, beat with sympathetic emotion. We ought to beware of confounding mechanical instinctive sensations with emotions that reason deepens, and justly terms the feelings of humanity' (*VRM* 89). Like Hannah More, Wollstonecraft equates commonplace charity with sentimentality—being moved by the tale or sight of poverty—as an instinctive reaction to distress. True benevolence and philanthropy, however, is 'not a condescending distribution of alms, but an intercourse of good offices and mutual benefits, founded on respect for justice and humanity' (*VRM* 39). Wollstonecraft is quite critical of charitable practices in both *VRM* and *Letters* because she thinks that virtue is acquired through the practice of reason, not an innate instinct as Burke believes. The practice of charity does not train reason and thus the poor remain ignorant, corrupted with sensual pleasures, exercising vice that 'degrade[s] humanity' (Wollstonecraft *VRM* 45). Charity, in the sense of giving money, degrades both the privileged's and the poor's sensibilities:

> I have always been an enemy to what is termed charity, because timid bigots endeavoring thus to cover their sins, do violence to justice, till, acting the demi-god, they forget that they are men. And there are others [...] whose benevolence is merely tyranny in disguise: they assist the most worthless, because the most servile, and term them helpless only in proportion to their fawning. (Wollstonecraft *Letters* 337).

Wollstonecraft's is not an uncommon criticism of charity: the same criticism had been articulated by political economists such as Patrick Colquhoun and Frederick Eden. She does offer a substitute for common forms of charity with something much more useful: enlightenment in the guise of the paternal hand leading the poor towards improvement. This is Wollstonecraft's vision of societal benevolence that would lead England to truth, virtue and liberty: 'Instead of the poor being subject to the griping hand of an avaricious steward, they would be watched over with fatherly solicitude, by the man whose duty and pleasure it was to guard their happiness' (*VRM* 93). Wollstonecraft's criticism of charitable endeavors hinges on rewards unearned by hard work, virtuous thought or moral action. It is a system that maintains corruption, and maintains class stratification in such a way as to stifle 'progress.'[16] As Wollstonecraft claims: 'It is not by squandering alms that the poor can be relieved, or improved—it is the fostering sun of kindness, the wisdom that finds them employments calculated to give them habits of virtue, that meliorates their condition. Love is only the fruit of love' (*VRM* 93). Throughout the treatise, Wollstonecraft shrewdly argues for justice and liberty that the 'rights of man' will offer England, and in her visionary turn toward the end, 'almost imagines' the possibilities of Price's 'universal benevolence.' Like the unrepresentable women in *VRW*, this vision of society is not yet describable. Or, perhaps Wollstonecraft's revisioning of societal relations must come after her revisioning of womanhood, her 'utopian' dream.

If the wrongs of women can be corrected, women's moral virtue will enable benevolence to naturally grow from their sympathetic hearts. However, not all women can foster sympathy and improvement. Middle-class women, rather than the poor or the upper-class women, are the ones to accomplish this because they are the most 'natural' (*VRW* 9). This statement has much political significance in the context of the earlier discussion of 'natural' and 'imaginary' woman and in the context of the rich and poor. She positions the 'middling class' in opposition to the upper classes particularly:

> perhaps the seeds of false-refinement, immorality, and vanity, have ever been shed by the great. Weak, artificial beings, raised above the common wants and affections of their race, in a premature unnatural manner, undermine the very foundation of virtue, and spread corruption through the whole mass of society! (Wollstonecraft *VRW* 9)

The language here, 'false-refinement,' 'artificial beings,' 'premature and unnatural,' signifies the Jacobin notion that the foundation England was built upon is weakening. Because of its system of hereditary wealth and privilege, discourses invested in this system display the ability to 'make us feel, whilst we are dreaming that we reason, erroneous conclusions are left in the mind' (Wollstonecraft 91). According to Wollstonecraft, the power structure of the state, supported by this kind of male discourse, is irrationally subjected to 'feeling,' misusing reason as a trick to justify its corrupt power.

In a strikingly class-conscious contrast of the middling classes to the upper and lower classes (unlike *VRM*, she rarely mentions the latter in *VRW*), Wollstonecraft gives her benevolent vision of the middling-class family who is the hope of mankind's salvation:

> Whilst my benevolence has been gratified by contemplating this artless picture, I have thought that a couple of this description, equally necessary and independent of each other [...] possessed all that life could give.—Raised sufficiently above

abject poverty [...] and having sufficient [means] to prevent their attending to a frigid system of economy, which narrows both heart and mind [...]. I know not what is wanted to render this the happiest as well as the most respectable situation in the world, but a taste for literature [...] and some superfluous money to give to the needy and to buy books. (emphasis mine, *VRW* 143)

The middling classes are 'artless': they have just enough money to be able to afford the little luxuries—giving to the poor and buying books. The implication of these little luxuries, as opposed to the conspicuous consumption of the upper classes and the 'abject poverty' of the lower classes which 'narrows both the heart and mind,' is that these acts (giving to the poor and all classes buying books, which are syntactically equated in their importance) ameliorate the middling classes and, in turn, the society as a whole. Thus, the upper classes, characterized as despots, and the middling classes, characterized by their interest in the 'progress of civilization' are, from the very beginning of Wollstonecraft's text, thrown into struggle because of historical necessity:

> Thus, as wars, agriculture, commerce, and literature, expand the mind, despots are compelled, to make covert corruption hold fast the power which was formerly snatched by open force. And this baneful lurking of gangrene is most quickly spread by luxury and superstition, the sure dregs of ambition. The indolent puppet of a court first becomes a luxurious monster, or fastidious sensualist, and then makes the contagion which his unnatural state spread, the instrument of his tyranny. (Wollstonecraft *VRW* 18)

The upper classes merely want to maintain their power, while the middling classes want to advance into a new age. Wollstonecraft's note to this passage points out that she believed society was at an historical threshold: through the spread of reason, 'arbitrary power' could be overthrown. The production of discourse was one of the ways in which 'covert' corruption of the state is spread and sustained, holding back what she calls the 'perfection' of man and the coming of a new historical epoch. The cause of women's education, and women's production of new discourses, is part of the 'progress of knowledge and virtue' enabling the advancement of English (and European) civilization. In other words, these distinctions between classes are based in part on how discursive power will be employed—who controls what is written and how it is read. The separation between classes is defined by the ability to use discourse (writing and reading it) to lead to this 'progress' of civilization, as *VRW* demonstrates. For Wollstonecraft that control over discourse, over literacy, is clearly a middling-class prerogative. Literacy as a social practice facilitates the transformation of the social structure as well as developing a middling-class reading culture as central to English culture.[17] Literacy is linked to the progress of mankind under the guise of universal benevolence; but it is equally about locating a new form of power that proves to be transformative in the sense that the ideologies of improvement and progress become the central foci of Wollstonecraft's, and others', discourses. Whether 'improvement' and 'progress' are ultimately achieved through discursive practices is another question that is left to be resolved at a future moment.

If, as Wollstonecraft claims, her favorite subject is the 'improvement of the world' (*Letters* 338), then the two *Vindications* provide a trajectory for that improvement through the rational cultivation of virtue in all parts of society: men and women, the upper and middling classes and the poor. However, it is by the universal benevolence of middle-class women, who traverse the private and public domains of discourse as the two *Vindications* suggest, that improvement will occur. What is produced by the end of *VRW* is a model of femininity that is capable of desiring improvement for herself and for society.

Producing the Benevolent Woman

Keeping her attention focused on reason and knowledge as the foundation of virtue, Wollstonecraft describes and then critiques the common eighteenth-century construction of womanhood because it inhibits the progression of knowledge:

> Ignorance is a frail base for virtue! Yet, that is the condition for which woman was organized, has been insisted upon by the writers who have most vehemently argued in favour of the superiority of man; a superiority not in degree, but essence; though, to soften the argument, they have laboured to prove, with chivalrous generosity, that the sexes ought not to be compared; man was made to reason, woman to feel: and that together, flesh and spirit, they make the most perfect whole, by blending happily reason and sensibility into one character. (*VRW* 63)

Again, women have been produced by 'false' discourses, enabling them to only 'produce sensation' (Wollstonecraft 60). The sensation produced is desire in the spectator, assumed to be male. Male superiority is garnered by absolute 'essence' of being, and not one gained by 'degree' of superiority; that is, merit. *VRW* demonstrates how to critique male notions of femininity by critiquing discourses on women's education; if and when feminine understanding is employed, then a whole woman—the sum of body and mind—would emerge. This woman would not be a 'weak being who must be restrained by arbitrary means, and be subjected to continual conflicts; but give [her] activity of mind a wider range, and nobler passions and motives will govern their appetites and sentiments' (Wollstonecraft *VRW* 82). The sum of body and mind leads women to become independent and self-disciplining subjects who would not then be dependent on the 'arbitrary means' of men (i.e. their discourses) or dependent on their sensory perceptions (i.e. male desire).[18]

Wollstonecraft's text denies women as 'sexual' beings in order to produce a desire for women that is not based solely on the feminine body. It is not necessarily a denial of the 'sexuality' of women, but a more 'useful' transformation of it. Sexuality, later on in her text, is constructed as the 'maternal' rather than the 'beautiful' (as Burke would define it) constructed by men. The 'maternal,' of course, connotes another 'productive' model of desire. The personal traits of 'modesty, temperance, and self-denial' which are the 'sober offspring of reason' are the starting point for her revolution in female manners (*VRW* 82). The purpose of her text is to present this model as desirable. Consequently, this divorce of the 'sexual'—the component tied to male gratification—from the feminine body, and the transcendent quality of the mind of woman over the materiality of her body, results in an introduction to a model of womanhood guided by internal restraints to serve a 'nobler purpose': productive as readers, writers, mothers, and citizens, each knotting private notions of moral improvement with public duties in civil society.[19]

But for this model to be perceived as 'desirable,' Wollstonecraft must persuade men and women, as Claudia Johnson has argued, that 'modest and rational woman is more, not less enjoyable to the senses' (45). This is the purpose of the third section of *VRW*: it is an act of mixing features and concepts to provide a discursive space for women's agency to write. This is what Wollstonecraft refers to as her 'utopian dreams' (*VRW* 36). But it is less a dream than an attempt to produce a new aesthetic model of the 'beautiful' to rival Burke's category which was widely invoked in the ideas and language of eighteenth-century conduct literature and the particular discourses Wollstonecraft chose to interpret in her text.[20] The third section, while less programmatic than contemporary critics would like, is an attempt to aestheticize feminine moral virtue, whereby sympathy can occur. Underpinning sympathy is the production of other discourses which will enable the amelioration of mankind—texts whose purpose is philanthropic.

If sexuality can be disengaged from the body, then the 'beautiful' and the production of desire have a different basis—to improve the mind by fostering truth. Wollstonecraft calls this basis the 'sacred offspring of sensibility and reason'— modesty, or what Price would call virtue. To illustrate the separation of the body from sexuality, Wollstonecraft separates modesty from chastity: 'for I doubt whether chastity will produce modesty, though it may propriety of conduct' (*VRW* 124). Virtue is then ascribed to modesty and modesty ascribed to beauty: 'It may be thought that I lay too great a stress on personal reserve; but it is ever the handmaid of modesty. So were I to name the graces that ought to adorn beauty, I should instantly exclaim, cleanliness, neatness, and personal reserve' (Wollstonecraft 128). Thus, the consequence of this is that 'the reserve I mean, has nothing sexual in it and that I think it equally necessary in both sexes' (Wollstonecraft 128). Virtue is both sexless and genderless.

But, if this is true, how is Wollstonecraft to posit a concept of feminine moral virtue? Morality has to be reinscribed in another domain of womanhood, which is associated with the body, but not reducible to it—the maternal: 'the grand duty annexed to the female character by nature' (Wollstonecraft 151). Morality and affection are domestically based in, though not limited to, the home. In a 'sentimental' evocation of domestic novels, Wollstonecraft evokes the reader's admiration of a mother with her children:

> I have [...] viewed with pleasure a woman nursing her children, and discharging the duties of her station with, perhaps, merely a servant maid to take off her hands the servile part of the household business. I have seen her prepare herself and children, with only the luxury of cleanliness, to receive her husband, who returning weary home in the evening found smiling babes and a clean hearth. My heart has loitered in the midst of the group, and has even throbbed with sympathetic emotion, when the scraping of the well known foot has raised a pleasing tumult. (142-143)

The mother attending to her babes should inspire affection in the husband and sentiment in the reader's mind.[21] The portrayal positions the mother at the center of the social system, the primary one to whom the father always returns. The continual pleasures of hearth and home, rather than immediate sexual gratification or a 'deferral and variety' of pleasures, holds the family together. Women produce babies and affection, becoming primary to this social system based on 'sympathetic emotion' instead of social restraint.[22] In Wollstonecraft's maternal image, however, women from different classes remain distinct, but they are 'harmonized' within the home. This middling-class woman is distinct from the working-class 'servant maid' who maintains the daily chores of domestic life, allowing the 'mother' to perform her most important task of nurturing and loving her children. In place of male educational discourses which produce images of women consumers and women as objects to be consumed, Wollstonecraft's educational project seeks to produce a model of women's productive capacities, by deploying her discourse, producing images of affective and sympathetic motherhood.

She achieves this model by combining 'sentiment' with political rhetoric, rewriting femininity as contingent upon 'affection'—the heart. This kind of femininity is 'natural.' The heart has the capacity to 'expand and feel for all that is human, instead of being narrowed by selfish passions' (Wollstonecraft 124). But that capacity can only be reached if the heart is rationally directed by the mind, which should 'frequently contemplate subjects that exercise the understanding without heating the imagination.' Thus, the concept of love, or 'natural affection,' is no longer 'imaginary' but practical, dedicated to the 'humane plans of usefulness' (Wollstonecraft 123) rather than to the 'exclusive affections' (Wollstonecraft 188) of romantic love of men and/or a mother's excessive love of her children. As a consequence of these exclusive affections, women's natural duties to her family and to society had been undermined. Exclusive affections flatter men and make them tyrants, and instruct children to reproduce the already corrupted gendered relations. 'True happiness' is then taken away from these weak mothers, spoiled children and husbands. Wollstonecraft claims that until a woman learns to regulate her heart's passion, society's children will suffer from vain indulgence reproducing their mothers' and fathers' weaknesses. Motherhood, again, is portrayed as a productive act, providing, as Mitzi Myers states, 'a persuasive rational for better education, as well as for civil existence and work' ('Reform' 210).

Wollstonecraft's portrait of 'true beauty,' then, reunites the parts of womanhood she painstakingly separated early on in her treatise: the mind, the body and the heart. Wollstonecraft calls this the 'beauty of moral loveliness' (149), the transcendent aspect of femininity. True and virtuous femininity as specified here will lead to the kind of universal benevolence that informs Wollstonecraft's writing. The specific effect produced by this reunited whole is unlimited sympathetic understanding and affection between women and men, and the cord of love which binds them together is their children: 'a child then gently twists the relaxing cord, and a mutual care produces a new mutual sympathy' (Wollstonecraft 152). Wollstonecraft's definition of 'natural affection' is also women's special ability to bind people together. Women's natural 'vocation' is to produce this sympathetic understanding and affection among people.

I previously stated that Wollstonecraft's 'beauty of moral loveliness' is based upon, but not limited to, the domestic. While she promotes the duty of motherhood to heroic proportions, she also makes it clear that the domestic is political and that this private duty has a public dimension for 'every family might also be called a state.' This is the liberty that women achieve in becoming virtuous beings. As we have previously seen, this allusion to the social and political structure is not merely an affective analogy. It is a transversive (perhaps even transgressive) theme in *VRW*. From the very beginning of the treatise, Wollstonecraft claimed that if the private virtues of the citizenry are corrupt— based on improper models of desire—then the whole body politic will be corrupt. Since this kind of 'beautiful' woman neglects her primary responsibility— childrearing—then she cannot, and should not, affect public matters, morals or policy. But Wollstonecraft's model of 'virtuous beauty' emphasizes production; women produce subjects, not just physically, but through their ability to write and 'teach' people how to be 'good' readers as she demonstrates through the form of *VRW*. Women produce 'good' citizens both physically and ideologically; women have a stake in guiding private morality as well as a stake in guiding public morality. Wollstonecraft's model of womanhood is both private and public, domestic and political, ameliorating the personal for the benefit of the public.

Thus, Wollstonecraft's vocation for women has, at its basis, a philanthropic function, which she hopes her treatise will construct. As she states in the address to M. Talleyrand-Perigord:

> If children are to be educated to understand the true principle of patriotism, their mother must be a patriot; and the love of mankind, from which an orderly train of virtues spring, can be produced by considering the moral and civil interest of mankind; but the education and situation of woman, at present, shuts her out from such investigations. (*VRW* 4)

The 'moral and civic interest of mankind' precedes and follows from virtue. Maternal duty precedes and follows from 'understanding the true principle of patriotism.' Thus, private, maternal love and the public 'love of mankind' are inseparable and, more importantly, 'naturally' linked like the cord that extends from mother to child. But just as she invokes the abstract principles from which her 'natural affection' emanates, she also brings the reader back to the historical predicament of the 'present' condition, or rather, the constructed subjectivity of women through masculine educational discourse. To enable 'improvement' of mankind, to enable 'love' of mankind, women must be able to improve themselves; only then will the natural benevolence of femininity enable true philanthropy to 'expand and feel for all that is human' (124).

Vocational Philanthropy and the Discourse of Improvement

Wollstonecraft sees herself as a visionary, exposing the historical problem of the position of women in a changing social and economic structure. One important reason this new aesthetic model could not emerge until the late eighteenth century, and why its fruition is 'put off' in her discourse until a future epoch, is because her new model of womanhood—the production of a new feminine ideology—is firmly anchored in bourgeois notions of rational equality of human minds, 'disinterested' virtue, and the values of merit and ceaseless improvement. These bourgeois notions were just then beginning to discursively contest the authority of older aristocratic privileges. Again, Wollstonecraft's Jacobin rhetoric is fused to her gender politics and therefore inextricable from it in both language and practice: 'But for this epoch we must wait—wait, perhaps, till kings and nobles, enlightened by reason, and, preferring the real dignity of man to childish state, throw off their gaudy hereditary trappings: and if then women do not resign the arbitrary power of beauty—they will prove that they have less mind than man' (Wollstonecraft *VRW* 22). Thus, Elissa S. Guralnick asserts that 'oppressed womankind serves in the *Rights of Woman* not merely as a figure for oppressed and impoverished mankind, but as a figure for all, high as well as low, who are implicated in social and political contracts which condone inequality of rank, wealth, and privilege' (159). While I agree with Guralnick that Wollstonecraft positions her 'feminism' in a broader political contestation, she does it from a perspective that is not egalitarian, but very class conscious. The equality of rational minds is taken to be a 'natural' and 'simple' principle in *VRW*, but the idea of equality is radically bourgeois at this point in history, and it is unclear how far 'equality' extends in her discourses. Thus, while Wollstonecraft speaks of, and primarily addresses, the middling classes as the most 'natural,' the privileged classes are her target of indignation because they are 'sentimental,' as in *VRM*, and man is her symptom of its corruption because he is effeminate, as in *VRW*.[23] Alternatively, the poor are corrupted and cunning, but deserve more sympathy because of the oppressive conditions they endure.

Wollstonecraft participates in producing a new system of aesthetic discriminations through new formulations of womanhood in *VRW*. For example, when Wollstonecraft discusses 'The Prevailing Opinion of Sexual Character' she mentions, with the decorum of a negative statement which proves the positive, a new conception of gender founded not on superiority in 'essence' but on equality posited, paradoxically as it may seem, in terms of 'degrees and kinds':

> should experience prove that [women] cannot attain the same degree of strength of mind, perseverance, and fortitude, let their virtues be the same in kind, though they may vainly struggle for the same degree; and the superiority of man will be equally clear, if not clearer; and truth, as it is a simple principle, which admits of no modification, would be common to both. Nay, the order of society as it is at present regulated would not be inverted, for woman would then only have the rank that reason assigned her, and arts could not be practiced to bring the balance even, much less to turn it. (36)

This language of 'degrees and kinds,' so prevalent in late eighteenth- and early nineteenth-century discourses, signals a change in classification systems.[24] These new systems are implicated in new aesthetic formation of gender and a new purpose for discourse, with their attendant ideological functions, which emphasize the connection between her philosophy of benevolence, her gender, and her Jacobin politics. Based on equalizing the genders in terms of their minds, and not in terms of bodies as formerly constituted in aesthetic and gendered discourses like Burke's *A Philosophical Enquiry into the Origin of our Ideas of the Sublime and the Beautiful*, she finds virtue as the 'common' strength. Moral virtue, founded on knowledge and rationality, is the 'kind' of 'simple principle' that can be shared between the sexes. Therefore, truth as a 'simple principle,' without the 'arts' of former aesthetic and gendered constructions, is the litmus test for the superiority of man, which, of course under the terms she coyly puts forth here, is ultimately doomed to failure.

However, the 'degree' to which women 'may vainly struggle for' strength of mind and moral fortitude is in proportion to the 'rank that reason assigned her' (Wollstonecraft *VRW* 36). 'Rank' no longer signifies an absolute economically privileged position; it signifies her 'natural' capabilities or talents. It is assumed that women, and men for that matter, will have different but natural 'degrees' of talents and capabilities. The point is to establish a basis of 'equal' opportunity, rather than a rigid state of 'equality,' between men and women. This notion of 'equality' echoes her Jacobin politics: individuals in society are equal if each has a fair opportunity to improve his/her talents and gain respect and merit due him/her. In the passage cited above, the limitations placed on women because of educational practices are unfair, because women cannot 'improve' on their natural talents. Thus, rather than leveling distinctions between the genders, she assumes a political paradigm of equal opportunity. Later on in *VRW*, merit replaces rank as the test of respect: 'the respect, consequently, which is paid to wealth and mere personal charms, is a true north-east blast, that blights the tender blossoms of affection and virtue' (Wollstonecraft 141). Affection and moral virtue, of course, enable the particular vocations ascribed to men and women.

Alone, the discussion of matters of affection and virtue would seem to be only an issue of gender or a private issue of familial relations. But again, the structure of the argument reveals a different context. This discussion of merit follows directly after Wollstonecraft inveighs against the aristocratic system of hereditary wealth and titles as irrational as well as corrupting:

> Hereditary property sophisticates the mind, and the unfortunate victims to it, if I may so express myself, swathed from birth, seldom exert the locomotive faculty of body or mind; and, thus viewing every thing through one medium, and that a false one, they are unable to discern in what true merit and happiness consist. (*VRW* 141)

Like women, the middling classes are duped into a 'false' understanding of merit and respect, which, again like women, usurps their 'rightful' place in the social order. 'True merit' consists of constantly ameliorating one's innate talents, expanding knowledge, and measuring those talents with others, in order to secure a 'progressive' state of the mind as well as civilization: 'disappointed as we are in our researches, the mind gains strength by the exercise, sufficient, perhaps to comprehend the answers which, in another step of existence, it may receive to the anxious questions it asked' (Wollstonecraft 109). Just a few sentences before, however, Wollstonecraft claims that 'vanity and vexation,' characteristics she associates with the upper classes, 'close every inquiry: for the course which we particularly wished to discover flies like the horizon before us as we advance' (109). Knowledge is crippled because the criteria of the inquiry are already tainted. The juxtaposition of these two sentences compares two social systems: the social system based on the stability of rank is stultifying and retards the 'growth' of the nation; the social system based on the desire to understand knowledge and the emergence of different 'degrees' of talents to produce it propels the society forward into a new age. The mind, thus, should always be in a state of improvement: knowledge builds on knowledge, strengthening individual understanding. One of the ways this is accomplished is by proper reading and writing which will inform and instruct mankind women (and men). Improvement thus requires the production of new discourses which, in turn, requires new generic mixtures in order to create spaces for discourses for different classes and genders. Consequently, the production of discourses which seeks to improve women, the middling and lower classes, and mankind in general, constitutes the goals of vocational philanthropy.

This 'progressive' notion of merit and knowledge is important because it hints at a moral rationale: the idea of social mobility and 'equal' opportunity, in which wealth and social respect is not equivalent to property rights or titles. One of Wollstonecraft's primary complaints about women and their place in society was that women were socially conditioned to avoid the 'race of life'—the ability to compete fairly for society's privileges—and thus never receive the rewards due to talent and merit.[25] Only a rational education and political rights could, as Isaac Kramnick states, 'fit them for the race'; but women had 'lacked any desire to improve [themselves]' (12). Wollstonecraft's *VRW* participated in changing that social conditioning by invoking the 'desire' in women to at least approach the starting-gate.

This idea of improvement is particularly accented in a *British Critic* review of *VRW*.[26] The review states: 'in that work, the grand principle is, that woman is not the inferior of man, but his equal in moral rank, walking along with him the road of duty, in which "they are both trained for a state of endless improvement"'(qtd. in Janes 303). Even though the reviewer, most likely a clergyman, was persuaded to dislike Wollstonecraft because of Godwin's portrayal of her in *Memoirs*, he seemed to have had no quarrel with the general proposition cited above. Accepting 'improvement' as a natural desire in persons and in the state, even though perhaps Wollstonecraft herself was not the most popular writer to express this desire, seems immediately to prove what she set out to help construct: to foster the desire to ameliorate women and in turn to ameliorate men and society in general.

In the last few pages of *A Vindication of the Rights of Woman,* Wollstonecraft reiterates:

> I have endeavored to shew that private duties are never properly fulfilled unless the understanding enlarges the heart; and that public virtue is only an aggregate of private [...] and that the most salutary effects tending to improve mankind might be expected from a REVOLUTION in female manners, appears, at least, with a face of probability to rise out of the observation. (192)

As a result of the 'revolution' of female manners, the private duties of the maternal are linked with the public duties of good citizenship through the 'love' and improvement of mankind. Her improvements for women, and the society in general, were yet only a proposition. What was needed, and what I think *VRW* and other discourses by women helped to produce, is a desire for that improvement. Wollstonecraft provides a sympathetic and benevolent woman with an agency to act, traversing the spheres of public and private. The fact that this treatise is, by her own account, unfinished is significant. This fact becomes, in the context of *VRW*'s primary argument, a metaphor for 'endless improvement.' Thus, reading and writing are intimately connected as well as necessary to the perpetuation of the desire for improvement within certain class and gender categories: that is the project of vocational philanthropy. Writing generates more and more writing in order to create a space for women's 'natural' and 'proper' desires—to ameliorate people—and more writing maintains new gender categories in relation to specific classes. More writing leads to more improvement; more improvement enables more writing. While fighting for 'equality' of a gendered kind, she succeeded in contributing to an 'equality' of degree of class. It is from within that 'degree' that her vocation as a polemical woman writer becomes clear: to ameliorate the condition of mankind.

Notes

1   Hereafter, all references to *A Vindication of the Rights of Woman* will be cited as *VRW*; *A Vindication of the Rights of Men* will be cited as *VRM*.

2   Regina M. Janes, 'On the Reception of Mary Wollstonecraft's *A Vindication of the Rights of Woman,*' *Journal of the History of Ideas* 39 (1978): 293. Janes states that rational education for women, though still debated, was an acceptable belief.

3   Isaac Kramnick, *Republicanism and Bourgeois Radicalism, Political Ideology in Late Eighteenth-Century England and America* (Ithaca: Cornell UP, 1990), claims that 'middle-class behavior (part of which was writing) reveals a patterned sense of common interests against superior to a class above and a class below [...]. They knew what they were doing and said what they were doing,' 27. This seems to be confirmed by Graff, *Legacies* 230-257.

4   See for examples, Mary Poovey, *The Proper Lady and The Woman Writer* (Chicago: U of Chicago P, 1984); Anna Neill, 'Civilization and the Rights of Woman: Liberty and captivity in the Work of Mary Wollstonecraft' *Women's Writing* 8.1 (2001): 99-117; Mitzi Myers, 'Reform or Ruin: "A Revolution in Female Manners"' *A Vindication of the Rights of Woman*, ed. Carol Poston, (New York: Norton, 1988): 328-343.

5   See for examples, Elissa S. Guralnick, 'Radical Politics in Mary Wollstonecraft's *A Vindication of the Rights of Woman,*' *Studies in Burke and His Time* 18 (1977): 155-166; Claudia Johnson, *Equivocal Beings, Politics, Gender, and Sentimentality in the 1790s, Wollstonecraft, Radcliffe, Burney, Austen* (Chicago: U of Chicago P, 1995); Wendy Gunther-Canada, 'The Politics of Sense and Sensibility: Mary Wollstonecraft and Catharine Macaulay Graham on Edmund's Burke's *Reflections on the Revolution in France,*' *Women Writers and the Early Modern British Political Tradition*, ed. Hilda L. Smith (New York: Cambridge, 1998): 126-147; Kathryn Sutherland, 'Writings on education and conduct: arguments for female Improvement,' *Women and Literature in Britain 1700-1800*. ed. Vivien Jones (New York: Cambridge, 2000) 25-45.

6   Mary Poovey, 'Aesthetics and Political Economy in the Eighteenth Century, The Place of Gender in the Social Constitution of Knowledge,' in *Aesthetics and Ideology*, ed. George Levine. (New Brunswick, NJ: Rutgers UP, 1994) 96.

7   Janes claims *VRW* would have been recognized in its own historical period as an educational treatise, 294.

8   For a discussion of Shaftsbury's concept of moral virtue, see Poovey 'Aesthetics' 83; Markley 210-230.

9   For useful a discussion on Shaftsbury's concept of 'disinterest' and its relationship to the discourse of sentimentality, see Markley 210-215. See also Janet Todd, *Sensibility: An Introduction* (New York: Methuen, 1986).

10 See Johnson 7. Claudia Johnson's reading of *VRW* emphasizes how men might have viewed the treatise and their portrayal within it. See Johnson 23-46.

11 Janes points out that the printed reception of *VRW* was generally positive by the moderate and liberal journals that reviewed it, 293. This would seem to indicate that people accepted the fact that a woman is 'capable' of employing reason. An exception

was *The Critical Review*, which scarified *VRW* because it rejected its premise that women were not primarily sexual beings and were capable of intellectual equality with men, see Janes 296-297. Janes also indicates that *VRW* was largely ignored by journals that were 'less politically or more conservatively committed,' 294.

12 Interestingly, Wollstonecraft did include two pieces by Madame Genlis in the *The Female Reader*.

13 As Mary Poovey states in *The Proper Lady*, 'revolution' commonly meant a 'gradual turning' 79. This definition would certainly fit into Wollstonecraft's visionary discourse. But given the historical context of this treatise, I think we should not discount the possibility that Wollstonecraft did take revolution to mean a 'sudden, momentous' change or a governmental overthrow, especially given her Jacobin politics and her support of the French Revolution.

14 See Guralnick 158.

15 See Julia Allen, 'The Uses and Problems of a "Manly" Rhetoric,' *Listening to Their Voices: The Rhetorical Activities of Historical Women*, ed. Molly Meijer Wertheimer (Columbia, SC: U of South Carolina P, 1997) 322-323. Allen claims that Price's philosophy 'divided mind from body' by claiming that virtue and knowledge are united in the soul. The body merely does the 'bidding of the soul.' This principle enables Wollstonecraft to detach virtue from the gendered body.

16 See Mitzi Myers, 'Politics from the Outside: Mary Wollstonecraft's First Vindication,' *Studies in Eighteenth-Century Culture* 6 (1977) 122.

17 See Graff, *Legacies* 246.

18 Johnson claims that since it was a 'republican manifesto' many of *VRW*'s readers were men, 24. According to her argument, only hypermasculinity will ensure feminine rationality, 45.

19 Susan Khin Zaw, 'The Reasonable Heart: Mary Wollstonecraft's View of the Relation Between Reason and Feeling in Morality, Moral Psychology and Moral Development,' *Hypatia* (1998) 86.

20 The characterizations of femininity within conduct literature that Wollstonecraft cites is consistent with the language used in Burke's *A Philosophical Enquiry into the Origin of our Ideas of the Sublime and the Beautiful* to describe the aesthetic category of the 'Beautiful.'

21 Myers points out this portrayal of motherhood elevates it to heroic proportions, 'Reform' 337.

22 Lucinda Cole discusses the discourse of sympathy in *VRW*, 107-140.

23 See Guralnick 161-162.

24 See Clifford Siskin, *The Historicity of Romantic Discourse* (New York: Oxford, 1988) 21.

25 Isaac Kramnick cogently summarizes the bourgeois radicalism of this position: 'the ideal of equality of opportunity and its rendition in the metaphor of life as a fairly run race was at its origins in the eighteenth century an effort both to reduce inequality and to perpetuate it. It was egalitarian at its birth because it lashed out at the exclusiveness of aristocratic privilege, but it sought to replace an aristocratic elite with a new elite, albeit one based more broadly on talent and merit. Equality of opportunity is a theory not really of equality but of justified and morally acceptable inequality,' 14.

26 See Janes 298.

Chapter 3

Beyond the Polite:
Philanthropy and the Politics of
'Popular' Tales

Burke supposes that there are eighty thousand readers in Great Britain [...]. Out of
these we may calculate that ten thousand are nobility, clergy, or gentlemen of the
learned professions. Of seventy thousand readers which remain, there are many
who might be amused and instructed by books which were not professedly
adapted to the classes that have been enumerated.
Richard Lovell Edgeworth, Preface to *Popular Tales*, 1806

As chapter 1 demonstrated, in the second half of the eighteenth century, and in the
last two decades particularly, the disunity of England's two 'nations'—the
privileged and the poor—had begun to be written about as a problem, rather than a
natural, albeit unfortunate, fact.[1] As many eighteenth-century political economists
observed, the level of independent poverty—surviving on a subsistence income—
had eroded to the level of dependent poverty: depending on the parish dole or
private charity for subsistence.[2] Because of legislative measures and the needs of
nascent capitalism in the mid- to late eighteenth century, social conditions were set
for laborers to be dependent on wages as well as on the parishes and private
philanthropy.[3] In order to alleviate the increasing dependence on the monetary
relief system, and to more efficiently accommodate a capitalist system, the
middling and upper classes increasingly focused their philanthropic efforts and
energies on 'improving' the lower orders' behaviors and morals through education:
teaching reading of 'appropriate' discourses. Harvey Graff comments that this was
an important function for the growth of literacy: 'education could be remolded and
redirected [...] to serve its new social roles [...]. The language of morality reveals a
continuity of concern for hegemony and control [...] and an emphasis in social
thought and perception on the moral failings of individuals and classes as sources
of society's severe problems'(264). The new late eighteenth-century 'self-help'
philosophy championed individual amelioration as the more appropriate solution to
the problems caused by material inequity. Charity had shifted from doling out
money to the production and dissemination of discourses designed to improve the
habits, values and behaviors of the lower orders, which compelled voluntary
changes in their behaviors, and enabled the middling classes to serve as their
guardians. This new philanthropic paradigm denotes the function of vocational
philanthropy; it would take as its aim a transformation in habits and behaviors in

order to restore the poor to a level of independent poverty, and the lower orders to a state of independent dignity.

Beth Fowkes Tobin and Dorice Williams Elliott have recently discussed how the middling classes, particularly women, positioned themselves as the 'superintendents' of the poor, by representing themselves as sympathetic and benevolent.[4] The relationship between the privileged and the poor was in the process of being reconstituted, at least in the eyes of the middling ranks, as a sympathetic bond: they perceived both classes as working towards the same goals to improve each other morally and economically. Within the middling-class discourses on poverty, this sympathetic bond became the basis of social harmony, a harmony which could be threatened by the lower orders' 'corrupted' beliefs and behaviors. The middling-class women, who were enabled by superior moral virtue, 'natural' benevolence, and economic power to discern the ills of poverty as a threat to the prosperity and health of the nation, were empowered to intervene in the poor's lives by personally directing the inculcation of new values and supervising their habits. This endeavor entailed a construction of ideologies through which the lower orders, and the middling and upper classes, could be united.

This ideological project was undertaken on a broad and ambitious scale by two women of the expanding upper middling classes: Hannah More and Maria Edgeworth. Because self-help philanthropy was authorized as the most useful means of charity, it became a medium through which middling-class women's 'virtue,' privilege and power were recognized and displayed. Thus, the movement towards self-help philanthropy at the end of the eighteenth century, which hinges on whether one is deserving of help or not, was co-extensive with the entrance of women into the 'vocation' of philanthropy.[5] Understanding More and Edgeworth as writers who participate in 'self-help' philanthropy enables us to see their writing as acts of charity: through reading, individuals can be improved, society can be harmonized. It enables us to see their writing as an earnest attempt to 'improve' humankind, a sympathetic outreach to those in need of guidance, but also as a way to politically mediate, through the practice of reading, the contentious oppositions arising in the society at large.

Though the audiences addressed by More and Edgeworth are not quite the same, together they represent a new reading public: the truly poor (laborers and the dependent poor) and the lower middling classes (yeoman farmers, tradesman, small merchants, small shop-owners).[6] Bringing readers from outside the 'polite' classes into the growing body of the English reading public enabled More and Edgeworth to produce the relations by which the new ideologies *could* work. The social relationship represented by the production of their tales—that individuals exist in a social spectrum which must be harmonized in order to function—is the 'imaginary' relationship that is represented in these tales. What can harmonize classes across the economic spectrum is reading, and reading fiction in particular; through reading, individuals can be disciplined in ways that encourage certain kinds of desires, discourage others, and ensure the lower orders as subjects who work to reproduce social relations envisioned by these discourses. Therefore, one of the primary goals of *The Cheap Repository Tracts* and *Popular Tales* was to inculcate the habit of reading as a means to discipline the laboring-class subject.

This effort by women writers to reenvision the relationship between the lower orders and the middling and upper classes in order to address the issues of appropriate behavior and provide a way to make sense of their position in a changing economic structure were manifested in the genre of the moral tale. This genre has long been a peripheral part of literary history, traditionally referred to as 'didactic' or 'minor' literature because it emphasizes the inculcation of moral ideas and behavior.[7] Using the word 'inculcate' makes this kind of discourse seem simplistic or ideologically repressive, but it was neither. Features of didacticism should not necessarily be confused with the overall complexity of these writings. The didactic is one element that supports the text's ideology. But because of these didactic features, the moral tale has been easy to dismiss as an unproblematic 'mirror' of social reality.[8] It has been subsumed by other kinds of 'developing' literary forms such as the social-problem novel.[9] However, assigning literary 'value' as a universal concept to texts like More's *Cheap Repository Tracts* and Edgeworth's *Popular Tales* is anachronistic. Since eighteenth-century literary value was defined by a text's ability to inculcate moral instruction, these tales comfortably fit the criteria for ethical, educational, aesthetic and social value used at the time of their writing.[10] It should be noted, though, that I am not attempting to claim that these texts have universal literary value or potential. I am interested in how these texts imagine societal relations, but this does not mean that the texts were 'coercive' dogma, preaching obedience and submission; they were, however, a new way for the poor to imagine their reality, offering them the opportunity to 'improve' their lot, but only when they begin to desire the middling-class values presented in these texts.[11]

More's and Edgeworth's endeavors were not an overt 'will to power' so much as an attempt, within a specific historical situation, to transform social relations for what they thought would be the benefit of mankind. While many scholars have written about Hannah More's *Cheap Repository Tracts* as a way to reform the nation, or alternatively, to refashion paternalism in order to accommodate a nascent capitalism, only the naturalizing of philanthropy as a feminine endeavor outside the political debate on the Poor Laws and the origin of poverty could have enabled More's and Edgeworth's discursive projects.[12] Thus, Mitzi Myers argues that More's *Tracts* redefined political and social problems as moral and religious ones that women specifically could solve ('Tracts' 274). Maria Edgeworth's more rationalist approach also transforms the same social and political problems into those that a practical education could solve, and that kind of teaching is defined as a feminine sphere of influence. Traversing the private/political terrain in this way was not an unusual goal of women's writing during this period. As Kathyrn Sutherland points out, 'women of all persuasions were engaged in fashioning from the rhetoric of popular democracy a discourse appropriate to their particular needs as women' (35). The language of morality (whether cast as religious and/or enlightenment rhetoric) that stems from the values associated with domesticity becomes the 'source of politically legitimating concepts like "the national family" and "love of country"' (Sutherland 38) and, I would argue, love of mankind. The language of morality in both their discourses suggests a perception of 'benevolence' which propels these women and their writing out of the 'properly' political, and public, realm and into the benevolent, and private, realm. 'Reform' is then naturalized as the ethical domain of women's endeavors. In doing so, More and Edgeworth and their writings suture the political/economic implications of their own texts.

Recent critics like Sutherland and Anne K. Mellor have attempted to restore Hannah More to her rightful place as an important 'revolutionary reformer' of the 'culture [...] of the English nation' (Mellor 14). This attempt describes her politics as a kind of feminism which 'advanced the cause of women's social empowerment' (Mellor *Mothers* 18).[13] While restoring the more 'radical' political, as well as ethical, dimension of More's writing, and hailing it as at least proto-feminist, these scholars seem not to question the ethics of More's political action in terms of class and its ideological effect on the poor; in fact, when class implications are considered, they are perceived as 'negative press' (Mellor 16) or, worse, a leftist displacement of the 'story of female experience' onto a 'narrative of the emergence of class consciousness or the struggles of working men' (Sutherland 30). Against earlier feminist and marxist interpretations of More's work based on her patriarchal complicity and her 'oppressive' project to control the masses, more recent critics who see her as a political and social 'reformer' seem to assume that feminine ethics are excluded from class politics, and that those ethical values which will reform the poor are not middle-class values, but universal ones that will unequivocally improve those laborers. Implicitly, they validate 'improvement' as positive, and becoming shareholders of 'middle-class' values as the goal; in other words, they naturalize those values as the ethical effect of women's politics, but negate the social and economic conditions that make 'improvement' of the lower classes necessary at that historical moment. To see these discourses as evidence of women's 'empowerment,' or feminist social engagement, is certainly correct, but that evidence needs qualification; it is not just a spontaneous overflow of ethical feeling, but rather that ethical feeling is imbricated in a network of complicated social conditions and relations.

What is suggested here is that the ethical values propounded by More and Edgeworth as 'natural' are the ideologies of capitalism that recent critics are also perceiving as 'natural,' and that women writers need not be complicit with patriarchy, or anti- or proto-feminist, to expound them—they must conform to the feminine construction of benevolence that is founded upon class difference. One need not overlook social and economic determinants to examine gender implications; one need not assume that women's ethics and benevolence were always disinterested (as Wollstonecraft claimed they were in *VRW*). If they are disinterested, then their effects have social ramifications that perhaps were not intended, but that does not mean they should not be examined. What is at stake in More's and Edgeworth's kind of philanthropy and social reform is the shift from one social system in which the lower orders' social betters are responsible for materially helping them (through charity, traditional 'use' rights, subsistence farming, etc.) to teaching them what the middling class perceived to be necessary changes in their way of life (proper middle-class values of sobriety, hard work, self-improvement) that would allow them to be 'independent' in a capitalist social system. In this way, gender and class, and all their political implications, are mutually dependent on one another for (re)construction at this historical moment.

The very point is that More and Edgeworth are empowered, as literate middling-class women, to construct and classify in their texts the ways in which the laboring classes are distinct from the middling and upper classes, and thus the ways in which they can be improved accordingly. They are represented as different in degree rather than kind, a Romantic trope. To be sure, the lower orders are represented not as the inevitable occurrence of economic conditions to be helped by philanthropy, but as individual subjects who can be morally improved or rewarded because of their improvement. The tales attempt, through their didacticism and mixed generic elements, to create an approximation of reality with which the lower orders can identify, inculcating a desire for moral improvement (which is rewarded with monetary improvement but only to a degree) and reconstituting their relationship with the middling and upper classes. How the middling class imagined the lower orders should behave and live in a revamped system of social and economic relationships and how the poor could imagine themselves are exemplified in these texts. The function of this kind of discourse is to interpellate individuals through ideology into a different imaginary system of social relations, producing subjects who think, feel and relate to other subjects in specific ways. More and Edgeworth attempted to forge a common language between the privileged and the poor through a type of narrative fiction that universalizes middle-class values, and makes them desirable for the poor and privileged alike.

Reading Hannah More's *Cheap Repository Tracts* and Maria Edgeworth's *Popular Tales* revisits an important episode in the history of women's philanthropic endeavors, women's writing and class relations. This kind of women's fiction, with its philanthropic function, was the medium through which the lower classes could be united in economic and ideological purpose with the middling classes. Thus, women's writings for the lower classes became a powerful source of social control as well as social reform. The task is to express certain values *as* 'universal' to the lower orders, without upsetting the existing social order of a gendered and class-specific language. This task is discursively difficult, socially precarious and historically dangerous.

Literacy and the Masses

The linch-pin of philanthropy and moral improvement of the lower classes is literacy. While there are relatively high rates of literacy for the upper and middle classes, there are indications that the overall rate of literacy for the laboring classes in the late eighteenth and early nineteenth centuries remained low and stable, if it did not decline.[14] There are a couple of possible reasons for this counter-intuitive phenomenon: first, that the population growth outstripped the capacity of educational programs to deliver literacy; and second, that industrialization put little value on literacy skill acquisition and was often disruptive to educational endeavors (Graff *Legacies* 317). Harvey Graff claims that while there is a negative correlation between literacy's relationship to work and economic development, there was also a need for the laboring population to be 'trained for factory work and taught industrial habits, rules and rhythms. Traditional social habits and customs did not fit the new requirements of industrial life' (*Legacies* 323). This kind of subjective reform became the impetus for philanthropy which centrally included the teaching of reading.

The prefaces to both More's and Edgeworth's texts indicate the broadening of the reading public that can access a variety of forms of literature, and that needs to develop reading habits in order to participate, to some degree, in English society. Hannah More's advertisement to the *Cheap Repository Tracts* states as its aim 'to improve the habits, and raise the principles of the common people, at a time when their dangers and temptations, moral and political, were multiplied beyond the example of any former period [...] ' (190).[15] More suggests that the 'improvement' of the poor and lower classes, specifically in terms of 'habits' and 'principles,' and not material improvement, was needed at this historical moment because of the political agitation in France, the dire economic problems the laboring and poor classes faced in England in the 1790s, and the circulation of 'radical' literature such as Thomas Paine's *The Rights of Man*.[16] In More's view, all these determinants signaled a state of social disunity and moral disintegration. The tales were needed to counteract these pernicious social and political elements if the moral health of the nation was to be regained.

Similarly, in the preface to Maria Edgeworth's *Popular Tales*, Richard Lovell Edgeworth, the author's father, addresses the 'seventy thousand readers' of the lower classes outside the 'ten thousand' polite readers who may be considered 'nobility, clergy, or gentlemen of the learned professions' (iii). These seventy-thousand readers are the population of England to whom the 'popular' tales are addressed and whom they supposedly represent within their pages. These tales represent an enlargement of the reading public to include yeoman farmers, manufacturing and agricultural laborers, clerks, etc. The Edgeworths recognized that 'the art of printing ha[d] opened to all classes of people various new channels of entertainment and information [...] in our days, instruction, in the dress of innocent amusement, is not denied admittance amongst the wise and good of all ranks' (Edgeworth vi). The Edgeworths believed a new narrative of moral improvement needed to be written, one that could be shared among the classes to improve the whole society. The admitted purpose of the tales, as of virtually all Maria Edgeworth's fiction, is to provide instruction to people who had not previously had moral guidance.

These addresses to the masses outside 'polite' Society, and the tales that follow them, contrast with the typical depiction of the lower orders in texts. After 1750, negative images of the poor as untrustworthy and lazy began to circulate in discourses (Valenze 40-47). Depicted as indolent, particularly vulnerable to leisure activities such as drink and profligacy, as well as vulnerable to superstitious beliefs, these undesirable activities and beliefs are portrayed as the cause of the poor's 'dependence' on the relief system and charity, preventing them from becoming independent workers. These images complicated the argument for literacy. The opponents of literacy (and to some degree charity and philanthropic institutions) argued that education would unfit laborers and the poor for their occupational roles, and increase sedition and atheism, thereby subverting the traditional forms of state, class and church authority (Graff *Legacies* 315). Proponents of literacy claimed that education would improve morality, making the laborers content with their position in society and thereby stabilizing the social hierarchy of England (Graff *Legacies* 315). What is at stake here is the concern with the effects of reading; it is important to those who possess literacy that the new acquisition of literacy and the practices of reading not disrupt social order. The power of print and the power of the practice of reading inform these two arguments about literacy. More and Edgeworth, who both believed in the reforming possibilities of reading, also embraced the argument for greater control of the lower classes through literacy and appropriate reading materials.

These tales, then, attempt to lay out guidelines for the 'correction' of the poor's moral deficiencies and, as the logic extends, financial problems without upsetting social order. In these tales, morality and economic strata are linked. Variances in material conditions are merely social differences, stemming from a god-given hierarchy and from the possession of particular levels of moral virtue. The well-being of the mind can then be regulated; worker exploitation, the problems of unemployment, and lack of food are backgrounded and rendered incompatible with the values illustrated in these tales. Thus, in effect, the criteria for determining which poor deserve middling-class help and guidance moves from the body (identifying a material position) to the mind (identifying rationality and morality).

In these tales, the lower classes are positioned in a particular social relationship to the middling classes. The relationship is largely constructed upon social sympathy which is based on aesthetic judgment: a member of the lower classes would be perceived as 'deserving' of improvement because his/her state evokes the 'proper' amount of sympathy in the viewer; or, he/she would be perceived as already as virtuous as possible, poor but existing independently in his/her own socioeconomic sphere. A person who diverges from this relationship altogether would be considered 'undeserving,' and is therefore thrust outside of the sympathetic bonds of social relations, requiring no further consideration from the privileged. Responsibility for the poor's existence is personalized and their impoverished conditions are borne solely on their own shoulders. The two collections of tales assume that, on the whole, it is the lower classes' morality, and not changing economic conditions, which threaten to dissolve the stability and unity of Britain.

This signification process reduces all relations of social and economic dominance to individual 'choice': those who choose to be moral citizens will be rewarded within the pages of the tales and those who do not will, in the end, still be poor and morally corrupt. In addition, these moral standards and codes for behavior were, for the first time as Richard Edgeworth's preface makes clear, to be articulated to the lower orders and shared between the upper and lower classes so that each understands their social position and its attendant responsibilities.

To achieve this moral hegemony, approved social attitudes and behaviors were portrayed in narratives thought to be comprehensible to the poor and the lower orders.[17] As Olivia Smith points out in *The Politics of Language*, 'the belief that the self and language coexisted in a simple and direct relation was the foundation of theories of universal grammar as it was studied in the last half of the [eighteenth] century' (21).[18] Knowledge of self and society is reflected by the level of formality or abstraction of language. According to the logic of the universal grammarians, the mind performs two basic functions: reflection and sensation. The linguistic difference which separates those who can 'express ideas which are not determined by time and place' and those who are 'imbruted' in the material world are broadly cognate to the division of the upper and lower classes, respectively (Smith 22). Because ideas about language in the eighteenth century rationalized and justified class division—those who are civilized and morally virtuous were defined against those who are vulgar and corrupted—attempts to interpellate the laboring classes through the use of literature was seen by many upper-class people as dangerous.[19] But, if the tales were to be a powerful source of social reform and control, then its mission to express 'universal' bourgeois values to the poor without upsetting social order was a necessary, though precarious, one.

To illustrate the precariousness of this problem, Smith examines attempts by radicals and conservatives alike to address a laboring-class audience in the 1770s-1780s.[20] The Association for Preserving Liberty and Property Against Republicans and Levellers was formed to counteract radicals like Thomas Paine, Daniel Eaton and Thomas Spence, who had been distributing political pamphlets to commoners. The writers in the Association's series *Liberty and Property*, of whom Hannah More was one, as well as the radicals had difficulty envisioning their laboring-class audience, as Smith makes clear in her reading of Daniel Isaac Eaton's journal, *Politics for the People*: 'initially the editor appears to be wary and uncertain of his audience. Material is carefully controlled and information is guarded; the audience is not represented and an appropriate language is admittedly absent' (85). Many of the tracts in the *Liberty and Property* series discouraged any reading by the laboring classes, even the bible, in order to counteract the pamphlets of radicals (Smith 69).[21] Smith contends that the writers of these tracts were 'unwilling to claim the audience's language as their own [...] the poor are effectively silenced and, as linguistic conventions defined them, capable of expressing only their wants and needs' (88). Since so much of this literature dealt directly with political ideals, writers groped for a language in which to express these abstract ideals to the poor, and consequently found their writing at odds with their politics (Smith 87). If the purpose of these tracts was to modify the poor's behaviors and beliefs, according to middling-class values, then a way to portray proper behaviors to the laboring classes in a language that appeared familiar and is comprehensible needed be found.

Women writing moral tales for the lower orders find that language. More's and Edgeworth's use of the moral tale bridges this discursive gap between the 'universal' values of the middling classes and the 'imbruted' nature of the lower classes. This type of narrative fiction is suited for philanthropic purposes, because the 'tale' was perceived as pedagogically useful and not highly literary.[22] In fact, middling-class women writers took the generic name 'tale' in order to affirm their fiction's 'realism.'[23] In order to make it appealing to the lower orders, this fiction combines particular discursive maneuvers, appropriating familiar generic elements from chapbook literature (which was commonly in circulation among the lower classes) and combining them with sentimental and pastoral elements from 'literary' texts.

Hannah More's tales were based on literature found in common chapbooks and broadsides.[24] The content of this cheap, lower-class literature had not concerned the middling classes prior to this period. For at least a century, the chapbook had been compiled from a substantial amount of literature in various forms: prose and metrical romances, chivalric and folk tales, fairy stories, songbooks, jest-books, riddles and humorous tales, godly and supernatural tales as well as descriptive non-fiction such as history, biography and travel (Pedersen 100-101). These tales constitute a significant contribution to what would eventually become working-class popular culture in the nineteenth century.[25] As Susan Pedersen explains:

> Its antiauthoritarian, subversive, 'world-turned-upside-down' aspect gave this literature its ideological coherence. Within these stories, the poor found unaccustomed power and good fortune: they could perform brave acts, find treasure, watch the rich hang, or marry their masters. However, these adventures should not be interpreted as a reflection of either actual material possibilities in the lives of the poor or a conscious radicalism in politics or ideas. For chapbook literature is, as a rule, innocent of ulterior motives, didactic or otherwise, and often without direct social relevance [...]. Popular literature, read—and often produced—by the common people, was a coherent genre, largely autonomous from elite contact or control. (105)

Pedersen claims these popular tales were formally the 'fantasy' literature of the day. But, they were by no means 'innocent of ulterior motives.' These tales had an ideological force among the literate lower classes that could not afford to buy a novel or, if they did, could not identify themselves within its pages. Appropriating the form of the tale was important if Hannah More were to rework the ideologies of an organic, self-sufficient society provided by this 'fantasy' literature. More provided a new and 'improving' function in the form of chapbook literature.

Paradoxically, as Gary Kelly explains, varieties of fiction written by middling-class women writers around the turn of the century also took the generic name 'tale' in order to affirm their fiction's realism: fiction construed as fact (Kelly 72-3). Jane Taylor's *Display: A Tale for Young People* (1815) explains this middling-class view of tales as opposed to novels:

> a tale is supposed to be a shorter and less labored production than a novel; that a tale is designed to relate the natural occurrences and simple incidents of life; while a novel sets real life and probability at defiance [...]. How comes it that novels are, with few exceptions, the most pernicious in tendency of any works; while, under the generic title of Tales, we have some of the most instructive and profound compositions in the language. (qtd. in Kelly 3)

Obviously, the tale connoted something very different to the middling classes by the turn into the nineteenth century. The tale is supposed to invest readers in the realism of simple, everyday life, while novels are overtly fictive and therefore not amenable to the purposes of instruction. This middling-class definition of the tale is interesting when considering the background of the generic category of tales in laboring-class popular literature. A literary gap appears between the two classes of writers and readers: a gap between the function of middling-class literature as a means to moral improvement, which maintains class stratification, and the function of laboring-class literature as a fictional means to transgress their class status. The generic and ideological gap between the upper and lower classes is bridged by vocational philanthropy: the intervention of women writers, like Hannah More and Maria Edgeworth, who create a form of 'improving' literature from a 'popular' literary form.

Through these narratives, a new set of behaviors for the laboring classes are aestheticized, so that the poor could be reeducated and reformed from within their social sphere. Moral tales by More and Edgeworth, for instance, are the medium through which the lower classes are tied in economic purpose and ideology with the middling classes. As Gary Kelly explains in *English Fiction of the Romantic Period 1789-1830*: 'Fiction could have an important role not only in depicting this "imagined community" and remaking all classes in the image of the professional middle classes, but it would also have an instrumental role in educating children and reeducating the upper, middle and lower classes to the name and nature of these new modes of individual being and social relationship' (72). A common language in which to envision a new social relationship and a common 'industrious' ideology by which to tie the two classes together had become necessary to consolidating political and economic hegemony in the late eighteenth century. Women writing moral tales for the poor thus play a major role in this reeducation of a new 'imagined community.' Women writers appear to participate in this public, ideological reformation as an act of private benevolence. By examining particular tales, I will illustrate how Hannah More's and Maria Edgeworth's moral tales attempted to 'reform' the underprivileged.

Hannah More and her Tales

Hannah More's *The Cheap Repository of Moral and Religious Tracts* (1795-1798) stands as the first attempt to create a body of literature on an international scale to be primarily read by the poor and laboring classes. As mentioned above, there had been other attempts by conservative and radical writers alike, such as John Wesley, and Hannah More's fellow Anglican Sarah Trimmer as well as moral tracts published by The Society for Promotion of Christian Knowledge (S.P.C.K.), to write for the lower classes on the subjects of morality and politics (Jones 138).[26] But More's *Cheap Repository Tracts* were by far the most successful of all these endeavors, not only in terms of distribution and sales, but in terms of finding a comprehensible narrative of a moral lower-class lifestyle.

While there were other contributions from prominent evangelicals and the gentry, Hannah More wrote at least fifty tracts during the *Cheap Repository*'s three-year existence (Pedersen 85). She was also primarily responsible for its design and distribution. Subscriptions were sold for at least the first year, but there is evidence that at some point subscriptions were no longer needed and the *Tracts* sold on their own for a profit (Spinney 302). More sold two million copies within the first year of publication; some were circulated within England, and some were exported to Ireland and America (Spinney 302, 309-310). At least a portion of the *Cheap Repository*'s success was owed to its distribution method. More appropriated the Association for Preserving Liberty and Property Against Republicans and Levellers' method: large numbers of tracts were given away at Sunday schools, taverns, workhouses, hospitals, and prisons; distributed to soldiers by their commanding officers; carried abroad by missionaries; and sold by hawkers, chapmen and booksellers (Spinney 309). Whether the lower classes bought them or read them is unknown, but they were well-circulated. In addition, many of the tracts were purchased by the middling and upper classes, and distributed to their workers (Krueger 111). A more expensive edition, printed on better paper, was then published to be sold, more or less exclusively, to the middling classes (Myers 'Hannah More' 266). By publishing different editions of the tales for different audiences, the tales serve as an ideological bridge between the two classes: as Mitzi Myers has pointed out, 'More was among the first to try her hand at interclass communication between England's "two nations"' ('Hannah More' 267). Interclass communication, perhaps, but this kind of discourse became an arena of class contestation because the relations between the two classes were specifically addressed and undergoing reconception. It is not an overstatement to say that 'More's Repository project proposes close to a total reconstruction of culture, a resocialization organized around the moral reform priorities of Evangelical womanhood' (Myers 'Hannah More' 269).

As Myers observes, this endeavor was taken on by a woman evangelist at a time of social upheaval and discursive contestation.[27] Her belief in 'practical Christianity' informs her well-chronicled devotion to philanthropy: 'Christianity practical and pure which teaches holiness, humility, repentance and faith in Christ, and which, after summing up all the Evangelical graces, declares that the greatest of these is charity' (Jones 83).[28] More's philanthropic work is realized in the Sunday school project, the Mendip Valley industrial schools, the English abolition movement, and discursive projects such as *The Cheap Repository Tracts* themselves. More's discursive project was a benevolent act that she felt was appropriate to her faith and her gender, rather than an assertion of her skill as a writer in the public spheres of discursive production (Smith 91). But while scholars have emphasized her religious motivation for 'reforming' the poor's habits and desires, I suggest that they are not reducible to religiosity. Emphasizing religion does highlight her 'private' benevolence, viewing her writing as a way of creating a feminine mode of discourse that is seen in opposition to both scientific rationalism and the emptiness of ecclesiastic rhetoric.[29] But this rationale belies its political effects and, perhaps, its political impetus as her advertisement points out. Given Edgeworth's similar project, too great an emphasis on her religious impetus would obfuscate how her discourse functions in a broader spectrum of similar discursive endeavors. Hannah More's investment in transforming the morality of the poor certainly stems from her association with Anglican Evangelicalism, but this impetus also gives her actions and endeavors a religious justification and intention despite its politics.[30] Her project enabled her to venture out into the public sphere under the aegis of benevolence. Consequently, More's belief that women are better suited to care for the poor reveals a political position in which both class and gender relations are at stake.[31] The ideology of feminine benevolence reconstitutes the middling-class woman as morally superior to either gender of the poor in need of guidance. This reconstitution of the middling classes' relationship to the poor is based on moral responsibility and sympathy, and not monetary exchange, and one that secures the privileged in their righteous position. More's agency to act politically is only permissible because of *The Cheap Repository Tracts'* philanthropic function and her belief that writing to reform the poor is her feminine vocation. In this context, we can look at the tales to understand the world More envisioned.

In order to guide the poor, More claimed she, as a woman, was capable of speaking to them in a simple and credible language. Her relationship to language was 'closer' to the poor's than men who attempted a similar endeavor simply because her mind, though on a higher moral level, was accustomed to 'simple' realistic narrative. Her familiarity with the lifestyles of the poor, gained through her experience superintending the Mendip Valley schools, enabled her to write about various trades, everyday village life and the common practices of working and poor people.[32] More believed that one of the 'characteristics of female genius' is the ability to create a 'vraisemblance to real life as to the events themselves [...]. It farther consists in the art of interesting the tender feelings by a pathetic representation of those minute, endearing, domestic circumstances, which take captive the soul before it has time to shield itself with the armour of reflection' (More *Essays* 551).[33] Women are thus perfectly suited to the task of writing pastoral forms which are used to 'instruct indirectly by short inferences.'

More also studied popular chapbook literature, adopting its format and producing a familiar quality to her tracts. But while More's improving literature adopted the chapbook format, the content of her writing radically differed from that in the popular version. Features of Evangelical culture such as sermons, the use of proverbs, and guidance by the clergy, become infused with features of popular chapbook literature in her tales—woodcuts, entertaining characters, 'realistic' depiction of laboring-class life and culture. The bridge across this ideological gap between polite and popular culture is found in the integration of the laboring-class generic form and middling-class content of the tales.

As Susan Pedersen and G.H. Spinney suggest, the intention of *The Cheap Repository* was not only an attempt to appropriate this form of literature for her own 'improving' purposes, it was a deliberate attempt to compete with and to outsell the popular literature Hannah More thought was indecent. Pedersen states that Hannah More rejected 'not merely the content of this popular literature but also the very existence of a popular culture autonomous from dominant society' which is of course defined by the middling classes (108). Thus, 'the model for moral reform put forward in the tracts' is an attempt to project a set of middling-class morals onto the lower orders, eradicating the autonomous existence of laboring-class popular culture (Pedersen 108).

Though *The Cheap Repository* was unquestionably well distributed to and possibly widely read by both classes, Pedersen points out that the persistence of popular penny publications in its traditional generic category of 'street-literature' survived and flourished in the popular literature of the nineteenth century (111).[34] Therefore, one stated goal of the more sober *Cheap Repository* and successive popular-moral tales—to eradicate traditional tract literature—had not been fully met. Thomas Laqueur argues that the *Tracts* seemed to have had no effect at all, because with the growth of literacy, there was also a growth of radical working-class literature (205). Yet, even Laqueur admits that the kinds of values represented in these tales were the same kinds of values that were increasingly adopted by working-class culture in the nineteenth century, and that these values were necessary to the 'industrial system and the interest of the bourgeoisie' (239).[35] It can be argued that *The Cheap Repository* had some impact on the reorganization of the social relations between the two classes, if only in the sense of converting More's peers to recognize the poor as needing amelioration and the poor to recognize themselves as people who are capable of amelioration.

The project of *The Cheap Repository* is therefore an ideological attack on the 'moral economy of the common people' much of which is represented in its tales; that is,

> the lottery-of-life mentality, tolerance of 'small sins' such as pilfering and poaching, the lower-class culture of amorous courtship and marriage after pre-marital pregnancy, interest in dreams and prophecies, the idea of the 'fair wage' and 'fair price' based on traditional relationships of social interdependence, and popular acceptance of the social structure of gentry hegemony and rural paternalism. (Kelly 61)

As will become clear in the reading of specific tracts, the moral economy Kelly refers to is exactly what is under reconstruction.[36] The popular acceptance of a capitalist system is the linchpin of Hannah More's, and even Maria Edgeworth's, philanthropic project. And our popular acceptance is what enables us to understand More as a 'reformer' of, rather than a participant in, the economic and political structure undergoing systemic change in the 1790s. But to see More as the righteous reformer, the ethical guardian, is to see her how history has taught us to see her: as the woman writer who defined, didactically or not, as Anne K. Mellor states, 'what we might now call 'middle-class values' as normative for the nation as a whole' (*Mothers* 25). While More may be undercutting the 'social prestige and political authority of the aristocracy' (Mellor, *Mothers* 25), she is also defining the mode of economic and political participation for the workers: that is, 'if workers would become sober, industrious, thrifty, healthy, and religious, then they could rise into the lower rungs of the middle class' (Mellor *Mothers* 22). If workers serve the needs of capital, then they could rise by the ideology of moral improvement. This statement takes at More's word that the workers are in need of 'reform,' and that these 'middle-class' values are more civilized, natural and inherently more desirable than the ones that the workers already have, and dissociates history from literature in a peculiar way. Reading the tales in this way, for content rather than ideological effect, leads Mellor to draw the conclusion of social mobility for everyone (albeit with certain limits for the workers) as the didactic 'message' of *The Cheap Repository Tracts*.

But the tales are more complicated than sending a 'message' of reform and serve a more important function in the redefinition of classes: simply put, the tales in their simple, didactic language change the stakes of desire for both the middling and laboring classes. Moral reform of the laboring classes will have three ideological effects. First, laboring-class subjects are reimagined as diligent workers and contented citizens. This entails that workers have less leisure time and, simultaneously, are less economically dependent on the parishes. Second, a new role is established for the middle class as 'social leaders' who have the authority to regulate the behavior of the lower classes; Mrs. Jones, More's alter ego in many tales, is most often the formal characterization of this notion. And third, all social relations are transmuted into interpersonal relations, but primary is the family.

To achieve these three ideological effects, Hannah More's tales in *The Cheap Repository* display certain characteristics. The first and most prominent is that they are mostly set in rural, not urban, England. This fact would support Gary Kelly's suggestion that the topos of rural simplicity became 'a source for a new model of the national community, a community thoroughly penetrated by professional and middle-class values [...]. If British society were to be remade in the image of the professional and middle classes, the country and village had to be so remade' (86).[37] This renovation must necessarily exclude the gentry, who had played, through village politics and land ownership, an important part in the lives of the lower classes under the old regime. But it can also be argued that the topos of rural simplicity is a nostalgic return to the idea of a benevolent rural patriarchy, in which the poor would have been supported by the landowners. Now, the caveat for the poor is whether or not they will be judged worthy to be helped to an 'improved' state. Given the transformation of agriculture and increasingly industrialized towns, of which More was well aware from the view of her home in Bristol, this conservative view of laboring life is somewhat anachronistic.[38]

The second characteristic of the tales: a middling-class observer or intermediary is present in the rural, laboring-class community that the tales depict. The observer or intermediary supervises the farm workers and shepherds to make sure they are industrious and God-fearing, intercedes in matters of rural justice and teaches the poor 'proper' obedience to social superiors, frugality and the distinction between 'right' and 'wrong.' These duties are conceived by More as 'true' charity: charity that helps the poor better themselves through moral instruction. These middling-class intermediaries are depicted as guests welcomed in the community by most of the laboring classes, except those who are characterized as unrepentantly immoral. And these guests only help those whom they judge worthy of help. They are the community's new and necessary social leaders, directing the 'deserving' poor and laborers to morality and self-discipline. The middling and laboring classes are thereby tied together in a mutually dependent, self-fulfilling, and, most importantly, harmonious relationship.

The third characteristic is the attainment of a moral, personal or religious reward for those who correct their immoral habits and attitudes in the course of the tale, always with the help of an intermediary, or for those who already live a dignified, industrious lifestyle. The reward is never purely pleasurable, nor is it purely material; it usually involves the opportunity of further improvement. Those same rewards are given to readers on an aesthetic and rhetorical level: pleasure that comes from reading the tales is the pleasure accorded to one who learns about his/her moral value and place within the family and, by extension, the society. The family is a figure for society in these tales: if one behaves appropriately for the betterment of one's own family, one will behave appropriately for the betterment of society. Conversely, immoral behavior, in the end, is always punishable, not by the law, the community or the middling-class intermediary, but by divine justice—for More, the ultimate legitimacy of the social and economic order.

Though all three above-mentioned characteristics are present in More's tales, different narratives work to inculcate different ideologemes useful to middling-class hegemony.[39] I have chosen to examine *The Shepherd of Salisbury Plain*, *Black Giles the Poacher* and *Betty Brown the St. Giles Orange Girl* because they depict different sets of values, use different rhetorical techniques to build a common narrative bond between the poor and privileged, utilize traditionally 'didactic' plots, and combine elements of didacticism, sentimentalism and pastoral in their portrayal of the laboring-class community and the middling classes' relationship to it.

The Shepherd of Salisbury Plain tells the story of a fifty year-old shepherd who supports his wife and family of eight children on a meager, but productive, living. The shepherd works as a common pastoral emblem who exemplifies 'the nobility of spirit that only rural hardship is capable of producing but whose efficacy can be spread' (Patterson 234). The narrative, however, does not focus directly on the shepherd or his trials and his forbearance, but instead focuses on a Mr. Johnson whom we are told in the first sentence is a 'very worthy charitable gentleman.' As readers, we see the shepherd through his eyes—he is our intermediary who will 'teach' us what is correct behavior. While traveling in Wiltshire, Mr. Johnson comes upon the shepherd who is at work tending his sheep. The patched coat the shepherd wears becomes 'plain proof' to Mr. Johnson of 'the shepherd's poverty,' and 'equally proved the exceeding neatness, industry and good management of his wife' (More 191). Mr. Johnson goes on with his observations:

> His stockings no less proved her good house-wifery, for they were entirely covered with darns of different coloured worsted, but had not a hole in them; and his shirt, though nearly as coarse as the sails of a ship, was as white as the drifted snow, and was neatly mended where time had either made a rent, worn it thin. This furnishes a rule of judging, by which one shall seldom be deceived. (More 191)

From the shepherd's clothing, Mr. Johnson draws positive conclusions about the morality and values of the shepherd. Elizabeth Kowaleski-Wallace observes that his clothing signifies 'the virtues that he has internalized. Poverty has not given way to slovenliness or wantonness [...] his wife's extreme diligence assures that her husband's body continues to be properly covered, neatly enclosed within the suit of clothes that testifies to an attentiveness to a certain kind of physical decorum' (76).

As with the shepherd's coat, his 'tremendous control over his bodily appetites,' when he 'denies himself a piece of bacon in order to pay a doctor's bill' (Kowaleski-Wallace 77) is portrayed positively. However, a laborer's bodily control is not the only issue at stake. The purpose of the tale is not just 'to celebrate the binding [...] of desire' (Kowaleski-Wallace 77), but to rework a relationship between the privileged and the poor, as demonstrated by the relationship between Mr. Johnson and the shepherd. This new relationship does not stem from the gratification of 'bodily desires' in some form of materiality, such as food, clothing and shelter. Rather, both the upper and lower classes should learn from this example of the poor in their virtuous, already contented state. A life lived closer to nature is not necessarily 'imbruted' or morally corrupt; it can mean 'simple' and 'pure,' and in that simplicity and purity is innate moral correctness.[40] The gratification for the reader, as well as for Mr. Johnson, comes in the example of a perfect 'rural domesticity' which enforces ideological closure: in this case, the respect for the middling-class's private property (the shepherd's small but well cared-for rented land and cottage), his domestic affections (his loving and frugal wife and eight children) and his sober work ethic (his occupation defines him as an individual).[41] The example of the shepherd's clothing is a consolidation and easily representable integration of these three primary ideologies.

Oddly, there is much conversation about his respect for the land and his industry in working it, while there is little actual representation of the shepherd's physical exertion. This substitution has an ideological effect: the oppressiveness of hard labor and material necessity is backgrounded, and labor as a means of inspiring competence, industry, contentment and morality is foregrounded. Labor is a primary mechanism of improvement for the poor, especially for men with dependents. Subsistence for the shepherd is a moral matter, dependent solely on recognizing that 'a laborious life is a happy one,' despite the fact that the family 'seldom ha[s] smoke in the evening, for we have little to cook, and firing is very dear in these parts' (More 191). The cottage they inhabit and the grazing land they rent is all they need, even though Mr. Johnson is at first appalled by the sight of his dwelling:

> 'What, that hovel with only one room above and below, with scarcely any chimney? How is it possible that you can live there with such a family?' 'O, it is very possible, and very certain too,' cried the shepherd [...] 'how many good Christians have perished in prisons and dungeons, in comparison of which my cottage is a palace! The house is very well, sir; [...] I should not desire a better; for I have health, peace, and liberty, and no man maketh me afraid.' (More 192)

Mr. Johnson makes the dire conditions of the shepherd's life seem ennobling. The shepherd's response is pride: he prides himself on his work and home, and therefore would not resort to stealing or beggary nor rely on the parish dole (More 192). The combination of the shepherd's pride and diligence demonstrates his respect for others' property as well as respect for whatever he has been able to provide with his own money.

Industry, rather than physical labor, is emphasized in this tale. Work is shared among all members of the household in numerous demonstrations of frugality, prudence and fortitude. The shepherd primarily supports his family by bringing home a 'shilling-a-day.' The father is portrayed as a wage-earner, wholly independent of parish relief, relying on his wits and hard work. But the burden of support is lessened by the almost leisurely depiction of his wife's and children's industry.[42] Because of Ellen's physical frailty, she is unable to do day-labor, so she cards cotton from the 'scattered pieces of wool the children pick out of the brambles' against which the sheep rub. The eldest daughter then spins it into thread and yarn. Through the women's collective frugality and work, the mother and daughters mend stockings and such, as well as knit 'chiefly for sale, which helps to pay our rent' (More 193). Similarly, the boys are set to work gleaning or picking stones, getting paid by farmers to keep birds off the corn and so forth (More 193). The parents take pride in breeding their children 'to such habits of industry' because 'anything is better than idleness' (More 193). Though there is an implicit gendered and generational division of labor, the family works as an organic unit, each member contributing to the financial support of the other members. The mutual interdependence of the family for subsistence binds them together, integrating industry and domesticity.

This portrayal emphasizes the patriarchical model of the family in which the father, as head of the household, has primary financial responsibility for the others, though other members contribute as well. If the mother were able to work outside the home, she might have assumed more of the financial burden; but there is no indication that she would have rivaled his superior position within the family. She would have merely been better able to help her husband and attend to her other domestic duties. Deference is always paid to the father as provider, both economically and, more important to the tale, spiritually. In his conversations with Mr. Johnson, we find out that he is the spiritual provider for the family who reads the Bible daily, who leads the family in prayer and who is a proven example of God's contented 'shepherd.' Christine Krueger notes the use of scriptural language, and the power of religious reflection, which serves as a commonality to unite both rich and poor (112).

Even more interesting than the pastoral values of the shepherd and his family is Mr. Johnson's response to the family: he is emotionally 'moved' by the example of their goodness. As he increasingly understands their simple lifestyle, he is 'transformed' by the experiences of these people. Within the logic of the tale, the laborers are not transformed by the relationship, but the 'very charitable gentlemen'—Mr. Johnson—is. The laborers are naturalized and constant, bare of material desires, and therefore closer to a state of grace. It is the middling class who must learn from the simply virtuous laborer. Throughout the tale, Mr. Johnson is inspired by the spiritual transcendence of their meager living conditions. He learns lessons that the shepherd and his family teach him: he 'secretly resolved to be more attentive to his own petty expenses than he had hitherto been; he resolved to be more watchful that nothing was wasted in his family' (More 193); he reminded himself, 'I will never waste another [shilling].' Mr. Johnson learns his lesson by the conclusion of the first part of the story: 'I see more and more that true goodness is not merely a thing of words and opinions, but a living principle brought into every common action of a man's life. What else would have supported this poor couple under every bitter trial of want and sickness?' (More 195). The shepherd's lessons have taught Mr. Johnson to observe what he and his own family lack in terms of 'goodness,' industry and sobriety. Hannah More thus illustrates that these are 'universal' values to be shared among all classes, but are particular to the 'naturally' virtuous laboring classes. In the end, it is Mr. Johnson who envies the shepherd's lifestyle, and not vice-versa. This maneuver dignifies the position of the poor within the society. The narrative celebrates the 'the binding of desire,' but it is interwoven with the narrative of the organic family, which now exists as a substitute for the organic community.[43] The observer in this tale exists to judge and verify the worthiness of the shepherd and his family. But Mr. Johnson finds his task a pleasurable one—he is reassured that these people are contented in this social arrangement. He, too, is to be rewarded for his endeavor; he is secure that his privileged social position will not be contested.

At the conclusion of the second part of the tale, the shepherd's goodness is so valuable to Mr. Johnson that he rewards the shepherd and his family by making the shepherd a master at a Sunday school and his wife a mistress at a small weekly industrial school teaching sewing, spinning, and knitting. This form of charity is given only to encourage work, and by doing that work, other laborers will be brought into the community that More's tale envisions. By accepting these new occupations, they can leave the small, crowded cottage formerly observed by Mr. Johnson. This constitutes the shepherd's paradox: the shepherd is rewarded for being good and self-reliant. He deserves help because he does not think he needs it, and therefore, does not ask for it. He waits to be rewarded. The effects of hard work are present in the shepherd's reward: '"I am not going to make you rich, but useful" states Mr. Johnson.' To which the shepherd replies 'Not rich? [...] How can I ever be thankful enough for such blessings?'(More 200). Social or economic inequality is not a problem to society if the poor and privileged understand their appropriate places in the society, as the example of the shepherd, his family and Mr. Johnson demonstrate. Conflict is nullified and wholly absent from the tale. Mr. Johnson vows to call on the new clerk and his family once a year or so, presumably for progress reports on the schools, but also because it is pleasurable to learn continually about 'true' goodness from these 'simple' people.

Black Giles, the Poacher is, in many respects, the antithesis of *The Shepherd of Salisbury Plain*. In the tale of the same name, Black Giles is used as a negative example of a man who, though certainly the head of the household, misuses his position in the family structure. The appearance of Black Giles' cottage draws an immediate contrast to the shepherd's:

> Poaching Giles lives on the borders of those great moors in Somersetshire [...].
> He lives at the mud cottage with the broken windows, stuffed with dirty rags, just
> beyond the gate which divides the upper from the lower moor. You may know the
> house at a good distance by the ragged tiles on the roof, and the loose stones
> which are ready to drop out from the chimney; though a short ladder, a hood of

mortar, and half an hour's leisure time, would have prevented all this, and made the little dwelling tight enough. But as Giles had never learnt any thing that was good, so he did not know the value of such useful saying as, that 'a tile in time saves nine.' (More 251)

In comparison with the description of the shepherd who works to make his cottage as comfortable and clean as possible for his family, Black Giles does not care for his family at all. This is the first moral litmus test Giles fails. The condition of his house proves he is lazy, filthy, and inattentive to others' needs and he misuses and mistreats his family. Again, domesticity and industry are linked, but this time the outcome is not as productive as it was with the shepherd. In the next paragraph, we find out that Giles thinks his desperate outward appearance is what will draw compassion from his betters:

> Besides this Giles fell into that common mistake, that a beggarly looking cottage, and filthy ragged children, raised most compassion, and of course drew most charity. But as cunning as he was in other things, he was out in his reckoning here; for it is neatness, housewifery, and a decent appearance, which draw the kindness of the rich and charitable, while they turn away disgusted from filth and laziness; not out of pride, but because they see that it is next to impossible to mend the condition of those who degrade themselves by dirty and sloth; and few people care to help those who will not helps themselves. (More 251)

The authoritative narrator instructs the reader as to which individuals 'rich and charitable' people determine are 'worthy' and 'unworthy.' Giles' 'cunning' is that he expects charity simply because he is poor. In this tale, the expectation of charity is equated with other crimes, such as poaching. Both are forms of thievery. Giles, unlike the shepherd, does not adhere to the middling-class perception of the 'deserving' poor: that they should be clean, as comfortable as their conditions permit, and always industrious. He is depicted as undisciplined, desiring what he has not earned by labor or by his goodness. As the passage indicates, any charitable person who witnesses Giles and his family can see he does not merit any help, because he does not exemplify the necessary qualities of 'worthy' poor men.

However, if the tale were as simple as a parable about 'what it means to want—and to obtain—what you do not deserve,' then it would likely end shortly after the first two paragraphs (Kowalski-Wallace 80). The object of the tale is to represent a world in which private property, protected by new laws (in this case poaching laws), is to be esteemed above all else, even if that means respecting the commons which were now enclosed as 'private property.' To illustrate the consequences to the poor if property is not respected, the tale uses a didactic formula: a series of contrasts: good vs. bad people, scrupulous vs. unscrupulous people, and the exploited vs. the exploiter. The first contrast to the dishonest Giles is Jack Weston, who we are told is 'an honest fellow in the neighborhood.' Jack is brought before a magistrate because he is 'accused of having knocked down a hare.' The magistrate adjudicating the case is Mr. Wilson, the tale's middling-class intermediary, who we are told is 'not only a pious clergyman, but an upright justice':

> Mr. Wilson was grieved at the charge; he had a great regard for Jack, but he had still a greater regard for the law. The poor fellow pleaded guilty. He did not deny the fact, but said he did not consider it as a crime, for he did not think game was private property, and he owned he had a strong temptation for doing what he had done, which he hoped would plead his excuse. The justice desired to know what his temptation was.—'sir,' said the poor fellow, 'you know I was given over this spring in a bad fever. I had no friend in the world but you, sir. Under God you saved my life by your charitable relief; and I trust also you may have helped me save my soul by your prayers and your good advice; [...]. I know I can never make you amends for all your goodness, but I thought it would be some comfort to my full heart if I could once give you some little token of my gratitude [...] I did not stay to consider whether it was wrong to kill a hare, but I felt it was right to show my gratitude [...].' (More 253)

Through his personal familiarity and conversations with Jack, Wilson discovers he was honest, but not knowledgeable about the new poaching laws. Though moved by Jack's good intentions, the readers are told that 'this worthy magistrate never suffered his feeling to bias his integrity; he knew that he did not sit on that bench to indulge pity, but to administer justice; and while he was sorry for the offender, he would never justify the offence' (More 253). The honesty of Jack's confession is valued by Mr. Wilson, but it does not diminish the severity of crime. This passage serves two ends. First, it obviously illustrates the judiciousness of the middling classes in distributing justice as well as charity. Only they are qualified to determine who is deserving of help; the worthy poor will appreciate this decision and, more importantly, passively accept whatever decision is made. In Jack Weston's case, he thankfully accepted the magistrate's decision, indicating his integrity.

Second, the tale emphasizes the rural community's adherence to the new game laws, effective after 1770, which effectively protected the property rights of the landed classes.[44] Even if catching a hare was what the poor Jack Weston thought was right according to traditional use rights of the commons, his intentions and actions according to the new middling-class law were wrong. So it is not just Black Giles who is villainous because he wants what he does not deserve (i.e. he cannot control his appetites), but all those who disrespect the right to private property. This right is elevated to a sacrament in a sermon-like speech made by Mr. Wilson: 'All property is sacred, and as the laws of the land are intended to fence in that property, he who brings up his children to break down any of these fences, brings them up to certain sin and ruin' (More 254). The insertion of religious authoritative discourse—a sermon by a clergyman, who is also the parish judge—asserts the unquestioned nature of private property, which in 1790s rural England was certainly questioned by the laboring classes. The principle behind 'private property' is at stake, rather than the relative consequence of Black Giles' or Jack Weston's poaching. Therefore, beyond the self-controlled, disciplined laborer which the shepherd exemplifies in the first tale, we are to understand other forms of transgression, such as poaching, as immediately caused by a lack of self-discipline and the 'right' principles. Within the narrative, legal and economic issues are

transposed into moral ones—the discourse of the sermon—that the reader must feel
to be 'right,' and thus identify with the morally-correct character, the clergyman
and magistrate Mr. Wilson, who is not poor.

However, though the tale portrays these negative examples, it still offers a
hopeful alternative, wishing to instruct the readers in proper behavior as is More's
'duty of a faithful historian' (More 254). Buttressed on one side by the description
of Black Giles and on the other by the fate of Jack Weston, a narrative is begun
about one of the Giles children, Dick, 'the best of Giles' bad boys,' and is
continued in part two of the story. Dick becomes the focus of Mr. Wilson's
attention for he has long been interested in 'snatching some of this vagrant family
from ruin' as a charitable endeavor (More 252). Black Giles, as head of his
household, taught his children idle habits and employments such as begging,
thievery, poaching, etc. and kept them out of Sunday school, Church and any
'useful' employment. His wife, Tawney Rachel (and the subject of another tale),
neglected her family by going 'about the country telling fortunes, and selling
dream-books and wicked songs' (More 253). Both parents corrupt the family,
legitimizing Mr. Wilson's intercession in the family through a series of incidents
designed to persuade the young Dick, and the reader, to change his corrupted ways.

In one of these attempts, Mr. Wilson employed Dick to plant a little field
of beans, hoping to teach him the value of work. We are told that Dick willingly
went to work, until Black Giles scolded him for working for the parson who
promised to pay Dick once the work was completed. Black Giles then gives his son
a misguided lesson: 'Come, give me a handful of beans, I will teach thee how to
plant when thou art paid for planting by the peck. All we have to do is to despatch
[sic] the work as fast as we can, and get rid of the beans with all speed; and as to
the seed coming up or not, that is no business of our's; we are paid for planting and
not for growing' (More 252). Ostensibly, this scene depicts Black Giles' lack of
industriousness, a quality which he wants to instill in his son. Readers should view
this scene with disdain, but readers also witness an interesting transposition in
social relations: the exploitation of the landowners by the laboring classes.
Essentially, Giles steals from the landowners because he does not plant crops,
either for profit or for food. Since their land yields food and work for day-laborers,
Giles perpetuates his, his family's, and his class' misery. Therefore, if the lower
orders are not supervised properly or do not possess the 'correct' qualities, then the
tale portrays the landowner, in this case Mr. Wilson, as a victim of the laborer's
laziness. Again, the scene justifies the intercession of the middling classes into the
lives of the laboring classes in order to correct this exploitation.

Eventually, Dick is won over by the goodness of Mr. Wilson. He attends
Sunday school, where he not only learns to read and spell, but learns the Ten
Commandments. Beth Fowkes Tobin points out that even though the Church
believed that human nature was essentially sinful, More believed reading and
reflection upon religious texts, 'will aid in self-examination' in which one's
behavior could be self-regulated and thus one's soul saved (84). Particularly
highlighted are the eighth (thou shall not steal); the fourth (thou shalt keep holy the
sabbath-day); the fifth (thou shalt honor thy mother and thy father—we are told this
is the only commandment in which Dick's heart 'did not smite him'); and the tenth

(thou shall not covet). Hannah More resolves the conflicts between the lazy workers and the virtuous landowners, by evoking god-given strictures. The commandments are used as rules for conduct which, if properly understood and practiced, would re-interpellate subjects, like Dick, as self-disciplined and self-controlling: useful to the new needs of a new economy.

Betty Brown, the St. Giles's Orange Girl is a final example from More's tracts. The narrative follows Betty, a young orphan, who could neither 'sew, spin, nor knot, nor wash, nor iron, nor read, nor spell.' The reason for Betty's lack of knowledge about respectable laboring-class tasks is because she was born 'before many good gentlemen and ladies began to concern themselves so kindly that the poor might have a little learning. There was no charitable society then as there is now, to pick up poor, friendless children in the streets [...]' (More 247). Again, More evokes the charitableness of the privileged at the beginning of the tale. Betty, though she 'always put herself in the way of doing something,' was misguided by impoverished circumstances and exploited by other laboring-class people. For example, Betty was employed by a cook-maid to sell 'the ends of candles, pieces of meat and cheese, the lumps of butter, or any thing else [the cook-maid] cribbed from the house' in which she worked to Mrs. Sponge, who kept an eating-house. Betty is 'faithful to both her employers, which is extraordinary, considering the greatness of the temptation and her utter ignorance of good and evil' (More 247). The implication is that she is faithful to the wrong people:

> Mrs. Sponge lent Betty the money to buy the oranges and a barrow to sell it from, taught her how to buy and how to sell the fruit. However, the unscrupulous Mrs. Sponge also took most of the money Betty made either from rent of the barrow, interest on her investment, rent from the room she let to Betty and the price for her meals. Betty became indentured to Mrs. Sponge, out of gratitude: Poor Betty's gratitude blinded her so completely, that she had forgot to calculate the vast proportion which this generous benefactress was to receive out of her little gains. (More 248)

Salvation occurs when Betty is spied by a genteel Lady who inquires about her situation. The Lady tries to explain to Betty that she is being taken advantage of: 'do you know that you have already paid for that single five shillings the enormous sum of 7*l*.10*s*.? I believe it is the most profitable five shillings Mr. Sponge ever laid out' (More 249). But again Betty's loyalty to her employer, as well as her dependence on Mrs. Sponge for lodging, food and the wheelbarrow, blinds her. The Lady then benevolently gives her advice, which is presumably more valuable than giving her five shillings would have been. Through self-denial, Betty Brown would be able to save enough to live 'independently and honestly':

> Only oblige yourself to live hard for a little time, till you have saved five shillings out of your own earnings. Give up that expensive supper at night, drink only a pint of porter, and no gin at all. As soon as you have scraped together the five shillings, carry it back to your false friend; if you are industrious, you will, at the end of the year, have saved 7*l*.10*s*. If you can make shift to live now, judge how things will mend when your capital becomes your own. You will put some clothes

> on your back; and, by leaving the use of spirits, and the company in which you
> drink them, your health, your morals, and your condition will mend. (More 249)

Again, 'good,' industrious working people are contrasted with other less scrupulous 'low' class people, such as Mrs. Sponge. Within the logic of the tale, exploitation only emerges in the form of intra-class relationships: good poor people are exploited by other greedy, lazy poor people. Middling-class people are portrayed as judicious, virtuous and helpful to the poor who are 'worthy' enough to accept their valued advice and learn from it.

Betty Brown, as someone who was only misdirected by others rather than really immoral herself, takes the Lady's advice and saves her money—to the condemnation of Mrs. Sponge. And of course the lady's advice is a corrective to 'these poor blinded creatures' (More 249). Towards the end of the tale, after Betty has proven herself to be a hard worker and a frugal and obedient woman, the benevolent Lady sponsors her attendance at Sunday school. Rewards abound when Betty Brown 'rose in the world' by keeping a 'handsome sausage shop' (More 250). Again, her rewards, though material, are attained because of virtuous personal qualities. Morality comes to be defined, in terms of the poor, as the ability to produce material benefit from those personal attributes. Therefore, through the logic of the tale, the only obstacle to material self-sufficiency is lack of moral fortitude: the restructured capitalist economy, even the criminalization of customary rights, is not an obstacle to self-reliance and subsistence. In contrast, virtue for the middling class is defined in terms of their ability to 'direct' the poor to financial independence—the only proper form of charity.

Hannah More's tales in *The Cheap Repository Tracts* promulgate the ideologies that labor is a source of moral improvement, and that the family, rather than class association, is a source of moral and financial responsibility and loyalty. For the poor, labor and domesticity are tied together; the productivity of one engenders the productivity of the other. Therefore, labor is not oppressive, but is the impetus to personal and domestic improvement. However, leisure is oppressive, because it exploits the landowner, and negates the responsibility and loyalty of each family member to the other. As figured within these tales, the efficacy of labor, which goes hand in hand with moral improvement, enables harmony within the family and between the classes. The condition of poverty is allayed by the personal improvement of the poor. The by-product of this ideological configuration is a sympathetic world in which moral regeneration of society is borne on the shoulders of laborers.

Maria Edgeworth's *Popular Tales*

The ideological purpose of *Popular Tales* (1804) is similar to that of Hannah More's *Cheap Repository Tracts*. Without the Evangelical fervor of More's endeavor, Edgeworth's tales are significantly different in intellectual tenor; however, both attempt to envision a way in which the un- and underprivileged can participate in the greater 'good' of the nation and, by doing so, politically mediate potential class conflicts. Edgeworth, a novelist and educational theorist, was well-versed in the economic, social and educational theories of her time.[45] Like *The Cheap Repository Tracts*, *Popular Tales* represents the middling-class concerns for property, prosperity, and individual improvement. For Edgeworth, though, the tales were an illustration of the rationalist, educational principles already established in *Practical Education*, but modified for older audiences.[46] Much of her fiction was created as a 'continuation of the scientific discussion by other means' (Omasreiter 195). These 'other means' are, presumably, the novels and regional tales she wrote. Concerned with trying to tailor an 'enlightened' education to the demands of an increasingly capitalist society, Edgeworth's tales linked the 'dissemination of the ethics of labor' with human happiness (Omasreiter 199). For Edgeworth, the practice of reading would motivate the improvement of her audience, by disseminating particular ideologies as a way to harmonize society.

Little is known about the publication history of the tales, but a review by Francis Jeffrey, editor of the *Edinburgh Review*, is useful for gauging their reception. He thought their didacticism one of their most important features. In his words they are:

> an attempt, we think, somewhat superior in genius, as well as utility, to the laudable exertions of Mr. Thomas Paine to bring disaffection and infidelity within the comprehension of the common people, or the charitable endeavors of Messrs. Wirdsworth [sic] & Co. to accommodate them with an appropriate vein of poetry. (qtd. in Butler 339)

The review positions *Popular Tales* as the mid-point on a discursive spectrum: on one side are the radical pamphleteers, and on the other are the poetic endeavors of poets like Wordsworth. Jeffrey considers both emotionally excessive. Rather than focusing attention on the individual as introspective, which is, in his view, potentially radical, he lauds the social utility of Edgeworth's tales and her attention to the 'real' world (Jeffrey, qtd. in Butler 340). This passage emphasizes the tightrope to be walked between attention to the 'real' world and the 'real' worth of the individual.[47] These tales fulfill a social need by teaching the lower orders what should be valued in their social sphere, and it seems to confirm what Mitzi Myers has claimed about this type of fiction: that didactic literature is 'emblematic of women writers' increasingly confident handling of social questions [...]' ('Tracts' 265).

The impetus for writing *Popular Tales*, as well as tales for children such as *Parent's Assistant* (1800), *Moral Tales* (1801), and *Early Lessons* (1809), comes from her desire to have a practical illustration of the beliefs and teachings described by both Edgeworth and her father in *Practical Education* (1798).[48] The goals of education and literature should ultimately be to cultivate 'taste and judgment' (Harden 24). Instruction and enjoyment, however, were not mutually exclusive which was another, more common, view of writers on education (Michaels 208). Still, in the eighteenth century literature was valued for its instructive quality and moral guidance. Based on the theories of Locke and Rousseau, the purpose of a practical education was to cultivate the rational qualities of the mind, allowing for proper judgment which will naturally advance the individual to a state of fulfillment. The Edgeworths saw education as the key to changing man's essential nature, which, as Locke had claimed, is formed by both circumstances and experience. But, education must always befit circumstances and experience. Literature, and fiction in particular, could represent and substitute for that experience. For these tales, as for Hannah More's tales, the pedagogical and aesthetic functions are linked.

In *Popular Tales*, Edgeworth universalizes rationality by extending it to the laboring and lower, middling classes. To do this, she presented her protagonists as positive examples of laboring life. The characters could start out with faults, but by the end transcend them and transform their lives. Instead of using an intermediary as More does, Edgeworth 'teaches' the reader how to reason. Her tales would, it was hoped, counteract their laboring habits and experiences, by being a substitute for them, by making them 'think' about the morality involved in their choices. The suggestion that the lower orders have the ability to apply reason and tailor their own conduct is dangerous at this point in history. Even Hannah More, who was widely criticized for advocating literacy among the poor, never went so far to say they could possess rationality; she thought they could possess only simple and natural virtue as *The Shepherd of Salisbury Plain* demonstrates. More's tales negate further necessity for reading: while they 'learn' proper values through them, they also learn to look to the middle classes for moral guidance. For Edgeworth, though, progressive theories of economics and education point to ways in which laboring-class subjectivity could be renovated to accommodate new social relations, centrally including a kind of 'enlightened' rationality gained through reading practices. If laboring-class people could think, they could 'freely' choose particular 'habits of action.' This is a recurrent ideological notion throughout *Popular Tales*. To Edgeworth, the freedom to choose was a progressive notion, but, paradoxically, the lower orders would have to be taught 'proper' limits to freedom of thought as well. As Alan Richardson has noted, 'Edgeworth's is an ambivalent ideology at odds with itself, caught between the nostalgia of tract writers like Trimmer and More for an earlier era's vertical social hierarchies and bonds of patronage and obligation, and the ethos of self-improvement and rugged individualism' (225).

One way to straddle this contradiction was to be a benefactor: a writer whose texts 'improved' individuals. Thus, she attempted to create an ethical code which could be constructed from within laboring-class subjectivity. Thus, based on the development of individual degrees of morality, the laboring classes had the illusory choice to either enter a mutually beneficial bond with middling class or reject it. This combination of pedagogy and economic stratification, not uncommon in the eighteenth century, was important for understanding the ideological work of the tales.

The instructive or didactic element is the generative point for all Edgeworth's fiction, and was not an element imposed on the story by either Edgeworth or her father at a later stage in the composition (Butler 237). Marilyn Butler observes that Edgeworth was in the 'habit of recording the "Object of the Story"' in her notebooks:

The sketch for *Tomorrow* (one of the *Popular Tales*, 1804) is followed by a typical note, headed 'Things to be done' –'to show that those who have the habit of procrastinating may lose fortune, fame, friends and happiness.' (236)

From this point, Edgeworth assembles 'data' in her notebooks which illustrates that 'objective': these included facts, anecdotes, and eccentric characters that might be used in her fiction (Butler 238). As Butler states, 'the most significant feature of this notebook [literary notebook of 1805-1807], as of those that survive from the 1820s, is that it does not record ideas, or sensations, but facts. It shows a mind alert to all kind of miscellaneous information encountered in everyday experience, in conversation, and in books' (239). Her composition method must certainly be attributed to her father's high esteem for experimental science and the scientific training he had taught her as young girl—observation, notation, experimentation.[49] Education was an experimental science to Edgeworth, and she was an educator and writer who could guide the experiential lessons of life through literature. Her approach to writing tales for the laboring classes parallels her educational theories for children. The theory behind educating children was to 'plant the seeds of science, morality, and other departments of thought in the small child's conscious or partly conscious mind' (Butler 64). This same theory—proper judgment, ingenuity and moral inculcation—is operable in her tales for the lower orders.

Popular Tales are harder to characterize as a group than *The Cheap Repository Tracts* because they encompass a wider range of readers: laborers, small merchants and shopkeepers, yeoman farmers, tradesmen, and clerks. And the tales as a group reflect this readership: manufacturing, service industry as well as traditional agricultural labor are represented. In More's tales, broader ideological concepts such as private property, proper domestic relations and labor productivity are represented in the mixing of discursive materials; in Edgeworth's tales, the laboring classes are taught to 'think' differently about their conditions of existence so they will be as content in their social sphere as the privileged are in theirs. Ideologemes such as 'free' choice and a limited kind of social mobility are illustrated through the plotting of the narratives. While emphasis falls on the individual's moral improvement, there is also the potential for limited social mobility—provided that the laborer internalizes middling-class values. This mobility would be considered a heinous transgression of civility to More's understanding of god-given social relations. But for Edgeworth, changing the social structure was premised on the progress of human knowledge, science, rationality. Rationality of mind was tied to the economic progress of production and trade. Thus, her enlightened belief in a limited social mobility guaranteed capitalist conformity to the progressive values of hard work, frugality, respect for private property and familial obligations.

While Edgeworth rejects paternalism and favors a self-regulating social and economic system based on the progress of the individual, an 'enlightened' middling-class benefactor, usually a merchant, manufacturer or large landowner, is again present, as in More's tales. However, the benefactor generally does not intercede in matters of justice or even give advice. Instruction occurs in the narrative sequencing of cause and effect: justice comes to those who learn from individual experience. The benefactor is an objective observer who exists to verify for the reader what the responsible course of action is, would have been or could be. This distancing of desire through sequencing enables her tales to act as a substitute for common laboring-class experiences in the sense that she encourages her readers to think about the morality involved in their choices. This sequencing suggests that the lower orders have the ability to apply reason. Rewards for proper moral behavior are again depicted, as in More's tales, if the 'right' course of action is taken. Again, however, the reward is never purely pleasurable, but enables those who act in the 'right' way to be 'content,' thus guaranteeing a degree of independent poverty to the worthy individual.

At various points in *The Lottery*, for instance, characters have choices to make. Choices are conditioned by a middling-class moral index of 'right' and 'wrong.' This is a different narrative structure from the tales that More presents. In More's tales, the poor either consistently make the 'right' or 'wrong' choice. In *Popular Tales*, the suspense (whether a character will make what is coded as the 'right' decision) and the pleasure of the narrative (the satisfaction when a character learns from terrible mistakes) are intertwined with the choices these characters make and the consequences those choices have. Consequences propel the plot. Unlike More's characters, Edgeworth's learn from their mistakes, not because someone like a cleric and a magistrate told them they were wrong, but because they assessed the consequences of their own actions and chose to change their habits. In other words, they learned how to redeem themselves through observing their experiences and rationally thinking about them. This is the lesson that the tales should 'teach' readers.

The characters' ability to measure their own failings would be impossible without positive and negative examples from which to choose. Generally, examples of moral fortitude, middling-class benevolence, and laboring-class indolence abound. Economic and social conditions exist because of an individual's habits of industry, and not because of economic and social conditions that precede the individual. In this way, the individual is preeminently responsible for his/her fate. Within the logic of the tales, a character can choose to improve or fall into idleness, but he/she must accept the current mode of social relations as natural. Therefore, free choice is already limited to those possible within this system, and limited again to those that are seen within the system to be moral actions for their class. To illustrate how free choice works, we will examine two of the tales.

The Lottery illustrates the pernicious effects of winning money, rather than earning it. In this tale, laboring-class economic prosperity is linked to labor, and labor is linked to moral worth. Therefore, those who gain economic prosperity by means other than labor are doomed to idleness and corruption because they have not been taught the lessons of labor—hard work, frugality, prudence and judiciousness. Even though economic self-reliance is achieved, financial prudence is not. In the end, then, this kind of economic self-reliance proves to be illusory. Class transgression is depicted as immoral and akin to beggary, which is socially abhorrent and irresponsible. This is the didactic element that propels the content of the plot. But how an action is proven to be moral illustrates the ideological work of the tale.

At the beginning of the tale, readers are introduced to the Robinson family: husband Maurice, a factory worker who was 'remarkable for his good conduct and regular attendance at his work'; his wife Ellen who was 'an industrious and prudent young woman'; and son George who was brought up by his mother 'to be honest, to speak the truth, to do whatever she and his father bid him, and to dislike being idle' (Edgeworth 161-2). Into this picture of domestic contentment, Maurice's cousin enters. Mrs. Dolly, we are told, is a 'laundry-maid in a great family, where she learned to love gossiping, and tea-drinkings, and where she acquired some taste for shawls and cherry-brandy' (Edgeworth 161). Mrs. Dolly's pretensions and vices disrupt the prudent and hard-working nature of the family. In the world of this tale, characters influence individual desires and vices; circumstances do not.

Judging who is a positive influence and which choices are correct are lessons the narrative teaches Maurice, the protagonist, but they are also lessons these texts essentially teach their readers. Recognizing positive examples from his own class (wife Ellen and friend William Deane), a negative example from his class (Mrs. Dolly), and living through the consequence of his own good or bad judgment, reinforces Maurice's belief, and the reader's, that he controls his own fate. His choices are to be coded as free, each with its own consequence. But for each episode in which a decision needs to be made, there is a tacit assumption that there is a correct choice. Maurice's failure to recognize that correct choice is portrayed as a particular problem of his moral nature. Moral improvement only occurs as a result of Maurice's freely choosing the only correct choice. The point is that individuals learn rational discernment, and by making the implicitly correct choice, they build moral fortitude. The illusion given is that the free personal choices an individual makes foster individual self-reliance and obedient citizenship.

Similarly, the reader participates in these choices by watching Maurice's life progress through the narrative. The reader learns to recognize which decisions are correct and moral, which are wrong and immoral. Edgeworth's characters, unlike More's, determine their own courses of action, and suffer the consequences of those actions. Through reading these tales, the readers, rather than having these experiences and suffering the consequences, can learn through generic cues to identify the right or wrong choices.

For example, Mrs. Dolly advises and eventually convinces Maurice to buy a lottery ticket against the advice of his wife Ellen and his upstanding friend William Deane. The reader has privileged knowledge that this is the wrong choice, because the narrative voice validates Ellen, his industrious wife, and Deane, 'the most industrious man in the parish.' Dean is also well-respected by both classes and, by the end of the tale, has made a living large enough to afford some comforts. He rivals Mrs. Dolly for influence in Maurice's life. Through this character contrast, reason always wins against pure desire. Deane, speaking as an enlightened member of the laboring class, argues reasonably against Dolly's advice:

> That when a man worked for fair wages every day, he was sure of getting
> something for his pains, and with honest industry, and saving might get rich

enough in time, and have to thank himself for it, which would be a pleasant thing: but that if a man, as he had known many, set his heart upon the turning of the lottery wheel, he would leave off putting his hand to any thing the whole year round, and so grow idle, and may be, drunken; [...] at the year's end, if he have a [lottery] blank, what is he to do for his rent, or for his wife and children, that have nothing to depend upon but him and his industry? (164)

As is no surprise to readers, this passage proves prophetic for the Robinsons. But the narrative does not proceed as simply as this passage implies. Since it is assumed that Maurice is the head of the household on whom his family is dependent, Maurice's reason and judgment are put in question through his decisions. The narrative is thus moved forward by the drama of choices: individual decisions propel the plot. First, Ellen gives her husband her hard-earned wages from spinning; he must then choose to buy either a cow, as she desired, or a lottery ticket, as Dolly wanted. Maurice, being of 'irresolute character,' vacillates between these two choices. But because of accidental circumstances, Maurice chooses to loan the money to Deane so that he can buy books for studying. Edgeworth makes it clear that this is to be perceived by the reader as a wise alternative and an investment in the future; books improve individuals. She accomplishes this by having Ellen and Maurice defend William Deane against Mrs. Dolly's rages:

Maurice declared he was the most industrious man in the parish; that his books never kept him from his work, but always kept him from the alehouse and bad company; and that as to his gimcracks and machines, he never laid out a farthing upon them but what he got by working on holidays, and odd times, when other folks were idle or tippling. His master, who understood the like of those things, said, before all the workmen at the mills, that William Deane's machines were main clever, and might come to bring in a deal of money for him and his. (167)

An investment in William's education eventually yields economic returns. Reading and skills training are valued as means to improve oneself, especially in a changing industrial age in which skilled labor becomes highly valued. But improvement can only occur if one is positioned as morally virtuous.

When faced with a second decision regarding the lottery, Maurice gives in and buys a lottery ticket. He and his family must contend with winning the hefty sum of 5,000 pounds, rather than losing money. This would suggest that risky decision-making and seemingly foolish choices pay off. However, Edgeworth portrays this as a rather vulgar class transgression that will not improve the participants or their lives, but will put their familial happiness in jeopardy:

'No more spinning-wheels!' cried Maurice; 'no more spinning! no more work! We have nothing to do now but to be as happy as the day is long. Wife, I say, put by that wheel.'

'You're a lady now; and ought to look and behave like a lady,' added Dolly [...].

'I don't know how to look and behave like a lady,' said Ellen, and sighed: 'but I hopes Maurice won't love me the less for that.' (169)

For the Robinsons, the lifestyle of the upper classes contradicts their 'nature' as laboring-class people. Since labor and happiness are directly correlated for the lower orders, money without labor can only lead to unhappiness. So, while on the one end, the lower ranks should live independently, on the other end, they should also not become so independent that they are taken beyond their class. While Maurice starts to live idly, as he thought a gentleman ought to, his wife wisely invests part of the winnings in a haberdashery and works prodigiously. Her husband, good-hearted but morally weak, gambles away the rest of the money. Ellen, however, makes the haberdashery a success through her frugality and diligence. As Edgeworth narrates the unhappy spiral of Maurice's fate, she illustrates that the lower orders have a natural propensity toward work which should not be interfered with:

> Maurice, who had been accustomed to be at work for several hours in the day, at first thought it would be a fine thing to walk about, as Mrs. Dolly said, like a gentleman, without having anything to do; but when he came to try it he found himself more tired by this way of life than he had ever felt himself in the cotton-mills at Derby. (173)

Only labor leads the lower orders towards happiness, self-respect and fulfillment; leisure leads Maurice to ruin. The more time passed, the less Maurice worked and the more unhappy he became.

Because of Maurice's idleness, the familial bonds to his family, formerly very strong and unified, deteriorate. Maurice frequently goes out and returns late at night, never attending to work in the haberdashery. Dolly spends much money on drinking sherry and buying expensive shawls. However, familial reunification comes when the money they had won is lost, along with their earnings from the shop, due to Maurice's gambling debts. Debt resolves the contradictory state in which they had been living. Ellen's relief is apparent when her husband confesses his gambling. She forgave him, claiming, 'we can work hard, and be happy again' (181). The family reunites in debt and the apparent happiness that overcoming strife brings. Labor promises to reverse the family's dissolution.

If the tale had ended here, however, it would have been the consequences of his gambling that urged him to recant his idle ways. But for Edgeworth, learning from experience must involve conscious thought and decision-making, and not merely financial and material deprivation from one's uncontrollable desires. The reader must be assured that his choices will be different next time. Assurance is given in the form of a chastisement from Mr. Belton, a rich carpet manufacturer, who employs the Robinsons' young son George as a record-keeper. He serves as the moral arbiter:

> 'It is not my intention,' said Mr. Belton, 'to add to your present suffering, Mr. Robinson, by pointing out that it has arisen entirely from your own imprudence. Nor yet can I say that I feel much compassion for you; for I have always considered a gamester as a most selfish being, who should be suffered to feel the terrible consequences of his own avaricious folly, as a warning to others.' (184)

Mr. Belton verifies the immorality of Maurice's choices and actions for the readers. As a member of the middling class, it is simply assumed that he has a superior character and possesses the ability and authority to discern the proper course of action. He values Ellen because she has been 'an excellent wife and mother'; therefore, she should not suffer 'by the folly and imprudence in which you had no share' (184). Because Ellen's character was irreproachable and because it was not her decisions that led to these disastrous consequences, Mr. Belton advances her money needed to pay off Maurice's debts so that she should not lose her home. He trusts that her 'industry and integrity' will lead her to repay him from the profits of her shop, leaving Maurice to suffer with the knowledge that he has driven his family into a debt that both he, Ellen and their son George must pay for. Effectively, this demoralizes and emasculates Maurice, undercutting his position in the family. He must prove that he is a 'worthy' husband, father, worker and citizen if he is to regain his former position as the beloved head of the household.

Mrs. Dolly does not fare nearly as well. Because of her drunkenness, she fatally falls from a horse. Upon her death, Ellen and Maurice find a lottery ticket in one of her expensive shawls. This is Maurice's final moral choice: should he live on false hopes of winning money or cash the ticket in and work hard to repay his debts honestly? Maurice, however, has learned his lesson, and proves his worthiness to his wife by selling the lottery ticket: 'how rejoiced he was when he had parted with his dangerous temptation, and when he had received seventeen guineas in hand, instead of anxious hopes!' (189). Maurice regains his valued position in the family because he is now 'worthy' of his family's respect and love.

Another, more pastoral, example from Edgeworth's *Popular Tales* is *Rosanna*. Edgeworth continues contrasting moral worth or, as she puts it in this tale, definitions of 'contentment.' The distinction separates those who are content to make the best out of their meager circumstances from those who are content to live slovenly without a chance for individual improvement: 'there are two sorts of content: one is connected with exertion, the other with habits of indolence; the first is a virtue, the second a vice' (195). Once again, characters represent this moral spectrum, because individual action determines one's fate and the course of the plot. The Gray family, of ancient noble Irish birth though their means are now very meager, represent the 'virtuous' side of contentment. On the other end, Easy Simon O'Dougherty—'a sort of a half or a half quarter gentleman'—has ruined his small landholding through his indolence.[50] And there are other variances in this didactic spectrum: the greedy 'middle-man' Mr. Hopkins; the vain, corrupt and nearly bankrupt parliamentarian Hyacinth O'Brien; and his faithful servant Stafford who marries Farmer Gray's daughter. Although the Grays are consistently portrayed as simple, good-hearted people who work the land, there is the suggestion that not everyone is exactly who they seem to be. O'Brien, though seemingly a wealthy landowner, had squandered his money by supporting his vanity. Easy Simon, though lazy, is always honest and a proud Irishman, refusing to dishonor his friends, the Grays. Because there are variances, rational discernment is necessary in order to determine who will be honest in business practices and who will not.

Rosanna, to which the title refers, is not a woman, but land on which a 'common oat-mill' and a tan-yard sit. Figuring the land as feminine is a very deliberate attempt to connect the love of the land, its productivity, and familial happiness. Rosanna is Easy Simon's patrimonial land, which he has let fall into decay because he believes the only way to get 'through this world' is to 'take it easy.' During the course of the narrative, Farmer Gray's sons rent these lands, repair all the unused, broken machinery, and make a success of both the mill and the tan-yard. Each son pays Easy Simon a portion from their profits, as well as their rent. Their hard work pays off for all interested parties: John and Robin Gray and the landowner Easy Simon. This is meant to depict how agricultural capitalism can work in a microcosm; it regenerates the land as well as the people who work and own it. For instance, the 'mud-walled' cottage and small farm, which the elder Gray rents and in which he began to raise his family, is described at the beginning of the tale as:

> a poor mud-walled cabin, facing the door of which there was a green pool of stagnant water; and before the window, of one pane, a dunghill that, reaching to the thatch of the roof, shut out the light, and filled the house with the most noisome smell [...]. The former inhabitants of this mansion had, it seems, been content without a chimney: and, indeed, almost without a roof [...] the farm consisted of about forty acres; and the fences of the grazing-land were so bad, that the neighbours' cattle took possession of it frequently by day, and always by night. The tillage-ground had been so ill managed by his predecessor, that the land was what is called quite out of heart. (196)

The regeneration of this impoverished land is linked to the regeneration of the family's 'nobility' of character, rather than its title; the poor are ennobled by working the land, as the wealthy are by owning it. A small investment in one's home and surrounding fields will yield great rewards. This reward comes from the individual's labor and financial prudence, and not from external sources. Through the 'contented' acceptance of a poor man's lifestyle by Gray and his family, they will reestablish a family estate, with hard work, frugality, ingenuity and diligence. As Gray says, 'No man [...] deserves to be called poor, that has his health, and the use of his limbs' (Edgeworth 197). Even though Farmer Gray has just enough money to support his wife and three children independently, their lives are fulfilled and comfortable, provided they viewed work in the proper manner: as a means to happiness and improvement. Having the proper values and viewing work in the proper context, the Grays cooperatively rebuild the house and make the land productive again:

> His house was soon new roofed and new thatched; the dunghill was removed, and spread over that part of his land which most wanted manure; the putrescent water of the standing pool was drained off, and fertilized a meadow; and the kitchen was never again overflowed in rainy weather, because of the labour of half a day to make a narrow trench which carried off the water [...]. The rooms also were cleared of smoke, for Gray built a chimney; and the kitchen window, which had formerly been stuffed up, when the wind blew too hard, with an old or new hat, was glazed. (198)

Edgeworth concludes her rather lengthy georgic description of the specifics of land improvement by stating: 'These may seem trifles unworthy [of] the notice of the historian; but trifles such as these contribute much to the comfort of a poor family, and therefore deserve a place in their simple annals' (199). This passage highlights a significant didactic element in the tale: the practicality of rural living. The tale self-consciously lists the detailed tasks to be accomplished on small farms and farmhouses in order to make the poor's living conditions comfortable, clean, and healthful. Of course, these tasks require much labor on the part of the family members, but this fact is elided. As realistic as the passage claims to be, work is never portrayed. Instead, readers are assured that all the family members really need to regenerate their lands is ingenuity and the desire to do so. As in Hannah More's tales, only the fruits of labor are illustrated: 'the house with the new roof,' etc. As the two contrasting passages cited above indicate, work is reified in its products, this time not only in terms of labor, but in terms of thought. Ingenuity is a substitute for labor. For example, Farmer Gray bargains with an army captain to buy the dung from soldiers' barracks at a fair price (202). In the next year, we are told the dung fertilized ten acres of grazing land for ten cows. Gray's wife and daughter Rose set up and manage the dairy in which they made butter and buttermilk, selling their products at the market price in a neighboring town. Farmer Gray's ingenuity is lauded in this description. It enables previously worthless materials to be transformed into valuable commodities which maintain and enhance the farm. One well-planned business decision could improve the land, increasing its value, productivity, and profits. The Grays are entitled to these profits and the comfort and happiness they bring.

But regenerating the land is premised upon an 'enlightened' landowner who encourages the workers' diligence and improvements. The landlord who owned Gray's land dealt fairly with his tenants, and allowed the land to be improved without charging higher rent or fees. Simon, though indolent, saw that he could not turn a profit from his land and made the judicious decision to rent it to Farmer Gray's sons. He allowed the Grays to work to improve the land, getting the mill running and clearing and renovating the tan-pits in the yard. In both these positive examples, land is more than property which is owned; it is turned into capital which can be valorized.

Sometimes, however, good-hearted, hard-working people who value their land are prey to less scrupulous people such as Mr. Hopkins. He wanted to buy the land from Gray's landlord cheaply, and charge an exorbitant rent (Gray's rent was apparently a fair market price), making his profits higher. This kind of rackrenting, in Edgeworth's view, is a heinous act which relates directly to his personal 'unhappiness,' rather than any economic motivation; social relations appear as personal relations. To illustrate this key point, Edgeworth relates his 'misery' to his lack of family:

> the rich Mr. Hopkins, who had scraped together in about fifteen years above twenty thousand, some said thirty thousand pounds, had never been happy for a single day, either whilst he was making this fortune or when he had made it; for he was of an avaricious, discontented temper. The more he had, the more he desired [...]. He had no wife, no children, to share his wealth. He would not

> marry, because a wife is expensive; and children are worse than taxes. His whole
> soul was absorbed in the love of gain. (211)

Hopkins could not be happy, because he was not productive. He acquired land, exploiting it and the people who rented it from him. He had no real love for the land and its potential, just as he had no real love in his life: any familial obligations or satisfactions. He could not be personally fulfilled by simply owning land because he had no rightful connection to it: he did not work the land and owning it was not a matter of family inheritance. There is only one proper relationship where agricultural production is concerned: between landowner and laborer, and both are tied to generative productivity. As it is portrayed here, agricultural capitalism is premised on the link between land and family. Their association makes their productivity, and improvement, a natural occurrence which fosters personal happiness and satisfaction. Hopkins is an interloper in a 'naturally enclosed' relationship between landowner and agricultural laborer.

This enclosed relationship, which Hopkins tries to disrupt, is portrayed as a complementary partnership that is grounded in friendship and in fulfilling mutual personal needs, and not in capitalist or imperialist economics; each helps the other by offering what he possesses. This is exemplified by the Gray-Simon alliance: the Grays offer their diligence and ingenuity; Simon offers his land. This portrayal of the relationship between landowner and labor effectively rewrites 'landed property as land, which becomes nature, and property, which becomes capital.'[51] Necessary to this new definition was the ideology that loving the land would lead laborers to improve it. In a capitalist economy, landowners could profit from these agricultural improvements, rather than indulging in rent-racking, especially in Ireland. This rewriting of the value of land and the way in which it affects the relationship between owners and workers is particularly important to Edgeworth. In the 1790s in Ireland, she saw that agrarian grievances among laborers were usually settled by violence towards landowners or their agents. The violence took the form of burning down houses, mutilating cattle and assaulting individuals (Butler 115). The Edgeworths therefore took an active interest in overseeing the operations of their estate: 'they took care to see that all [Richard Lovell Edgeworth's] tenants were kept regularly employed, well housed, and effectively secure of their land' (Butler 115).[52] Both Edgeworth and her father were critical of the absentee landlords who did not take the same care with their estates.[53]

Therefore, no space exists for middle-men who enter this 'natural enclosure.' 'Middle-men,' usually former agents for the large landowners, serve only themselves, financially gouging both the landowner (by buying the land under its market value) and laborer (by charging exorbitant rents). This inhibits production of food and cloth, processing of grain, and other goods that can be culled from the land. Someone like Mr. Hopkins does not work the land, producing products from it, and does not have a rightful title to it. He is naturally villainous, someone who is guided by his consuming desire to acquire land, in contrast to the naturally good Grays, who employ hard work and good management of their resources. But Hopkins is also pitiable because he cannot share, or enjoy, his life with others, because the only lasting pleasure is the pleasure of production: the regeneration of the land which is tied to the generation of family. The landowner is not an exploitative agent if the land is rightfully owned, as in the case of Easy Simon. The assumption is that 'true' landowners are only interested in making their land more productive and would, therefore, support the workers and their efforts: the people who worked their land reflected something about the morality of the landowner's family, their heritage and their pride.

Once Mr. Hopkins realizes that the Grays had considerably increased the value of their land in a short time without missing rent, material, or equipment payments, he resorts to other measures to ruin the Grays. He 'saw [...] that he could at a small expense turn the course of the stream, and cut off the water from the mill' (213). To achieve this goal it is necessary to obtain a field adjacent to the Grays' growing estate. That field was owned by Easy Simon. Simon, acting as he often does without thinking of the consequences of his decision, sells the land to Hopkins for 'the immediate want of a horse' (218). The injustice of this sale should be readily apparent to the readers because of the running commentary on Hopkins' lack of any positive qualities; he is, in fact, characterized as the 'oppressor of the poor' (242) because he does not recognize and applaud the work habits of the Grays. The Grays appeal to the upright magistrate, Molyneux, who is a landowner campaigning for a seat in Parliament, to plead the case of the Grays against the 'villainy of Hopkins.' They hope to recover their rights to work the land. Farmer Gray does this so that his

> boys shall have justice [...]. I am not fond of law, God knows! I never had a lawsuit in my life; nobody dreads such things more than I do; but I dread nothing in defence of my sons and justice [...]. The labour of their lives shall not be in vain; they shall not be robbed of all they have: they shall not be trampled upon by any one living, let him be ever so rich, or ever so litigious. (237)

Gray is primarily concerned with leaving his children a legacy of hard work (not property), which the improvement of the land represents. The loss of their ability to continually improve the land would signal the demise of their place in the social structure, corrupting their 'natural' talents by making them idle and dependent. Constant improvement is the element valorized by a capitalist work ethic for the laborers. Inherent in this new concept of land as private property, the land, individual morality and domesticity are joined as productive pleasures to be continually ameliorated.

Eventually, however, the good Grays (the laborers) win out over the evil Hopkins (the middle-man). Molyneux, recognizing the values the Grays possess and the injustice that was being perpetrated upon them, intercedes on their behalf. He finds a loophole in the contract between Easy Simon and Hopkins. Easy Simon had forgotten to renew his title to the land that he sold to Hopkins, which was renewable for life; he had thus de facto forfeited his ownership to the landholding. This meant that the sale of the land adjoining the Grays' was null. The freehold reverts to the landlord in Dublin who renews it again to Simon, with the promise that Gray would oversee the operations of the mill. Ultimately, the restoration of the lands to the hands of the Grays produces 'peace, industry, family union, and love, in the happy cottage of Rosanna' (Edgeworth 243). Molyneax only verifies for the reader the 'truth' of the situation; he is not a benefactor who gives rewards. Rewards are products of the laborers work, and the benefit of an ideology that links improvement with morality.

Both *The Lottery* and *Rosanna* are emblematic of the kinds of tales found in Edgeworth's *Popular Tales*. These enable the ideology that continual improvement in terms of the land and morality should be the primary force of laboring-class life. In the first tale, improvement stems from learning the correct choice to make: prosperity is a matter of individual determination. In the second tale, improvement is connected to a generative function: labor increases the accumulation of human happiness, in terms of both economy and personal fulfillment. And labor and the habit of reading hail the laboring-class individual into a subjective position in which desire is a matter of free choice, ingenuity and self-determination. Edgeworth represented the practical applications of this kind of ideology in these texts: to position the poor within the framework of the changing economic order, and to give them the values that they need to reenvision their social reality.

Hannah More's *The Cheap Repository Tracts* and Maria Edgeworth's *Popular Tales* address fundamental issues that confront the un- and underprivileged: how to exist in a changing economic landscape that includes loss of land and use rights to commons, and a changing social landscape that includes the ideal, if not the reality, of social improvement and/or mobility. On the one hand, both projects represent real economic problems facing the lower middling class, laborers and the poor, and attempt to teach each how to accommodate themselves for survival in a changing legal, economic, and social landscape. The tales disseminated ideologies that might alleviate the threat of the laborers' unrest, and conduct the poor's energies into productive activities, leading to a progressive version of middling-class social relations: i.e. that individual improvement leads to social and economic improvement and happiness. Far from being repressively didactic, these efforts represent those outside elite circles as respectable, as independent and always improving individuals, and create reading fiction as an ideological practice by which individuals can improve themselves. By constructing narratives that can be shared among the upper, middle and lower orders, the relationship between them is reworked so that it is represented as harmonious. The ideologies that the tales produce through their generic features—the affection for private property, domestic affection, and an improving work ethic—construct the foundation for what the middling class believe will be harmonious relations between the poor and the privileged.

On the other hand, the tales reveal Hannah More's and Maria Edgeworth's perceptions of their feminine duty: to respond to a real and perplexing eighteenth-century problem of poverty in a way that indicates an intersection, or merging, of philanthropy with women's writing. For More and Edgeworth, the moral aspect of individual amelioration and greater domestic responsibility cannot be separated from the economic concerns of labor, property and capital. Moreover, reading literature—especially of the kind produced for an emerging non-polite readership—becomes a social practice that has great cultural power at this time. The spread of reading and literary practices grows out of a benevolent impetus associated with women's philanthropic work. More and Edgeworth are ideological producers whose writing created the 'imaginary relations' of a reformed social system that could reconcile the poor and the privileged and quell political and social upheaval. By writing texts, the most productive philanthropic endeavor could be accomplished: the political harmony of English society.

Notes

1   See David Owen, *English Philanthropy 1160-1960* (Cambridge, MA: Belknap, 1964).
2   See Gertrude Himmelfarb, *The Idea of Poverty: England in the Early Industrial Age* (New York: Knopf, 1984) 5. For a more expansive description of the lives of the poor, particularly those on parish relief, see *Chronicling Poverty: The Voices and Strategies of the English Poor, 1640-1840*, eds. Tim Hitchcock, Peter King and Pamela Sharpe, (New York: St. Martin's, 1997).
3   See Himmelfarb 41; Roger Wells details the problems of famine and war in *Wretched Face*, and discusses the problems of the enclosure and its effect on the poor in 'The Development of the English Rural Proletariat and Social Protest, 1700-1850' *Class, Conflict and Protest in the English Countryside, 1700-1880*, eds. Mick Reed and Roger Wells, (Savage, MD: Frank Cass) 1990.
4   See Tobin, *Superintending the Poor.*
5   Owen states that towards the end of the eighteenth century, the poor had to illustrate that they 'deserved' improvement in order to receive monetary and other forms of relief (98). Women, simultaneously, increasingly participated in the amelioration of the poor. See F. K. Prochaska, *Women and Philanthropy in Nineteenth-Century England* (Oxford: Clarendon, 1980) 40-41; and Janet Todd, *Sign of Angelica* 205-6.
6   David Cressy, 'Levels of Illiteracy in England 1530-1730,' *Literacy and Social Development in the West: A Reader*, ed. Harvey J. Graff, (New York: Cambridge UP, 1981) 105-124 and R.S. Schofield, 'Dimensions of Illiteracy in England 1750-1850,' *Literacy and Social Development in the West: A Reader*, ed. Harvey J. Graff, (New York: Cambridge UP, 1981) 201-213, give raw data on the extent of literacy in eighteenth- and nineteenth-century England.
7   This literature is characterized as primarily 'didactic' by critics such as Gary Kelly and Mitzi Myers because of its rather simplistic fictional style, though they both admit that these tales had an impact on the history of fiction. See Kelly, *English Fiction of the Romantic Period, 1789-1830* (New York: Longman, 1989) 61-62, and Mitzi Myers, 'Hannah More's Tracts' 264-284.
8   Scholars such as Victor Neuberg, Margaret Spufford and Susan Pedersen view the tales as important only as an historical document without considering the generic elements which make it powerful ideologically. See Victor Neuberg, *Popular Literature: A History and Guide* (New York: Penguin, 1977); Margaret Spufford, *Small Books and Pleasant Histories* (London: Metheun, 1981); and Susan Pedersen 'Hannah More Meets Simple Simon: Tracts, Chapbooks, and Popular Culture in Late Eighteenth-Century England' *Journal of British Studies* 25 (January 1986): 84-113. Christine Kruger has noted that More's writing has usually been treated as 'derivative of male conservatives,' and she can therefore be easily dismissed as a marginal writer. See *Reader's Repentance* (95-6). Edgeworth's *Popular Tales* has had scant treatment. The one exception is Alan

Richardson who discusses two of Edgeworth's *Popular Tales*, 'Lame Jervas' and 'The Grateful Negro' in some detail. See Richardson, *Literature, Education, and Romanticism, Reading as Social Practice 1780-1832* (New York: Cambridge UP, 1994).

9   See Ivanka Kovacevic, *Fact Into Fiction* (Leicester: Leicester UP, 1975); and Joseph Kestner, *Protest and Reform: The British Social Narrative by Women, 1827-1867* (Madison: U of Wisconsin P, 1985).

10   The connection between aesthetics and ethics is an important one for eighteenth-century philosophy and literature. See Janet Todd, *Sensibility* 23-31.

11   Whether or not the laboring classes conformed to these middle-class desires is questionable. One could claim, for instance, that these texts did not quell the food riots of the early nineteenth century. Thomas Laqueur goes farther and claims that the literature used in Sunday Schools (though the texts I am discussing in this chapter have a broader circulation) had very little 'direct political propaganda.' He claims the material was first religious, second a 'part of working-class culture of self-improvement with its concern for history, the natural sciences, and 'useful' knowledge.' Third, it advocated 'honesty and kindness.' But, and I would agree, Laqueur comes to the conclusion that the Schools *did* 'promote certain values often associated with industrial society.' Yet, he dismisses More and other writers like Sarah Trimmer as having any substantial effect on the culture of the industrial society. See Thomas Laqueur, *Religion and Respectability: Sunday Schools and Working-Class Culture, 1780-1850* (New Haven: Yale UP, 1976) 203-214.

12   Most recently Anne K. Mellor has defended Hannah More's *Cheap Repository* on the bases of her association with the Clapham Sect, which developed the concept of 'Christian capitalism,' and in this way Mellor sees More as 'attempt[ing] to define a moral method of capitalist investment and consumption,' *Mothers* 32. For examples, see also Dorice Williams Elliot, *The Angel Out of the House*; Christine Krueger, *The Reader's Repentance*; Mitzi Myers, 'Hannah More's Tracts for the Times, Social Fiction and Female Ideology,' *Fetter'd of Free? British Women Novelists, 1670-1815*, eds. Mary Anne Schofield and Cecilia Macheski (Athens, OH: Ohio UP, 1986); Kathryn Sutherland, 'Hannah More's Counter-Revolutionary Feminism,' *Revolution in Writing: British Literary Responses to the French Revolution*. ed. Kelvin Everest (Philadelphia: Open UP, 1991) 27-63. Similarly, Elizabeth Kowaleski-Wallace's *Their Fathers' Daughters: Hannah More, Maria Edgeworth and Patriarchal Complicity* (New York: Oxford, 1991) discuss the two writers within the context of their complicity, not necessarily with paternalism, but with the masculine discourse which formed their understanding of gender and class relations.

13   Sutherland 51.

14   See David Cressy 'Levels of Illiteracy'; R.S. Schofield, 'Dimesions '; Harvey Graff, *Legacies* 313-314.

15   This advertisement comes from the bound edition that was sold to the middle and upper classes, and not from the chapbook version bought by or given to the lower classes.

16   For an elaboration on the threat of 'radical' working-class literature, see Graff *Legacies* 324-325.

17   This process of reaching moral hegemony is connected to the process of interpellation, which acknowledges the complexity involved in transforming individuals, through ideology, into specific kinds of subjects. See Louis Althusser 'Ideology'127-186.

18   Murray Cohen, *Sensible Words: Linguistic Practice in England 1640-1785* (Baltimore: Johns Hopkins UP, 1977) 89-109, 120-136.

19 Olivia Smith, *The Politics of Language, 1791-1819* (Oxford: Clarendon, 1984) 3.
    Laqueur also points out that literacy, particularly writing, was considered controversial;
    but he points out that it was the control over the laboring-class's literacy that was
    contested by clergy, politicians and interested citizens. See Laqueur *Religion* 124-145.

20 See Smith 68-109.

21 Hannah More contributed 'Village Politics' to the *Liberty and Property* series.

22 Smith attributes the success of *The Cheap Repository Tracts* to the fact that she is a
    woman writer who is 'outside' the traditional eighteenth-century discursive spectrum,
    91-92.

23 Kelly, *English Fiction* 72-73.

24 *Chapbooks of the Eighteenth Century*, intro. John Ashton (London: Skoob Publishing,
    1882).

25 Neuberg claims that 'such publications [were] more important in the formation of the
    mass reading public than anything else that was available to the poor in the eighteenth
    century,' 121.

26 Even Patrick Colquhoun in *A Treatise on Indigence* suggested a newspaper to be
    distributed to the poor with 'good instruction and useful information.' These
    newspapers would include short essays 'enlivened and rendered interesting by the
    introduction of narrative' on a variety of topics such as 'stealing corn on the pretense of
    gleaning'; 'combinations of workmen'; 'providence and economy,' 97.

27 For the influence of Evangelicalism on her personal life and on her philanthropic work,
    see Patricia Demers, *The World of Hannah More* (Lexington: U of Kentucky P, 1996)
    76-118; M.G. Jones's biography, *Hannah More* (London: Cambridge UP, 1952); and
    Charles Howard Ford, *Hannah More: A Critical Biography* (New York: Peter Lang,
    1996). For a critique of her work with respect to her strict religious beliefs, see
    Elizabeth Kowaleski-Wallace, *Their Fathers' Daughters* 56-93. For the association
    between Evangelicalism and emerging bourgeois consciousness, in which Hannah More
    could be positioned, see Issac Kramnick *Republicanism* 1-70; Briggs, *A Social History*;
    Ian Bradley, *The Call to Seriousness: The Evangelical Impact on the Victorians*
    (London: Jonathan Cape, 1976); and Leonore Davidoff and Catherine Hall, *Family
    Fortunes: Men and women of the English middle class, 1780-1850* (Chicago: U of
    Chicago P, 1987) 71-192. While it is obvious her religious convictions influenced her
    writing and actions, I believe they have been overemphasized as the impetus of her
    philanthropy to the exclusion of other political, economic, and ideological factors.

28 See M.G. Jones, *Hannah More* 89, for Hannah More's diary entry for July 8th, 1803.

29 See Krueger 110.

30 More did not wholly identify herself with Evangelicals or the Anglican church; in fact,
    she had many friends among dissenters, such as William Wilberforce, which troubled
    many associated with Anglicanism. Her association with dissenters influenced her in
    matters of philanthropy as much as Evangelicalism. See Jones 97-101.

31 As More states: '[Women] are peculiarly fitted for [philanthropy], for from their own
    habits of life they are more intimately acquainted with domestic wants than the other
    sex; and in certain instances of sickness and sufferings peculiar to themselves, they
    should be expected to have more sympathy [...],' *Strictures on a Modern System of
    Female Education* in *The Complete Works of Hannah More* (New York: Harper &
    Brothers, 1835) 332.

32 See Demers 100-109. For a counterpoint, see Kowaleski-Wallace's interpretation of the
    Mendip Annals 63-74.

33 For her other views on writing, see Hannah More, 'Essays on Various Subjects' in *The
    Complete Works of Hannah More* (New York: Harper & Bros., 1835) 548-561.

34 Kelly points out that even though *The Cheap Repository* ceased to exist, its 'real task' was to 'erase what was seen as the seed-bed of Jacobinism—the popular oral and print culture, the traditional, centuries-old 'moral economy' of the common people.' Its persistence beyond the crisis of the 1790s is a testament to its effectiveness in doing just that. See Kelly 62.

35 Oddly, though, Laqueur makes the claim that these were not middle-class values.

36 See Gary Kelly, 'Revolution, Reaction and the Expropriation of Popular Culture: Hannah More's *Cheap Repository*' *Man & Nature* 6 (1987): 147-159.

37 Kelly points out that the topos of rural simplicity was an important element of sentimental fiction in that it was 'a refuge from the political struggles of the [1790s], and a source for a new model of the national community, a community thoroughly penetrated by professional and middle-class values,' *English Fiction* 86. See also Raymond Williams, *The Country and the City* (New York: Oxford UP, 1973) 96-119.

38 See Roger Wells, 'The Development of the English Rural Proletariat and Social Protest, 1700-1850,' in *Class, Conflict and Protest in the English Countryside, 1700-1850,* eds. Mick Reed and Roger Wells (Savage, MD: Frank Cass, 1990) 33.

39 I use 'ideologeme' to describe the narrative structures by which certain class specific values, ideas, opinions, etc. are manifested as abstract, universal concepts. See Fredric Jameson, *The Political Unconscious: Narrative as a Socially Symbolic Act* (Ithaca: Cornell UP, 1981) 87.

40 This is an eighteenth-century pastoral trope that is elevated by the discourses of Romanticism, particularly in Wordsworth's portrayal of rural life such as in 'Michael: A Pastoral Poem,' 'The Brothers,' 'The Leech Gatherer,' and his comments in the preface to *Lyrical Ballads*.

41 For a similar view on the promotion of the concept of private property, see W. Thomas Pepper, 'The Ideology of Wordsworth's "Michael: A Pastoral Poem"' *Criticism* 4 (Fall 1989): 373-4.

42 As John Barrell suggests in 'Sportive Labour' arduous manual labor is increasingly difficult to represent once the comic mode of labor as leisure was no longer acceptable to a more sober agricultural economy. The problem was that 'the image of wage-laborers, selflessly and irremissively engaged in the back-breaking work of the fields, was everywhere hinted at, but was very hard to represent if the duty of the poor to labor was successfully to be recommended to the polite and vulgar alike,'126. The solution that emerged was to represent labor by its effects: 'a large family, a neat cottage—or something which is about to be begun or has just been finished.'

43 Barrell states that because of the growing awareness of rural poverty, it was necessary to persuade the poor to identify themselves as members of their own family unit first, and not as members of a common class, 121. This tactic had two advantages: first, a male farmworker would be conceived as the head of the household and the 'breadwinner,' inspiring him to work harder to support his family; and second, the family would be as little dependent on the parish as possible. These two tactics secured a dutiful, and patriarchal, image of the father.

44 See E.J. Hobsbaum, *The Age of Revolution, 1789-1848* (New York: New American Library, 1962) 184-185, 190-191.

45 See Omasreiter 195; see also Marilyn Butler's biography, *Maria Edgeworth* (New York: Oxford UP, 1972); and Kowaleski-Wallace 95-108.

46 See Richardson for a discussion of the Edgeworths' *Practical Education* and its place within the educational theories of the late eighteenth century, 128-135.

47 Marilyn Butler comments that Jeffrey's reviews are valuable because he writes 'as a humane, forward-looking, but essentially Philistine bourgeois, and so mirrors the tastes of the average cultivated middle-class reader of the early nineteenth century,' 340.

48 Often, *Popular Tales* are lumped in with the moral tales for children, probably because of the didactic element in both.

49 Butler calls Edgeworth's scientific method the 'intellectual stamp of her generation,' 66.

50 Easy Simon would be considered a freeholder of land.

51 See Pepper 376.

52 From the time that Edgeworth was fourteen, she accompanied her father on his visits to the peasantry who were his tenants in the countryside of Edgeworthtown. She was therefore intimately familiar with the workings of large estates and the people who labored on them; see Butler 84-88.

53 This is the theme of many of her better-known and well-received novels, such as *Castle Rackrent* and *The Absentee*.

Chapter 4

Reforming Fiction and the Middling Classes: Maria Edgeworth's *Belinda*

> These books are written chiefly to the young, the ignorant, and the idle, to whom they serve as lectures of conduct, and introductions into life. They are the entertainment of minds unfurnished with ideas, and therefore easily susceptible of impressions; not fixed by principles, and therefore easily following the current of fancy; not informed by experience, and consequently open to every false suggestion and partial account.
> Samuel Johnson, *The Rambler* #4, 1750

When Samuel Johnson warned the reading public of the pernicious effects of fiction in *The Rambler*, he was guarding his society against a relatively new form of discourse that was rivaling older literary forms and ways of reading. It was a warning that Maria Edgeworth heeded over a half century later. How could fiction be made productive of higher judgment and morality, rather than merely pleasurable? Just as her *Popular Tales* depicted the ameliorative possibilities for the laborers and petit bourgeoisie, her novels attempted to lay out the ameliorative possibilities for the middling class, and particularly middling-class women. By critiquing the upper classes' morals and manners, Edgeworth distinguishes the middling-class values needed to ensure social hegemony, and envisions a space in which women exist at the center of a domestic sphere that is central to civil society. Vocational philanthropy in this context is a process by which Edgeworth's readers learn the values that will guide their moral improvement so that 'not just any feeling, but the right feeling must be aroused by good literature' (Mellor *Mothers* 94). 'Right' feeling implies an ethical responsibility to improve the lot of those who are morally corrupted, disengaged from family, and unproductive members of society, even if those people exist in one's own class.

Johnson's warning is a testament to the eighteenth-century notion of the influence of fiction: the power of fiction to influence the minds of its readers, its power to be a force for the improvement of their morality or a force for their corruption. As Jacqueline Pearson points out, 'Anxieties clustered especially around the power of reading to affect the emotions. Supporters of sentiment argued that imaginative reading had positive functions to "humanise the heart," though rationalists viewed it more negatively, fearing it might develop "the heart prematurely" and lower the tone of the mind' (42). With the rise of circulating libraries, in which many types of fiction and novels comprised the most popular reading material for the middling classes, the fear of fiction heightened. Gary Kelly points out that since the seventeenth century, fiction had been 'associated with the aristocratic and gentry values and culture' and describes this fear of fiction as rife with class tension: 'the principal danger [...] was that novels would become an instrument of ideological penetration by what was seen [by middle-class commentators] as decadent aristocratic or gentry culture, depicted as either glamorous libertinism or its transmuted form of sensibility or sentimentalism [...]. Such penetration [...] would help to ensure the continued ideological and social hegemony of the upper classes' (*English Fiction* 7). Fiction was caught up in class contestation. Could it represent the values of the emergent middling classes?

In addition, though fiction posed a danger to both men and women, it was thought that the novel held strong emotional appeal for women especially: women were thought to identify with the 'imaginary' and sentimental characters, and thus they would easily fall into emotional excess and immoral conduct.[1] The consequence of this identification was a disruption of women's more important domestic duties; the fear was that an overflow of feelings for characters created wasted energy that left little time and sentiment for 'real' familial obligations (Gallagher 275-277). A plethora of warnings in conduct books, sermons and moral treatises appeared to counteract the pernicious effects of fiction, and to urge other areas of endeavor to take up women's leisure time. Maria Edgeworth understood the appeal of fiction, especially to middling- and upper-class women who were, as Mary Wollstonecraft thought as well, not educated to think rationally. So, in effect, the problem of the genre of the novel was also a problem of gender.

In Maria Edgeworth's estimation, fiction had become, as Catherine Gallagher has recently suggested, 'antiproductive' literature in the sense that the story exceeded the moral exemplar (273-275). The danger for young girls and women alike, as the Edgeworths point out in *Practical Education*, is enjoying fiction too much:

> Besides the danger of creating a romantic taste, there is reason to believe, that the species of reading to which we object has an effect directly opposite to what it is intended to produce. It diminishes, instead of increasing, the sensibility of the heart [...]. The imagination, which has been accustomed to [...] delicacy in fictitious narrations, revolts from the disgusting circumstances which attend real poverty, disease, and misery; the emotions of pity, and the exertions of benevolence, are consequently repressed precisely at the time when they are necessary to humanity. (428)

Good fiction should guide the reader towards sympathy and benevolence rather than sentimentality; it should refine those qualities so that readers would not 'revolt' from the hardships found in 'poverty, disease and misery.' For the Edgeworths, sensibility without the mediating exercise of reason leads to an 'excess' of imagination (*Practical* 421). In the advertisement to the 1801 edition of

Belinda, the first of many editions, Edgeworth offers the work to her readers as a 'Moral Tale' because she does not wish to acknowledge it as a novel. By this time, Edgeworth had already begun a successful writing career, building her reputation as a writer on educational issues and instructional tales by publishing *Letters for Literary Ladies* (essentially an educational treatise in epistolary form) in 1795, *The Parent's Assistant* (a collection of moral tales for children) in 1796, and *Practical Education* (an educational treatise co-authored with her father Richard Lovell Edgeworth) in 1798. Her first novel, *Castle Rackrent*, is the exception. It is her first attempt to use the novel form, but publishing it anonymously in 1800 suggests ambivalence about the reputation of the novel and its purpose. At first, she hesitated to consider 'novels' as part of her oeuvre, even though she reissued *Castle Rackrent* under her name the following year, along with the publication of *Belinda* and the *Moral Tales* collection. By publishing *Belinda* in this discursive context, and with its advertisement disclaiming the very genre of the novel, Edgeworth distinguishes between two categories of fiction: the novel, which inspires much 'folly, error and vice' and the 'moral tale' that she has written in which 'feelings [...] are laudable.' As the advertisement suggests, Edgeworth agreed with many eighteenth-century critics who thought that novels encouraged sentimentality, overstimulating the passions without an appropriate improving function. Edgeworth describes an 'addiction' to 'common novel-reading' as a vice among women (*Practical* 380-381)

However, Maria Edgeworth's hesitance to acknowledge Belinda as a novel, though it does roughly conform to what we would now identify as a novel of manners, also signals an historical gap in our perception of the novel.[2] How to combine 'feeling' with 'truth' became a generic, as well as moral, problem of Romantic discourse in general, but of the novel in particular. As the popularity of the novel 'rose' towards the end of the eighteenth century, this problem became an urgent concern for writers interested in moral education, like Edgeworth.[3] As Terry Eagleton has suggested, Edgeworth had a 'clear generic dilemma': 'the very form she deploys is complicit with the conduct she seeks to reform' (168). Form and 'reform' are in contradiction. The challenge before Edgeworth, then, is to attempt to make *Belinda* a different kind of fiction: one that has an ameliorative purpose for the middling classes and one that will distinguish them from the 'leisure' classes. In order to do this, 'feeling' and 'truth' must work together, forming a moral compass for the reader, and mediating the 'fictionality' of the novel form. This mediation of fictionality tangentially links *Belinda* with the expressive realism of the early nineteenth century, but yet retains the didactic function of moral instruction from the eighteenth century. My argument is that Maria Edgeworth helps to reenvision the purpose of the novel at a transitional historical moment in 1801: she reshapes the novel's ideological function—to reform readers, particularly women, so that truth always leads to feeling and feeling always leads to truth. In this way, proper reading guides moral improvement, not just for the laboring classes, which one might expect to need improvement according to middling-class notions of frugality, cleanliness, hospitality, entertainment, etc., but also for the middling classes who have not yet been 'enlightened' and who could fall into the pleasure traps of the upper gentry and aristocracy. For Edgeworth's program for fiction entails an attempt to improve all classes and both genders.[4] By using the discourse of the novel to reform, redeem and improve the middling-class female reader, Edgeworth takes the philanthropic step that Wollstonecraft claimed was needed to right the wrongs of woman: to make women rational beings so that women can begin to 'love [mankind], from which an orderly train of virtues spring' and consider the 'moral and civil interest of mankind' (Wollstonecraft *VRW* 4).[5] For Edgeworth, education that highlighted 'proper' reading was the most effective and efficient way to promote the 'love of the sympathy of our fellow-creatures' (*Practical* 344). As we will see in the reading of *Belinda*, Edgeworth takes direct aim at aristocratic libertinism and sentimentalism in an attempt to reform the fictional form in which these decadent values are produced.

The novel's ability to conjure an excess of emotion that will lead readers morally astray is supported by the criticism *Belinda* received upon publication. After much praise for her previous works, both *The Monthly Review* and *The British Critic* criticized the 'improper' actions taken on the part of the heroine Belinda; among other actions, she appears to shun her first love, and encourage a second suitor to whom she does not have quite the same emotional attachment (Butler 494).[6] Apparently in response, Edgeworth substantially revised the first edition, publishing the second edition in 1802, and revised it again a third time for inclusion in Anna Leititia Barbauld's *British Novelists* series in 1810. Marilyn Butler deems these changes necessary in order for Edgeworth to 'conform' more strictly to the turn-of-the-century assumption that the purpose of narrative is to illustrate 'moral truth' (314) or, as J.M.S. Tompkins states, to be an 'exemplum anchored to a text' (72-3). Butler finds Belinda's 'heavy-handed didacticism' a major fault of the novel, and perceives didacticism as a generic element that the reading public, Edgeworth, and other writers and critics of her day misguidedly included in their definition of 'good' literature. But it is exactly this element that defined Edgeworth's writing, and her popularity, throughout the period. A growing expectation on the part of critics was that didacticism should be a distinguishing feature of women's writing;[7] we know that it was one feature of her writing that critics applauded.[8] Since Edgeworth was predominantly concerned with providing educational theories and examples to a middling-class reading public, didacticism becomes her heuristic tool with which to 'teach' readers how to understand themselves as women who share similar manners and morals. As Murray Cohen points out, readers at this time were 'expected to respond to a series of charged expressive scenes or to identify (with) several distinctly affected characters…their judgments [are] guided by their responses rather than their knowledge' (105). Edgeworth guided her readers' responses in order to create a readership whose shared experiences consolidate them into a category or a 'class' of people who have specific moral and social responsibilities: that is, to facilitate the reformation and improvement of those around them through sympathy and benevolent feeing.

This vocation is the very same one Edgeworth took on as both a woman and as a writer.

Therefore, in order to understand how Edgeworth negotiated this feeling/truth dilemma in her novels, we must reexamine an important generic element in Edgeworth's fiction: didacticism. I am using didacticism to refer to a textual strategy rather than as a description of her texts.[9] Edgeworth's fiction is more than the sum of its moral. So, to restate my argument in a slightly different way, the novel form Edgeworth used to construct *Belinda* prepared readers to recognize themselves as particular kinds of gendered and classed individuals, to feel responsible and rational love for others, and to center propriety and moral value as the constituent factor in individual and, concomitantly, societal improvement. In this sense, then, Edgeworth's strategy initiates a new discourse of fiction, for a purpose that I call philanthropic. The novel sought to teach individual readers how to learn from feeling (an eighteenth-century function for the novel) rather than teaching readers to feel (a nineteenth-century novel function). But, her novel also taught individual improvement from feeling—the aspect which ties the two centuries together. Edgeworth's *Belinda* negotiates this historical and generic turn.

The element of didacticism in Edgeworth's novel, by closing off certain kinds of interpretation, creates a heuristic reading strategy; it enables readers to discover truths about the characters' moral virtue as the novel progresses through a series of generic excerpts. Didacticism carefully directs readers to the appropriate moral and aesthetic responses, which enable the reader to learn from those responses—the rhetorical mode. This strategy, in effect, 'teaches' the reader to more properly direct her own thoughts about, and aesthetic responses (truth and feeling) to, the text. Crucial to this heuristic reading strategy is Edgeworth's main character, Belinda, who serves as the reader's surrogate. In order to teach middling-class women readers how to read and reform themselves, Belinda mediates between the reader and the text, guiding the reader to a kind of self-discipline, which enables the reader to identify only with the appropriate female character. In *Belinda* that self-disciplining process—reconciling truth and feeling—is part of the novel's generic structure and its new ideological function. Form will be reconciled with reform.

Positioning *Belinda* as the Reader's Surrogate

As the title *Belinda* indicates, the positioning of the title character is important to the novel's structure. The novel has a tripartite plot structure: the first involves Belinda Portman's education as a young woman under the guidance of the corrupted Lady Delacour, and her ultimate rejection of fashionable society in favor of a more rational, domestic milieu exemplified by the Percivals; the second involves Belinda's and Clarence Hervey's plan to morally reform Lady Delacour and eventually to reconcile her with her daughter and with the newly reformed Lord

Delacour; the third involves Clarence Hervey's reformation because of his love for Belinda. His virtue had been morally compromised because of an association with Virginia de Saint Pierre, a young maiden whom he was 'bringing up' to be his wife. At the end of the last volume, we see the promise of domestic bliss for Hervey and Belinda.

However, the narrative is discontinuous and un-unified, each volume having a different plot. Using episodic chapters, the plots, though interwoven, seem disparate from each other, and yet they are interconnected through Belinda, even though each plot and each episode is not about her. The narrative hinges not on romance as the plot, as a novel like Austen's *Emma* does, but on the character of Belinda as the pivotal structural element of the novel. It highlights the idea of femininity as integral to the 'natural' relationship between people and between events. As both Elizabeth Kowaleski-Wallace and Gary Kelly have noted, *Belinda* is not about Belinda as a feminine heroine;[10] the title character is simply the formal element which ties the plots together and makes the novel's ideas about gender, class and morality cohere.

Therefore, while Belinda's relentless moral goodness bothers many critics, it is necessary for Edgeworth's didactic purpose: she is the reader's surrogate for the middling-class woman. From the very beginning of the novel, Belinda is the 'natural' innocent, whose mind is to be exercised by the events in the novel, much like the reader's. In the first volume, Belinda is faced with two contrasting examples of womanhood and class position: Lady Delacour and Lady Anne Percival. She listens to both, and judges each by the happiness she possesses and brings to others. This is a usual didactic formula, which Edgeworth uses often in her *Moral Tales* and *Popular Tales* series. But Belinda is depicted as having the ability to rationally think through others' actions, perceive what is seemingly imperceptible to others and make sober choices for herself which affect others' lives. She, in a sense, has an innate ability to 'read' others correctly, revising her ideas on femininity as the reader reviews them. As a character, she intuitively knows which actions are 'natural' and 'proper,' and which actions are 'improper,' and attempts to think them through to their consequences with the help of the omniscient narrator:

> Belinda, the more she reflected, the more she was surprised at her aunt's having chosen such a chaperon for a young woman entering the world. When the understanding is suddenly roused and forced to exert itself, what a multitude of deductions it makes [...] For the first time in her life [Belinda] reasoned for herself upon what she saw and felt.—It is sometimes safer for young people to see, than to hear of certain characters. (Edgeworth 61)

Because of Belinda's deductions about Lady Delacour's character, the reader can understand her dissipation and the logical sequence of motivations by which her 'vanity had led her…into follies and imprudence, which had ruined her health, and destroyed her peace of mind' (Edgeworth 62). Through Belinda's eyes, readers are invited to see through Lady Delacour's 'act' and readers are taught to read her actions as a lesson in how *not* to behave. Of course, Belinda has little knowledge of any other kind of living outside courtly life. But she steadfastly resolves not to be corrupted by worldly desires. Edgeworth's portrayal of the courtly excesses of wealth leaves little for Belinda, and the readers of the novel, to aspire to. And this is the very point. As in sentimental novels, this Society becomes, in Edgeworth's terms, an 'exercise' for the reader's moral sensibility.[11] Belinda intuitively possesses knowledge about virtue, prudence, and modesty—all of which were lost on anyone else she had known in her life until she meets Lady Anne Percival, the novel's representation of bourgeois femininity and of the possibilities of domestic life.

In contrast to the courtly excesses of the Delacours, the Percivals embody Edgeworth's vision of ideal middling-class domesticity. Readers are introduced to the Percivals by the image of Lady Anne Percival surrounded by her children, which is reminiscent of Mary Wollstonecraft's image of maternal domesticity in *A Vindication of the Rights of Woman*:

> [Mr. Percival and Clarence Hervey] found Lady Anne Percival in the midst of her children; who all turned their healthy, rosy, intelligent faces towards the door the moment that they heard their father's voice. Clarence Hervey was so much struck with the expression of happiness on Lady Anne's countenance, that he absolutely forgot to compare her beauty with Lady Delacour's [...].
> Whether she were handsome by the rules of art, he knew not; but he felt that she had the essential charm of beauty, the power of prepossessing the heart immediately in her favour. The effect of her manners, like that of her beauty, was rather to be felt than described [...] but in Lady Delacour's wit and gaiety there was an appearance of art and effort, which often destroyed the pleasure that she wished to communicate. –Some people may admire, but none can sympathise with affectation. (Edgeworth 89)

Here, Lady Anne's 'natural' beauty and affection for her husband and children is measured directly against the portrayal of Lady Delacour's affected beauty and her inability to provide a suitable and happy home for her husband and only child; the domestic is characterized in opposition to the courtly. Lady Anne's worth to her family is reflected not only in her contented countenance, but in her ability to attract her husband back to the domestic sphere where her affection possesses the heart, where her 'natural' beauty and manners are felt by her husband and Hervey, and where her ability to care for and superintend their many children can be displayed. The domestic self in this context is one who produces feeling—and apparently children—and thus the motivation of subjects is the domain of the feminine.

To have the reader sympathize with this feminine model, exemplified by Lady Anne, is important. Sympathy is the foundation upon which the sentimental novel is constructed. Sympathy is defined in the eighteenth-century sense of the 'inclination to sympathize with others, and to receive by communication [others'] inclinations and sentiments (Todd 27).[12] Linking sympathy with the domestic sphere ensures a private but productive feminine role. The feminine model is privatized as the basis for social harmony from which 'true' moral virtue emanates. Thus, according to this portrait, the feminine plays the pivotal role in the family; she is the person to whom all others cohere.[13] And family, as Mitzi Myers has argued, is the 'prototype of community and a reformed British cultural identity' ('Shot from Canons' 202).[14]

Edgeworth is conscious that she must convince her readers that the domestic sphere portrayed here is one that is desirable as well as 'natural.' Accordingly, what is at stake here is how one perceives 'pleasure': will it take the form of 'sense' or the form of rational sympathy? The response to the question comes in the form of a narrative intrusion that makes a direct appeal to the audience:

> Those who unfortunately have never enjoyed domestic happiness, such as we have just described, will perhaps suppose the picture to be visionary and romantic; there are others, it is hoped many others, who will feel that it is drawn from truth and real life. Tastes that have been vitiated by the stimulus of dissipation might, perhaps, think these simple pleasure insipid. Every body must ultimately judge of what makes them happy, from the comparison of their own feelings in different situations. Belinda was convinced by this comparison, that domestic life was that which could alone make her really permanently happy. (Edgeworth 204)

Julia Douthwaite claims that eighteenth-century readers would have recognized this kind of narrative device as one borrowed from romances.[15] So the narrative interruption, within the context of a domestic tale, underscores the rewriting of the romance, and the pleasure that accrues to the reader from reading it. Because an array of character types appear in *Belinda*, a variety of conflicting desires will exist to tempt the characters' virtue, such as aristocratic excess in the Delacours, Mr. Vincent's gambling, and Harriet Freke's crossdressing. The overall ideological implication is Edgeworth's recognition that even though the domestic pleasures are the natural ones, they are not necessarily the ones that the characters, and readers, will perceive as most desirable because their tastes have already been corrupted by Society.[16] Therefore, the novel is structured so that the character ad exemplum can teach what is a natural desire for the reader/subject to feel. Edgeworth's interruption of the narrative on the virtues of domestic life, and Belinda's personal choice, is not enough to make the reader desire that life. If it were, perhaps the charges of Edgeworth's didacticism would be true. But it is the complex structure of the narrative which facilitates Edgeworth's heuristic strategy of desire: the truth the reader discovers is her own desire for what is both 'romantic' and 'real' in the narrative. By reading correctly, she discovers this desire, and she knows she has read correctly because she feels this proper desire. In other words, the act of reading directs the reader's attention to choices, but also limits them by prescribing moral worth and happiness as already domestically preconditioned.

Belinda's intuitive knowledge about virtue takes its shape in the forms of domestic ideology represented by the Percivals, but she possesses this knowledge even before its example emerges in the narrative. Belinda is the 'subject presumed to know': she is the character who is always-already fully interpellated into a middle-class domestic ideology before that ideology is established in the societal structure and narrative typology.[17] This does not mean she possesses greater self-knowledge; she does not understand herself on a level that distinguishes her from others. Readers 'presume' that she intuitively understands how to feel, think and behave in a way that is consistent and coherent—without conflict. The knowledge she is presumed to possess about the world stands at a distance from the novel's other characters, and perhaps even the reader of the novel as well. For example, the other characters who have moral failings like Lady Delacour or Clarence Hervey must either learn or fail to learn from their own mistakes. Belinda does not. It is not that she is incapable of learning the errors of her ways; she simply does not make any mistakes that she must learn from (Mellor *Feminism* 40). She is already as virtuous as she will ever be, which is the very quality about Belinda that irks many contemporary readers.[18] However, in order for Belinda to serve as the intermediary between the novel and the reader, she, as the representation of the illusion of proper middling-class femininity, must appear as the measure of morality. In contrast, Lady Delacour and Hervey use the manners and moral codes of fashionable life but also have real domestic desires, leaving them 'conflicted' as characters, and consequently the characters contemporary readers find more 'human' or 'interesting.' Nonetheless, Belinda is a more important structural element in the novel: Belinda enables readers, as well as the other characters, to reform themselves.

For the other characters, Belinda serves as a constant against which to view others' actions, but also enables changes within the limits of the novel's form. Without her as the pivot point of the novel, there would be no coherence to it, structurally or ideologically, nor would there be any impetus for the characters to change. For example, Belinda is the only character to whom Lady Delacour wants to confess her social and moral transgressions because she knows Belinda is 'unworldly'—she possesses no knowledge of the worldly manners, so she is uncorrupted. She presumes Belinda possesses something more valuable to her— virtue and moral integrity—which a regretful Lady Delacour has long ago given up. Belinda is an illusion of feminine consistency that only appears to the reader when contrasted with someone like Lady Delacour. Belinda represents, to the reader, an interpellating force that allows each character to discover his/her mistakes, actions, and inaction and to re-envision themselves within a new set of social relationships. The novel thus becomes self-reflexive: while Belinda improves the characters which surround her in the fictional world of the novel, reading *Belinda* will improve readers, particularly feminine readers, because they will identify with the constancy of the title character's ideological position as the reader's surrogate. This is Edgeworth's attempt to ensure the appropriate reading of the novel.

To illustrate, Lady Delacour desires to rectify the trauma of her 'inner conflict,' her one attribute that makes her both appealing and repulsive to readers. Belinda is the mechanism that enables her to 'cure' herself (quite literally in terms of her health), but also enables her to enter into middling-class womanhood. Belinda is the anchor to whom Lady Delacour attaches herself—for dear life in terms of the narrative, but also ideologically. To use the previous example, when Lady Delacour confesses her transgressions to Belinda she produces knowledge about herself—her motivations (vanity), her influences (her friendship with 'feminist' Harriet Freke) and her regrets (the loss of her husband's love and her inability to care for her daughter). The transference of this knowledge is interesting because it produces a kind of narrative revision for both characters. The 'profit' Belinda reaps is to 'think for herself,' and Lady Delacour's transgressions are met with Belinda's ideal difference. Two alternative images emerge for the reader to make sense of: Lady Delacour's character is an example of feminine corruption and redemption and Belinda is an example of an incorruptible womanhood because of her ability to reason. I should point out that Belinda's ability to 'profit' from Lady Delacour's history, though, is not characterized as change or development; it serves to condition the reader's reading of the novel—allowing the reader to pull the 'truth' from the emotional context of the scene and from the difference in feminine images. As the reader's surrogate, Belinda's example of 'think[ing] for herself' about Lady Delacour and her revelations encourages the reader to examine the two contrasting images. The reader's ability to reason is thus engaged, but because the reader identifies with Belinda's constancy, the reader 'profits' from Lady Delacour's history, as well as Belinda's response to it. The reader's rationality, through the direction of the main character, is exercised by reading.

As the truth of Lady Delacour's corruption is articulated through the generic element of the confession, she relieves herself of the burden of her mask— her unnatural actions, which is, of course, premised upon the artificiality of aristocratic vanity and excess. But Belinda already understands this character's duplicity; the articulation of her repressed truth only serves to reify Belinda as the element which stands beyond Delacour's discourse: beyond form—Delacour's mask of self-delusion—and the content—her unnatural acts. It enables Belinda to be perceived by readers as an 'ideological illusion,' one who always-already reconciles, for the reader, the disjunction between form and content, and enables reform from perversity. Belinda cannot give Lady Delacour absolution, but her confession enables the narrative of her moral revision. Belinda helps Lady Delacour to 'heal' herself. Readers, if they are assuming the virtue of Belinda to be valuable, will understand the need to heal this conflict fairly early on in the narrative.

Belinda is complex model of femininity; she is the central symbolic point around which a middling-class ideological web pivots: she represents an illusion of feminine consistency and moral purity. Other characters learn how to remedy their particular moral dilemmas because of the strident goodness of Belinda. Thus, Belinda does not 'develop' or learn anything, because she already knows all she needs to about moral action; that is Edgeworth's very point. And it is this point that she wants her readers to discover through the heuristic mode of reading. While the value and function of reading fiction is very much in question by the end of the eighteenth century, Maria Edgeworth demonstrates that feminine moral virtue can be valorized by reading fiction. Fiction can valorize moral virtue by giving it a new narrative, a moral narrative that conditions interpretative possibilities.

Reforming Fiction to Reform Society

By giving moral virtue a new narrative, Edgeworth establishes a new ideological purpose for the novel: to inculcate moral reform by establishing codes of morality and manners which could be shared by an emergent middling class—a reading class. The new narrative, and its ideological purpose, is positioned in terms of class conflict: to stem the tide of pernicious, aristocratic desires and excesses, *Belinda* must promote the novel form as a genre in which 'truth,' constituted by more 'natural' domestic relations of society, can be represented by using a compilation of generic forms designed to draw attention to the novel's fictionality.[19] A variety of generic elements are used to piece together the episodes of each of the three interweaving plots: the generic elements range from adventure and romance narratives, gothic devices such as 'the mysterious boudoir,' confessionals, and satires on books like *A Vindication of the Rights of Woman* and *Emile* (as we shall see later on). If, as Catherine Gallagher claims, Edgeworth's fiction is a 'productive' force for the 'general good' (258), one of its most productive aspects is that it helps create a space for heuristic forms of fiction.

The heuristic aspect of novel writing defines 'the sort of reading' that produces 'reliable domestic women who would in turn raise useful productive children' (Gallagher 275).[20] Productive novel writing creates readers who are taught to read in particular ways so that (women) readers can feel, think, and act differently: i.e., these texts produce an ideology of middling-class femininity and readers who comprehend that ideology—Edgeworth's philanthropic, though discursive, goal. Moreover, *Belinda* creates a kind of domestic discourse that will enable the continued production of this ideology, making it seem natural. The only way to do this is by distantiating certain generic elements to expose their fictionality and then creating a coherent structure that makes the ideology posed— middling-class feminine virtue—seem natural. This is why a novel's structure is so important in Edgeworth's theories about fiction, and why fiction is so important to Edgeworth that she labors to produce so much of it in a span of twenty-five or so years.

Since the reputation of the novel had fallen into ill repute during the late eighteenth century, Edgeworth's attempt to write in the genre was nothing less than a reclamation project. Assuming that the majority of novel readers were women, literary critics and medical writers were particularly concerned with the genre's apparent ability to arouse

> 'strong passions' and le[a]d to unsteadiness of character and other nervous disorders [...]. The medical literature on this point echoed, moreover, several

decades' worth of attacks on the novel, all centering on the genre's peculiar
emotional power over women and the disruption of their domestic lives.
(Gallagher 277)

The emotional absorption in the lives of imaginary characters was perceived as
sentimental and pernicious, threatening the reader's rational capacities, wasting her
emotional energy, disrupting her duties to her family and household on which the
family's social and economic position rested.[21]

Edgeworth was keenly aware of the novel's effects on the moral virtue of
the individual, and this is the subject of her first independent literary work, *Letters
for Literary Ladies* (1795). Edgeworth was also well read in the moral/political
economy of her own time; her reading included Adam Smith (Belinda is, in fact,
reading *A Theory of Moral Sentiments* when Harriet Freke interrupts her), T.R.
Malthus and others, and she obviously discussed issues of political economy and
scientific progress with her father's associates from the Lunar Society. As a variety
of commentators have observed, while Edgeworth is the illustrator of these
economic and social principles, their impetus comes primarily from her father.[22]
According to Edgeworth herself, these economic and educational theories serve as
the raw material for her tales: 'In the lighter works[...] I have only repeated the
same opinions [i.e. R.L. Edgeworth's] in other forms [...]' (qtd. in Butler 272).[23]
Whatever the impetus, feminine virtue and duty for Edgeworth was always a matter
of class propriety. Women who do not emotionally sympathize and identify with
others, and women who cannot control their passions, like the aristocratic Lady
Delacour in *Belinda*, cannot be productive mothers who raise useful children and
who are productive citizens—an emerging middling-class ideal necessary to the
Edgeworth's vision of a reformed society.

Following from the theories she and her father espoused on education and
political economy, her fiction was not only an educational endeavor, but also a
philanthropic vocation. For Edgeworth, education was a process 'for the practical
purpose of being able to master the social and economic reality of life' (Omasreiter
198), and thus the purpose of knowledge is to be a productive member of society,
in which one's work would contribute to human happiness. Happiness could be
understood in the eighteenth-century sense of prosperity or 'the attainment of what
is considered good' by society.[24] This stricture could be applied to her productivity
as an author; her labor is only profitable insofar as it contributes to the greater
good. As political economists of the time claimed, including her father R.L.
Edgeworth, social institutions do not keep one from achieving prosperity, the lack
of productive activity prevents the individual from achieving happiness.[25] If
Edgeworth's reasons for writing are to 'make [her] readers more "productive"
members of society' (Gallagher 263), then her intention to produce writing for
women places them, as well as herself, in a position to affect the social relations
(both class and gender) of England. Writing is a productive act that affects human
happiness. The valorization of the productive members of society is fortified by the
production of the novel, or as Edgeworth would say, the moral tale.

For the middling classes, valorization was particularly important, for Edgeworth argues for the professionalization of the gentry in most of her works (Kelly *Novelists* 74). Gary Kelly has recently commented that Edgeworth and her father espoused social reform of all classes that would lead to greater economic production and prosperity (Kelly 'Class, Gender' 90). But it is the 'enlightened professional and manufacturing middle class rather than the mercantile and commercial petty bourgeoisie,' not unlike the Edgeworths themselves, who would lead this reformation (90). This reformation hinged on what Kelly calls the 'discourse of merit,' which would serve to both preserve the hierarchical order (with the enlightened middle classes achieving the leadership role) and to harmonize social order through middle-class cultural hegemony—merit serving as 'moral, intellectual and cultural capital' (89). Kelly goes so far as to say that Edgeworth's fiction was 'an educational plan for training in merit' (91). While the spirit of the statement is certainly true, her fiction needs more explanation than Kelly's description.[26] For example, as Edgeworth's *Popular Tales* makes clear, the landed gentry, agricultural capitalists and manufacturers have a responsibility to withhold charity, and to encourage the idea that the pleasure of productive work should be its own reward for the most diligent laborers. Laborers, in turn, had a moral responsibility to labor for the 'general good.' Both are rewarded in this mutually fulfilling relationship. Labor, for the lower orders, became the measure of an individual's worth and virtue, and merit became the means to happiness—familial, economic, moral. The same is true for the emergent middling classes, but not because merit and improvement are universal. As my chapter on the *Popular Tales* demonstrates, this notion of the effects of labor, and merit, is a middling-class production. One important way that this ideology was promoted is through discursive acts—like Edgeworth's tales, whether they were for the populace or for fashionable Society.[27] The ability to value labor, to reward diligence and reformation, and to act in accordance with economic prudence would consolidate the enlightened middling classes and harmonize the laboring classes with the middling classes.

However, as *Belinda* demonstrates, the value of labor is gendered. A middling-class woman's labor is manifested in the children she raises, not only physically, but by disciplining them with the ideas necessary to reproduce these emergent middling-class values:

> The children were treated neither as slaves nor as playthings, but as reasonable creatures; and the ease with which they were managed, and with which they managed themselves, surprised Belinda [...]. Without force, or any factitious excitements, the taste for knowledge, and the habits of application, were induced by example, and confirmed by sympathy. (Edgeworth 203)

Of course, this subjective discipline can only occur if the 'proper' domestic arrangement is established. The Percivals' home, of course, is the example of the productive domestic arrangement that leads to disciplined, self-reliant, active, but sympathetic individuals; the Delacours' home is its antithesis. Clarence Hervey, a gentleman playboy, must be 'taught' by his love for Belinda to desire the 'correct' domestic arrangement, exhibited by the Percivals, by the end of the last volume. Class consolidation and domestic duty coincide with individual morality and the general 'good.' The 'love of mankind' and the 'love of man' are ideologically linked.

The novel form that Edgeworth produces with *Belinda* illustrates these general, abstract notions of 'love of man' leading to 'love of mankind' in concrete terms. This may be why the episodes and plot lines appear discontinuous and disunified. The social milieu that the novel presents is not consistent, but rife with gender and class tensions, moral dilemmas, and pleasure traps. The shifting generic elements that Edgeworth employs to illustrate the various characters is reminiscent of picaresque fiction, highlighting particular situations in which a character's moral integrity is tested and then judged. However, in Edgeworth's novel, it is not Belinda whose moral integrity is in question, ever. We assume that she is virtuous, and will thus make the proper choices in each episode. The shifting generic elements enable her to demonstrate these choices in different contexts, while they enable the reader to follow her rational thinking without becoming emotionally tied to a particular situation. For instance, after the confessional 'Lady Delacour's History,' the narrative switches to courtly concerns of fashion and display in 'Birthday Dresses' then turns to 'Ways and Means' in which Belinda illustrates modesty and financial prudence; the narrative then finds the example of domestic contentment in the Percivals in 'A Family Party' then switches to 'The Mysterious Boudoir,' a parody of the gothic in which rooms hold secrets that must be discovered and servants perpetuate rumors that are 'born and bred in a kitchen, or servants' hall' (Edgeworth 122). Here Belinda's rationality will

> Put a stop to a number of charming stories by this prudence of yours—a romance called the Mysterious Boudoir, of nine volumes at least, might be written on the subject, if you would only condescend to act like almost all other heroines, that is to say, without common sense. (122)

Using Belinda as a guide to moral propriety, and proper reading of circumstances, the reader acclimates herself to the perspective of the already-interpellated subject, journeying through the various plots and episodes; thus, the readers can share the same manners and moral judgments without being tempted to identify with the 'wrong' characters. This subject position is unlike, for example, Jane Austen's *Emma* who presumes she knows social propriety but who continually commits social transgressions; in *Emma*, the reader's position is not commensurate with Emma's. The readers already know that Emma is misinterpreting others' actions, feelings and motivations. They know this because *Emma* positions readers as group who share similar manners and have a better moral understanding of Society than does Emma. The pleasure in reading *Emma* comes from the gap between what the reader knows and what Emma does. In *Belinda*, however, the point is to teach how to profit by reading, by producing an ideal readership that can share a middling-class perspective, thereby creating a reading audience for novels like *Emma*.

In addition, Edgeworth utilizes generic mixing to criticize other discourses, and not simply to 'reveal' something about a character in order to push the plot along: she parodies other educational discourses to demonstrate the problems their theories pose to the new society Edgeworth envisions. In this way, the episodes become social satires and criticisms of particular discourses. The episodic chapter involving Harriet Freke, entitled 'Rights of Woman,' is a particular example of this type of satire. Harriet Freke, Lady Delacour's crossdressing friend-turned-enemy, is portrayed as an aggressive, combative and witless woman, who cannot control her overly stimulated passions. By engaging in an argument with Mr. Percival and Mr. Vincent in front of the observant Belinda, Harriet Freke mimics feminist rhetoric empty of its philosophy:

> 'This is just the way you men spoil women,' cried Mrs. Freke, 'by talking to them of the delicacy of their sex, and such stuff. This delicacy enslaves the pretty delicate dears.'
> 'No; it enslaves us,' said Mr. Vincent.
> 'I hate slavery! Vive la liberte!' cried Mrs. Freke—'I'm a champion for the Rights of Women.'
> 'I am an advocate for their happiness,' said Mr. Percival, 'and for their delicacy, as I think it conduces to their happiness.'
> 'I'm an enemy to their delicacy, as I am sure it conduces to their misery.'
> 'You speak from experience?' said Mr. Percival.
> 'No, from observation. –Your most delicate women are always the greatest hypocrites [...].'
> 'But you have not proved the hypocrisy,' said Belinda. 'Delicacy is not, I hope, an indisputable proof of it?' (Edgeworth 216)

Though it seems so, Edgeworth may not be directly attacking Mary Wollstonecraft or her ideas. Many late eighteenth- and early nineteenth-century novels responded to Wollstonecraft, or her disciples, by introducing protofeminists, like Freke, into their novels to challenge, debunk or agree with her views (Johnson 195). Wollstonecraft and Edgeworth share similar educative goals, including the belief that women must be well-educated and rational if they are to resist aristocratic court culture which could only transform them into coquettes, as Lady Delacour illustrates (Kelly *English Fiction* 80). Colin and Jo Atkinson argue that Freke is a version of the 'masculine-woman stereotype and the Dreadful Warning figure in the didactic plot' (115).[28] The point of Edgeworth's satire is that this (or any) kind of radical discourse, or radical rhetoric, has a negative effect on women who have not yet learned to reason for themselves; in fact, it instills greater 'irrationality' in women. Edgeworth is careful to illustrate that Mrs. Freke lacks reasons for these 'feminist' views when Percival pushes her by asking her to prove them. She cannot give examples of her views, or give 'proof' of how 'overturning' the 'decent drapery of life' (217) would secure a better life for women. Protofeminist rhetoric gives Freke license to behave licentiously—rejecting all propriety of feminine conduct (she is a crossdresser, after all), masquerading as a Jacobin, and declaring herself an enemy of the 'artificial' constraints of men—all of which are just as bad, if not worse, than courtly culture. In contrast to the Percivals, Mr. Vincent and Belinda, Freke's behavior is portrayed as shocking and deviant to the domestic ideal:

> 'To cut the matter short at once,' cried Mrs. Freke, 'why, when a woman likes a man, does not she go and tell him so honestly?'
> Belinda, surprised by this question from a woman, was too much abashed instantly to answer [...]. (Edgeworth 216)

Belinda's intuitive femininity and her ability to reason, garnered from her reading, save her from Mrs. Freke's seduction. Throughout the scene, Edgeworth makes an implicit connection between reading and learning to reason—Belinda is reading a philosophical work, Adam Smith's *A Theory of Moral Sentiments* (Edgeworth 214).

These shifting genres position the reader within different discourses, teaching the reader how to extricate herself from the emotive responses to each genre.[29] Again, Belinda as the reader's surrogate ties the generic elements together in order to do two things simultaneously: first, to produce a feminine ideal for the reader's moral approbation; and second to reclaim the genre of the novel by distantiating questionable elements, tacitly critiquing and satirizing them. Moral reform is thus linked with reading. Using Belinda as a guide to moral propriety and proper reading of circumstances, the reader acclimates herself to the perspective of the already-interpellated subject represented by Belinda. Thus, readers can share the same manners and morality without being tempted to identify with the 'wrong' characters. In *Belinda*, the point is to teach readers how to 'profit' by reading, thus producing an ideal readership that can share the same middling-class perspective and 'happiness.'

Another example of this kind of satire is found in the Hervey-Belinda romance plot in volume three. It involves Clarence Hervey's educational experiment with a young farm maiden, Rachel, whom he renames Virginia St. Pierre.[30] The origin for this plot line is Thomas Day's adoption of a foundling, Sabrina Sidney, to be raised in accordance with Rousseau's principles on women's nature.[31] It is used in the novel as a 'feminist' criticism of Sophy in Rousseau's *Emile* as well as a parody of romance novel reading. Hervey, while living in France 'just before the revolution when luxury and dissipation were at their height' (Edgeworth 343), formed the 'romantic project of educating a wife for himself' by reading the works of Rousseau:

> this eloquent writer's sense made its full impression upon Clarence's understanding, and his declamations produced more than their just effect upon an imagination naturally ardent. He was charmed with the picture of Sophia, when contrasted with the characters of the women of the world [...]. (Edgeworth 343)

Hervey is excessively, and sexually, stimulated by the aesthetic qualities of Rachel: in a retired part of New Forest he saw a

> young girl watering the rose trees, which grew round the cottage [...]. The setting sun shone upon her countenance, the wind blew aside the ringlets of her light hair, and the blush of modesty overspread her cheeks, when she looked up at the stranger. In her large blue eyes, there was an expression of artless sensibility, with which Mr. Hervey was so powerfully struck. (Edgeworth 344)

As her dying Grandmother tells Hervey, Rachel is 'innocence itself' (347). After the Grandmother's death, and a promise to her that he will not 'ruin' her, he took this girl to be educated to eventually become his wife on the model of Rousseau's Sophy, claiming that

> sensibility [...] is the parent of great talents, and great virtues; and evidently she possess natural feeling in an uncommon degree; it shall be developed with skill, patience, and delicacy; and I will deserve, before I claim my reward. (Edgeworth 348)

Hervey, attached to more sentimental than rational ideas at this point in the narrative, changes her name to Virginia St. Pierre because she reminds him of the description of Virginia in M. de St. Pierre's romance (Edgeworth 350). Virginia was then secluded from all intercourse with the world, just as she had been in the forest, except for Mrs. Ormond, her governess, and Mr. Moreton, an elderly clergyman, both of whom are in charge of her moral development.

While Virginia had an instinctive taste for natural beauty, and was exceptionally ignorant of the luxuries and artifices of world, she also could not write nor read particularly well. The former pleased Hervey; the latter disturbed him. He could not have a wife who did not read literature because she 'could never be a companion suited to him,' however beautiful she was (Edgeworth 355). After several attempts to teach her how to read, she failed to acquire an active imagination and a cultivated taste for literature. He realized that Virginia's virtues sprang from 'sentiment' rather than reason. Without reason, she would not be able to cultivate an 'active understanding, knowledge of literature, or the power and the habit of conducting herself' properly (Edgeworth 359). These are the very qualities that Belinda intuitively possessed: 'on Belinda's prudence [...] he gradually learned to feel a different, and higher species of reliance' (Edgeworth 359), and he began to desire a different kind of woman than the one he imagined in his reading.

The failure of Hervey's experiment criticizes fashionable Society for its artifice, but also criticizes pure innocence as vapid. Moreover, any kind of pure aesthetic of 'the Beautiful,' as Edmund Burke would have it, is viewed as morally suspect. Virginia's physical nature is highlighted as her source of value by the male world, to the neglect of her mind. According to Edgeworth's theories of education, if a woman's mind is not rigorously exercised by entertaining ideas, and her sensibility is never tested, both her mind and sensibility cannot be strengthened;

therefore, the woman will remain an impressionable child. Consequently, this kind of education produces a dangerous kind of woman, whose feelings are easily aroused by sentimentality: the kind of woman who reads romance novels. This is exactly the kind of woman Virginia becomes:

> [her] mind was either perfectly indolent, or exalted by romantic views and visionary ideas of happiness. As she had never seen anything of society, all her notions were drawn from books [...]. Reading had become her only pleasure. (Edgeworth 359)

Reading romances excited pleasure, not rational thinking. The narrative turns from a criticism of educational theories and discourse, to a diatribe against reading romance novels. Edgeworth claims that these novels are counterproductive to the inculcation of virtue because the sentiment is not aimed at a particular object, which needs amelioration, relief or sympathy. Feeling must be accompanied by a kind of rational activity, otherwise it is wasteful. As one of Edgeworth's characters in *Letters for Literary Ladies* explains, that reading novels '[...] should, I think, always be associate with the active desire to relieve. If it be suffered to become a passive sensation, it is a useless weakness, not a virtue' (134). As an illustration of this faulty feminine model, Virginia falls in love with a man portrayed in a picture. Her emotional response is stimulated not by a real person, but a projection of her romantic imagination and thus leads to comic confusion for all:

> [...]Who is this man? and where is he to be found?[...].[interrupted Clarence.]
> [...]I do not know who this man is, I assure you; nor where he is to be found.'
> 'And yet you love him?'
> 'I only love his figure, I believe,' said Virginia [...].
> 'If you permitted this man to kneel to you, to kiss your hand, surely you must know that you love him, Virginia?'
> 'But that was only in a dream [...].'
> 'Only a dream! But you met him at Mrs. Smith's, in the New Forest?'
> 'That was only a picture.'
> 'Only a picture—you have never seen the original?' (Edgeworth 442)

Absurd as it seems, this parody illustrates the thought at the time that the kind of sentiment aroused by novels, according to many influential writers, 'caused convulsions of the passions and fractur[ed][...]the [female] personality' (Gallagher 277). Virginia's extreme reaction to a portrait animated by her images of romantic heroes makes clear that novel reading, particularly romances, engenders an enervation of the mind: it wastes the reader's energy making her incapable of thinking rationally. More importantly, it disrupted her most intimate ties—to a potential spouse, as it does in *Belinda*.

However, at least a part of Virginia's emotional involvement with novels occurs because she is not trained to read critically and be reasonable. Edgeworth obviously does not believe fiction is absolutely pernicious, but she does think that women are not taught to detach themselves emotionally from the imaginary world novels represent. Edgeworth's novel, and particularly this volume of it, is an attempt to counteract this reading problem, to provide a structure in which to move in and out of emotional scenes, so that the reader exercises nonsentimental reading habits (Gallagher 277). This heuristic reading strategy disciplines the reader. The shifting genres enable her to experience the character type, such as Virginia with her overwrought imagination or Clarence Hervey with his romantic imagination, for a brief time, and then have it comically exposed and rationally disavowed by a comparison to Belinda. Edgeworth's parody of Sophy in *Emile* not only illustrates the problem, but also attempts to contain it within the pages of a different novelistic discourse—the moral, or domestic, tale. As a consequence, the novel form is domesticated by Edgeworth to combat the imaginations of women who may not yet be trained to read properly.

Edgeworth's *Belinda* uses a mix of generic elements in order to teach the middling-class woman reader a new way of reading; that is, she is encouraged to feel, but those feelings must be tied to the moral truths contained in the narrative. Only then could she be assured of the proper effect of her reading—its ameliorative effect. This kind of ameliorative discourse blends the didacticism of the moral imperative of eighteenth-century novels with the pursuit of proper feeling in many nineteenth-century novels. Edgeworth's novel is distinctive in its function, aiming to reform the reader by teaching her how to read a different form of the novel, constructed by existing forms. However, by doing so, Edgeworth redefines the function for novels for her historical moment in 1801. Her novel form is one that propels 'proper' novel reading; so much so that we have forgotten that we ever needed to be taught how to regulate feeling with regard to narrative form. We have also forgotten that this novel function was a function of women's novels.[32] Edgeworth reconciles the novel's form and individual reform: the moral tale and the novel were no longer in contradiction.

Notes

1   For an overview of the 'dangers,' particularly for women, see John Tinnon Taylor, *Early Opposition to the Novel: The Popular Reaction from 1760 to 1830* (New York: King's Crown Press, 1943). See also J. Paul Hunter, *Before Novels: The Cultural Contexts of Eighteenth-Century English Fiction* (New York: Norton, 1990). Hunter's chapter on 'Didacticism' is important in order to understand the eighteenth-century emphasis on 'moral guidance' and how that emphasis finds its way into what we now understand as the 'novel,' 225-302.

2   Edgeworth's use of the term 'tale' has been interpreted as prudish. Mitzi Myers points out that Edgeworth was making a philosophical claim for her fiction; that it is at once moral and intellectual as well as 'wittily ironic.' See Myers, '"We Must Grant a Romance Writer A Few Impossibilities": "Unnatural Incident" and Narrative Motherhood in Maria Edgeworth's Emilie de Coulanges,' *The Wordsworth Circle* 27.3 (1996): 151-157; and 'Shot from Canons; or, Maria Edgeworth and the Cultural Production and Consumption of the Late Eighteenth-Century Woman Writer,' *The*

Consumption of Culture, 1600-1800: Image, Object, Text, eds. Ann Bermingham and John Brewer (New York: Routledge, 1995).

2   For an account of expansion of fictional work produced by women throughout the eighteenth century, see Turner 34-39. Turner notes that this discursive production culminated in a dramatic rise in the 1780s and 1790s. For an account of expansion of the publication of novels particularly, see James Raven, *Judging New Wealth: Popular Publishing and Responses to Commerce in England 1750-1800* (Oxford: Clarendon, 1992) 31-41.

4   Teresa Michals makes an important point about Edgeworth's notion of class specificity in 'Commerce and Maria Edgeworth's *Nineteenth-Century Literature,* 49.1 (1994): 3. She states that for Edgeworth each individual is 'a type within a system of classification that is at once moral and social' indicating both Edgeworth's scientific methods of analysis and her social position within bourgeoisie culture. As Michals points out the term 'class' in the eighteenth century can refer either to 'status or to character, either to a fixed social position based on the ownership of property or to a collection of personal traits shared by a group of people. Usually, however, it means both,' 3.

5   As Caroline Gonda has pointed out, 'to be a heroine of sense is something of a contradiction in terms' (212). Yet this is essential to both Wollstonecraft and Edgeworth's political/domestic projects. See Gonda, *Reading Daughters' Fictions 1709-1834: Novels and Society from Manley to Edgeworth* (New York: Cambridge UP, 1996).

6   For an overview of Maria Edgeworth's critical reception, see Butler, 338-51.

7   See Turner, 53-56.

8   For a fuller account of Belinda's post-publication history, see Butler, Appendix C, 494-499. For the original text from *Monthly Review,* see *Belinda,* ed. Eilean Ni Chuilleanain (Vermont: Everyman, 1993) 462-464. Mitzi Myers extensively discusses Edgeworth's critical reception in our day by both traditional and feminist scholars compared to her reception by her contemporaries in 'Shot from Canons.' Ina Ferris discusses the reviews of Edgeworth's oevre, and sees in the trajectory of the reviews an increasing 'restiveness and resentment' which underlies 'official approval' of Edgeworth's fictions. Her point is that the 'didactic' purpose of her fiction comes to be seen by 1817 as 'limiting' for the novel as a genre because it lacks 'passion and depth.' See Ferris, *The Achievement of Literary Authority: Gender, History and the Waverley Novels* (Ithaca: Cornell UP, 1991) 61-72.

9   Anne Mellor characterizes Belinda, following Jane Spencer's lead, as a didactic novel in which 'the author functions as moral teacher, racing the development of her youth to a mature, acceptance of the status quo and role of dutiful wife,' *Romanticism and Gender* (New York: Routledge, 1993) 40. Mellor goes on to say that although this is the tradition, feminist tracts made it possible to critique the status quo, and instead argue for the 'insistence on the domestic affections as the basis of all public and private virtues and happiness' (41). In this way *Belinda* represents a new Romantic ideology of femininity (44).

10 See Kowaleski-Wallace 129-130; and Gary Kelly, *English Fiction* 50. See also Heather MacFadyen, 'Lady Delacour's Library: Maria Edgeworth's *Belinda* and Fashionable Reading' *Nineteenth-Century Literature* 48.4 (1994): 423-439.

11 On this point about sentimental novels, see Kelly, *English Fiction* 50.

12 For a fuller discussion on the sentimental novel and its relationship to sense, sensibility and sympathy, see Todd's *Sensibility.*

13 Kowaleski-Wallace 121.

14 See also Myers, ' Reform or Ruin.'

15 Julia Douthwaite, 'Experimental Child-rearing After Rousseau: Maria Edgeworth, *Practical Education* and *Belinda,' Irish Journal of Feminist Studies* 2:2 (1997): 46.

16 Kowaleski-Wallace 122.

17 Slavoj Zizek uses the Lacanian concept, the 'subject presumed to know,' to clarify how the process of interpellation (in an Althusserian sense) produces subjectivation. See Zizek, *The Sublime Object of Ideology* (New York: Verso, 1989) 181-190. As readers, we will 'presume' that Belinda comprehends the moral implications of the follies of those around her, and chooses to stand beyond their follies, transgressions, and compulsions. We presume she does this because she understands a moral truth that we, as readers, do not (cannot) yet see.

18 Gary Kelly calls Belinda 'preternatural,' *English Fiction* 80. Elizabeth Harden in *Maria Edgeworth's Art of Prose Fiction* (Paris: Mouton, 1971) calls Belinda a 'lifeless model of perfection' (91). Even Edgeworth herself was not necessarily fond of the character she created, 'I really was so provoked with the cold tameness of that stick or stone Belinda, that I could have torn the pages to pieces' (Letter to Margaret Ruxton, December 1809), *A Memoir of Maria Edgeworth with a Selection from Her Letters*. ed. Frances Edgeworth, vol 1. (London: Joseph Masters and Son, 1867) 229.

19 Marjorie Lightfoot claims *Belinda* is a generic reinterpretation which classifies Edgeworth's genre mixing for the purposes of satire. Though in the end I disagree with her reading of *Belinda*, it is nicely argued. See Marjorie Lightfoot's '"Morals for those that like them": The satire of Edgeworth's *Belinda*, 1801' *Eire-Ireland: A Journal of Irish Studies* 29:4 (1994) 117-131.

20 Catherine Gallagher uses 'productive' in the sense of producing 'subjects' through reading, which is of course coextensive with an author's discursive labors. See Gallagher, *Nobody's Story: The Vanishing Acts of Women Writers in the Marketplace 1670-1820* (Berkeley: U of California P, 1994) xx-xxiv.

21 For an account of attacks on women's reading, see Peter de Bolla, *The Discourse of the Sublime: Readings in History, Aesthetics and the Subject* (Oxford: Basil Blackwell, 1989). For an examination of reading practices during the period in question, see Jon Klancher, *The Making of English Reading Audiences, 1790-1832* (Madison: U of Wisconsin P, 1987).

22 See Marilyn Butler 13-77; Kowaleski-Wallace 95-7; Ria Omasreiter, 'Maria Edgeworth's Tales: A Contribution to the Science of Happiness' in *Functions of Literature: Essays Presented to Erwin Wolff on His Sixtieth Birthday*, ed. Ulrich Broich, et. al. (Tubingen: M. Niemyer, 1984) 195-200. Gallagher also discusses Edgeworth's various disclaimers of her own writing, 273-275.

23 Butler argues convincingly against the notion that Maria, despite her assertions to the contrary, was a mouthpiece for her father's 'scientific,' 'educational' and 'professional' ideas.

24 See "Happiness," *The Oxford English Dictionary*, 1989 ed.

25 This is a paraphrase of T.R. Malthus' theory of 'generative' production in *Essay on the Principles of Population* (1798), ed. Philip Appleman (New York: Norton, 1976).

26 Another take on this 'discourse of merit' is what Teresa Michals has called 'personal credit' of the family. Michals, in an interesting reading of Edgeworth's fiction, uses the trope of commerce to reconcile the contradiction between economic individualism and corporate identity of the family. See Michals, 'Commerce and Character in Maria Edgeworth' *Nineteenth-Century Literature*, 49:1 (1994): 11-20.

27 Gary Kelly has claimed that Edgeworth's writing rests on an 'educational plan for training in merit' 91. See Kelly, 'Class, Gender, Nation, Empire: Money and Merit in the Writing of the Edgeworths' *The Wordsworth Circle* 25.2 (1994): 89-93.

28 For an extensive discussion of the Harriet Freke character in *Belinda*, see Colin B. Atkinson and Jo Atkinson, 'Maria Edgeworth, Belinda and Women's Rights' *Eire-Ireland: A Journal of Irish Studies* 19:4 (1984): 100-115.

29 My claim is an adaptation of Gary Kelly's claim that gothic romance was not a coherent genre; it was an 'ensemble of themes and formal elements which could be taken over and adapted in whole or part by other novelists,' *English Fiction* 49.

30 Douthwaite's 'Experimental Child-reading' discusses Rousseau's and the Edgeworths' educational theories with regard to the 'new' science of empiricism, 38-40.

31 Mitzi Myers extensively discusses the 'pre-text' of Day's experiment with the young woman, and how it figures into Edgeworth's subtle critique of patriarchal, oppressive culture. See 'My Art Belongs to Daddy? Thomas Day, Maria Edgeworth, and the Pre-texts of *Belinda*: Women Writers and Patriarchal Authority' *Revising Women: Eighteenth-Century 'Women's Fiction' and Social Engagement*, ed. Paula R. Backschieder (Baltimore: Johns Hopkins UP, 2000) 104-146.

32 Clifford Siskin has called the tendency of literary history to leave out writing by women, especially and particularly during the Romantic period, 'The Great Forgetting.' See Siskin, *The Work of Writing* 193-227.

Chapter 5

'More Than Half a Poet':
Dorothy Wordsworth's *Grasmere Journal*

Dorothy Wordsworth calls herself 'more than half a poet' while gazing upon the moon on White Moss Common (126-7), but her aesthetic contemplation only lingers long enough for her transcription of the scene in her journal, or so she writes:

> [...] as I climbed Moss [sic], the moon came out from behind a mountain mass of black clouds [...]. Once there was no moonlight to be seen but upon the island-house [...]. 'That needs must be a holy place' [...]. I had many very exquisite feelings, and when I saw this lowly Building in the waters, among the dark and lofty hills, with that bright, soft light upon it, it made me more than half a poet. I was tired when I reached home, and could not sit down to reading, and tried to write verses, but alas! I gave up expecting William, and went soon to bed [...]. (126-7)

Her inability to produce poetry is particularly highlighted in this passage; her ability to articulate this inability, though, is what is so interesting. The ability to write a passage recounting momentary aesthetic contemplation about the 'island-house,' but paradoxically her inability to write 'verses,' is an example of the productive activity in the *Grasmere Journal*. Writing is depicted as a natural extension of vision, but, at least for a woman, that ability to see does not necessarily transcend, or need to transcend, the material. However, it is her poetic inarticulation that has fostered much critical interest in Dorothy Wordsworth's writing and in *her* as a representation of early nineteenth-century womanhood. While Dorothy Wordsworth also wrote poetry, most scholarly attention has been paid to her journals, and then to only the slim selections of the *Alfoxden* and *Grasmere Journals*.

The reason we read these two slim selections is because they exemplify the kind of benevolence to which women were to ascribe. In the *Grasmere Journal*, we see the results of this philanthropic ideal. Dorothy Wordsworth maintains a superior benevolent, middling-class position in relationship to the laboring classes, whose appearance weave through the entries, because she can articulate their level of material needs and determine their worthiness for personal amelioration.

Similarly, she maintains her value to her brother in their household and in the Wordsworth circle, because of her inscription of her continual improvement of their home and his manuscripts. The *Grasmere Journal*, particularly, serves as a record of this feminine, benevolent, middling-class subjectivity and her philanthropic efforts, both of which are structured by an ideology of improvement.[1] This subject position and her articulation of her actions enables her to draw distinctions between different levels of literacy for the poor and for women, and between the georgic of domestic production, which centrally includes writing, and the aesthetic production of literature, a professional endeavor. Unceasing improvement is ensured by the construction, within the journal genre, of gender and class limits, enabling aesthetic and professional intervention to complete, and therefore improve, Dorothy Wordsworth, William Wordsworth, their writing, their home and the poor of Grasmere.

Therefore, Dorothy Wordsworth's writing is an interesting extension of the notion of literacy as a form of social control, which manifests itself in the private realm but with public consequences:[2] both domestic supervision and philanthropic work have become discursive work, and are seen as the domain of the feminine. These are considered 'labors of love' rather than labors necessary to ensure the survival of the family. Thus, Dorothy Wordsworth's discursive work is positioned against the material work of the laboring classes and, conversely, the professional or aesthetic work of her brother's literary endeavors.[3] While many other scholars have commented that benevolence is 'natural' to the middling-class woman's private sphere, it is that 'naturalness' which is to be put in question. The *Grasmere Journal* is a site of philanthropic intervention, positioning feminine writing as social practice: literacy is a special feminine duty that links together self-supervision, supervision of others and the supervision of the household. This duty reinforces the social function of improvement of the self particular to the literary culture that shapes Romanticism.

The Journal and Benevolent Femininity

Dorothy Wordsworth's texts disclose the benevolent ideology of 'Lady Bountiful,' but it is transformed because of the way she privately practices philanthropy, and because of the medium though which we come to know about it—her journal. The journal defines behaviors, values, and acts which will improve individuals, perhaps not monetarily but morally. In contrast to associated philanthropy of the mid-eighteenth century, 'self-help' philanthropy in the late eighteenth and early nineteenth centuries offered opportunities for women to enter a growing arena of public involvement.[4] The *Grasmere Journal* is evidence, a record if you will, of this relatively new function for philanthropy and for a discourse which helps define it. The 'private' genre of the journal demonstrates philanthropy as an internalized, 'natural' part of benevolent, middling-class, feminine identity.[5] Thus, individual amelioration is at the heart of private philanthropy—both for the philanthropist and her object of improvement.

The ideology of improvement structures the journal, but the genre also creates spaces of gendered inarticulation, which is necessary to understand first. In the White Moss Common excerpt quoted above, for example, writing is recounted as a constituent part of middling-class life, but her poetic inarticulation is a productive site of her writing because it tells us about gendered distinctions of discursive value. Her process of 'making sense' of her 'real' life categorizes discourse into very literally private/feminine and public/masculine realms of articulation. In fact, this is one of the purposes of the journals themselves: to catalog, to order, to reinforce what is proper for women and valuable about middling-class culture (what we have learned to call the 'real') and what is the stuff of more 'contemplative' and 'aesthetic' concerns. In her journals she categorizes the paths of usefulness for women, which centrally includes prose writing and philanthropy, and the paths of 'aesthetics' for men, which centrally includes poetry. She calls herself 'more than half a poet' and, therefore, so do we.

Consequently, the way criticism has treated Dorothy Wordsworth has all to do with the way she represents herself, her writing, and her brother in her journal. Scholars have labored to understand the function of the *Grasmere Journal* and of 'Dorothy Wordsworth' as a representation of nineteenth-century womanhood. Whether as a domestic subject, novice writer or helpmate, scholarship has focused primarily on her failure to realize herself, develop her talent, or establish her own home. We perceive Dorothy Wordsworth as William did, and therefore draw many parallels between them: the accuracy of Dorothy's 'real sketches' which William uses to create his poetry;[6] the 'subverted genius' who allowed her devotion to William to subvert her own creative powers;[7] the 'domestic dome' which encompasses Dorothy's material labors and William's literary endeavors.[8] Dorothy Wordsworth has also been used as an example of an early nineteenth-century woman with a suffocated unconscious who either could not (due to social sanctions) or would not (due to psychological sanctions) compete with her brother William in the public sphere of literary discourse;[9] she thus subverted the development of her literary talents by nurturing his.[10] Other scholars have looked at her writing as an exercise in the 'rhetoric of feeling' in which her writing actively asserts her own identity in defiance of William's portrayal of her.[11] However, reading the *Grasmere Journal* as a record of what Dorothy Wordsworth failed to do, of what she helped William to do, or even reading the journal as a covert act of defiance, misses the journal's most important *productive* function; Dorothy Wordsworth produces a function for women's writing, as well as a way of reading, which still shapes the critical evaluation of her and her texts.

I am not claiming that these readings are incorrect; in fact, they are the correct *effect* her journals seek to produce. While all of these analyses attempt to understand the feminine 'experience' of the late eighteenth and early nineteenth centuries, an important connection is missing between her writing (the journal) and her life (the apparent content of the journal): that is, the relationship between genre and what Dorothy Wordsworth chooses as the 'real' of her life produce 'Dorothy Wordsworth'—the benevolent, domestic model of womanhood who is the ideal collaborator for William.

Dorothy Wordsworth emerges as a woman who very literally reads and writes herself into literary existence just as a new social function for femininity is emerging: her most prominent form of literary production—the journal—is most functional to the task. Much in the mode of Hannah More's and Mary Wollstonecraft's vision of femininity, D. Wordsworth formed the emblematic middling-class woman of her day: sympathetic, charitable, and preeminently domestic.[12] These qualities become naturalized in the *Grasmere Journal*'s ideological work, because the realms in which they are depicted are the 'private' culture of the middling-class woman: family, charity and domesticity. As in the journal, these three realms almost blur into one another because they seem to us to be a 'natural' cultural consequence of femininity at that time. But it is the generic logic of the journal that weaves together these three realms, constructing them into the feminine subject who is Dorothy Wordsworth. Through these qualities, she literally writes a 'real' self that is at once domestic (useful and practical), tied to family (beloved) and philanthropic (charitable). To this end, her work becomes vocational much in the same way that W. Wordsworth's poetry has been described.[13] To D. Wordsworth, familial and social amelioration become her vocation: her feelings, duties, and beliefs all correspond to what she thinks is her special feminine capacity to rationalize, sympathize, and normalize the social sphere she supervises. But this social sphere does not only include the Wordsworth circle; it includes townspeople, servants and beggars that dot the landscape of the Lake District.

These laborers and beggars are not coincidental to the content of the *Grasmere Journal*; they are not, in other words, merely part of the scenery that D. Wordsworth comments on. These people enable her to play a particular 'philanthropic' role, one that appears seamless within the journals—so seamless, in fact, that few scholars have commented upon why these people appear, except to note where W. Wordsworth has taken the beggars or other transients out of D. Wordsworth's original (con)text and used them for his poetic material. However, the passages which deal with the social meaning and effect of poverty on people, specifically, are the key to understanding the triad of a specific kind of feminine subjectivity, one that exhibits familial love, charity and domesticity based on class difference.

Take, for example, the May 27th, 1800 excerpt from the *Grasmere Journal*:

> On Tuesday, May 27th, a very tall woman, tall much beyond the measure of tall women, called at the door. She had on a very long brown cloak and a very white cap, without bonnet; her face was excessively brown, but it had plainly once been fair. She led a little bare-footed child about 2 years old by the hand, and said her husband, who was a tinker, was gone before with the other children. I gave her a

piece of bread. Afterwards on my road to Ambleside [...]. I saw her husband sitting by the roadside [...]. The man did not beg. I passed on and about 1/4 of a mile further I saw two boys before me, one about 10, the other about 8 [...]. They were wild figures, not very ragged, but without shoes and stockings [...]. They continued at play till I drew very near, and then they addressed me with the begging cant and the whining voice of sorrow. I said 'I served your mother this morning'. (The Boys were so like the woman who had called at the door that I could not be mistaken.) 'O!' says the elder, 'you could not serve my mother for she's dead, and my father' on at the next town—he' a potter.' I persisted in my assertion, and that I would give them nothing. Says the elder, 'Come, let's away', and away they flew like lightning. (47)

While the boys beg at Matthew Harrison's house, D. Wordsworth confirms her suspicion that the boys had been lying because she 'met in the street the mother driving her asses; in the two panniers of one of which were the two little children, whom she was chiding and threatening with a wand' (47). This passage highlights the degree to which D. Wordsworth can distinguish between 'beggars' who are truthful but hungry, and beggars who are simply lying and trying to manipulate the more privileged people in the Wordsworths' position. She claims that the 'very tall woman' was 'without bonnet' indicating her poor condition, and that she had 'once been fair' but now was 'excessively brown' leading one to conclude that she is a transient. She does not mention whether this woman actually 'asked' for a piece of bread or some charity, and this seems important to D. Wordsworth. For the boys, the woman's children, actually asked for charity, characterized by D. Wordsworth as the 'begging cant and whining voice of sorrow.' Based on this puerile display and her description of the boys as 'wild' but obviously poor—'without shoes and stocking'—she decides not to 'serve' the boys by stating that she 'served' their mother this morning; her duty had been done. Her duty is not necessarily the act of giving food or money, but the decision as *to* whom to give food or money. This decision, of course, is an act of power. As Dorice Williams Elliott has pointed out, in the 'economy of charity' women maintain a position of power and authority only if the 'poor *remain* poor' (186). D. Wordsworth's decision maintains her commitment to helping the poor—the mother was 'served'—but is equally committed to keeping a 'paternalistic' or, rather, maternalistic relationship towards the poor.

The decision is based on the inarticulation of needs, rather than the articulation of them. Inarticulation, in the *Grasmere Journal*, does not signify a denial of needs, but higher moral integrity, which proves that you deserve what you did not ask for, but what you still really need. It is much like the Shepherd's paradox in Hannah More's moral tale *The Shepherd of Salisbury Plain* which portrays a self-reliant, good shepherd who deserves help because he does not think he needs it.[14] Thus, a distinction is made between people who deserve to have their needs satisfied and those who do not; this decision is based on whether and in what ways those needs are articulated. In the passage above, distinctions are stated in terms of growth: the mature, appropriate behavior of the poor adults receives D.

Wordsworth's attention and reward; but the immature and boisterous children receive her indignation. But this also creates a cultural distinction between those of the middling classes and those of the lower classes: the middling classes can desire things which exceed material necessities, like the Wordsworths who own their land (although by bequest) on which they set up a home, have enough food to give away, and have the time to attend to 'luxuries' like personal hygiene and decorous refinements like wearing a bonnet. The poor and the lower orders, however, must attend to more basic material gratifications like the beggars who roam the landscape struggling to satisfy their 'real' material needs. The distinction is borne out in the description of the beggars, which highlights what is missing, according to D. Wordsworth's perspective, from what should normally be apparent—a bonnet, shoes, stockings, food, and fair skin. She constructs the beggars as the antithesis to middling-class life, but who, nevertheless, must be integrated into its cultural and discursive landscape.

D. Wordsworth's description is in sharp contrast to W. Wordsworth's rendering of the exchange. In his poem 'Beggars,' the lack of material necessities is not highlighted; the reader is moved to feel pity for some lost time or landscape, and not for the beggars' poverty. The 'I' in the poem admits to the same skepticism about the woman's story: '[...]—On English Land/ Such woes I knew could never be,' and yet he gives her charity anyway because she 'was beautiful to see; a Weed of glorious feature!' (W. Wordsworth 243). The poem's function is to 'improve' or exercise the middling-class reader's aesthetic sensibilities while the journal entry recounts an actual occurrence of philanthropy. By reading W. Wordsworth's poem, the reader is impelled to feel; by reading D. Wordsworth's journal entry, the reader is impelled to believe in the writer's benevolence and judicious action. The latter teaches one about appropriate and inappropriate behaviors; the former teaches one how to feel. Action and feeling are therefore separated according to gender: literary women are proprietors of behavior while literary men are proprietors of feeling.[15]

D. Wordsworth's journal entry goes beyond simply accepting beggars as a natural part of the landscape, or turning them into aesthetic objects designed to evoke pathos as W. Wordsworth does. The passage is, on the one hand, one example within the *Grasmere Journal* of a retelling, or cataloging, of D. Wordsworth's charitable acts to those beneath her in economic and social status whom she deems worthy; that worthiness is based on the correct kinds of 'articulation' by the lower orders and whether their behavior evokes the correct kind of sympathy from her. D. Wordsworth's narration of her rational ability to discern truthful needs and the moral integrity to decide to act is designed to provide testimony of her own feminine virtue. But on the other hand, the passage constructs significant class distinctions that are based on cultural perceptions of the effects of poverty. Because the genre of the journal has a real referent, one that is not transformed by the imagination into a 'higher,' aesthetic perception of consciousness (again, this is a gendered distinction of genre that D. Wordsworth makes in her journals), the journal can describe distinctions between an inarticulate class, or one that does not articulate their needs properly, and a literary culture in which writing, reading and propriety in conversation are central to social and economic life. Thus, for D. Wordsworth, philanthropic feeling, as well as charitable giving, has at its center distinctions of class and gender based on literacy.

Obviously, Dorothy Wordsworth understood the societal ramifications of poverty, just as she understood her feminine, middling-class position and her role within the culture of philanthropy. Before any of the journals were written, she wrote to her friend Jane Pollard in 1789 about the establishment of her Sunday school where she instructed children 'only' in 'reading and spelling and they get off prayers hymns and catechism' (*Letters 1787-1805* 26). William Wilberforce, an avid supporter of Hannah More's philanthropic endeavors, had apparently underwritten the financial expense of D. Wordsworth's enterprise (26). She had intended 'a more extensive plan' which would include teaching 'spinning, knitting &c in the week days, and I am to assist her on Sundays, when they are to be taught to read' (26). But the school was not to materialize. As Lucinda Cole and Richard Swartz have noted, D. Wordsworth's interest in Sunday schools continued throughout her life: she encouraged their establishment and occasionally taught reading.[16] In addition, in 1808 D. Wordsworth's narrative *George and Sarah Green* was undertaken to financially support the orphaned children of the Greens, the Wordsworths' neighbors at Grasmere. Her hope was that through the subscriptions, a modest education might be enabled and the children would be placed in 'respectable' families until they were fit to go into service or be apprenticed (*George and Sarah Green* 18). Given the context of these other philanthropic endeavors, the entries in D. Wordsworth's *Grasmere Journal* that deal explicitly with portrayals of poverty have less to do with fodder for W. Wordsworth's poetic imagination, or, as Anita Hemphill McCormick has argued, D. Wordsworth's identification with the powerless and displaced poor, and more to do with constructing a particular representation of middling-class benevolent womanhood.[17] How she establishes this representation of womanhood as 'representative' of vocational philanthropy through the *Grasmere Journal* is the special 'subject' of the genre.

The genre is particularly useful to the benevolent identity she produces within the pages of the *Grasmere Journal*. Since her *Alfoxden* and *Grasmere Journal* have served William Wordsworth well with 'many verbal sketches of natural appearances which recur in [William] Wordsworth's and Coleridge's poems' (Abrams 313) and many of her narratives of the poor were used for W. Wordsworth's poetic production, how can the *Grasmere Journal* function as a 'private' document of subjective experience?

As is often mentioned, D. Wordsworth herself designates a reader for her work at the beginning of the *Grasmere Journal*:

> I resolve to write a journal of the time till W. and J. return, and I set about keeping my resolve, because I will not quarrel with myself, and because I shall give Wm. pleasure by it when he comes home again. (37)

D. Wordsworth assumes that her journals will be of certain and particular value to her brother: that is, 'pleasure' will come to William through the act of reading her journals.[18] 'Pleasure' will remind him of the value of 'home' when he returns to Grasmere; 'home' is explicitly linked to the presence of 'Dorothy' (W. Wordsworth's family) and with writing. This is why she does not 'quarrel' with herself—the point of writing is not to reflect upon herself, but to present in her writing an opportunity for improvement. In presenting herself in this way, the 'pleasure' that W. Wordsworth and we, as readers, take from the journals becomes a twofold rhetorical move. Pleasure comes from the material improvement of his life as a result of her labors of love, but pleasure is also an aesthetic effect that comes from *reading* about and enjoying 'Dorothy' as the feminine center of the domestic and community circle. The *Grasmere Journal* heuristically teaches him to recognize the feminine position as domestically and communally valuable, while he is occupied with other, more aesthetic, matters. Her writing creates for W. Wordsworth a vision of home to which he can return again and again in his poetry, and a vision of woman as a natural, sympathetic being who improves man, family, home, and the lowly.

Therefore, D. Wordsworth's *Grasmere Journal* defines different sites of discursive intervention for herself and for William. The genre creates spaces of gendered 'inarticulation.' It is true that D. Wordsworth's articulations have limits, limits of capability, of subjectivity, and of discursive value, but they are productive acts of power. Improvement requires limits. The journal as a record-book makes sense of home life so that W. Wordsworth can be comforted by remembering home, so that he can fill in the gaps of her narratives in the journals, be moved to (re)write poetry, plant a garden, remember a scene when they walked in the fields—in other words, to improve his poetry, his home, himself. That it seems to us a 'beloved' response to take care of W. Wordsworth, his wife, children and household, that it seems to us a benevolent response to help the needy, that it seems to us a rational desire to transcribe and criticize his poems, and read literature with and to him are all effects that her discourse seeks to produce. These are Dorothy Wordsworth's articulations, her writing, which gives William 'pleasure.' The question is not necessarily whether the journals are 'real' transcripts, or if they are a testimony of who Dorothy Wordsworth is as a 'real' individual. These questions are beside the point. The journal produces a kind of writing that ensures that an individual, whether it is the beggar, William or Dorothy, has depths that are hidden and capacities that need patient improvement.

The ideology of improvement structures the entries of the *Grasmere Journal*. If we look at the *Journal* in this way, we can see how D. Wordsworth has been read as a 'subjected,' 'suppressed' or 'repressed' female, or as Anne K. Mellor has argued, as 'a model of alterity' (157), because the feminine subject produced within that journal is necessarily constructed as always incomplete. Within the journal, D. Wordsworth writes herself as a subject that will always be in a state of 'becoming': to grow, to improve or to help others improve.[19] But paradoxically, because of her inarticulation—about her 'real' feelings, her 'real' thoughts—readers look for what she is not—as D. Wordsworth does with the beggars. She is a model of femininity that is defined in terms of the possibility of 'improvement,' of 'completeness,' of 'development'; therefore, D. Wordsworth seems 'real.' D. Wordsworth is 'more than half poet' who 'recollects' her 'own visions' but one who is not able to turn them into poetry:

> I was not quite well. When we passed through the village of Wensley my heart was melted away with dear recollections—the bridge, the little water-spout, the steep hill, the church. They are among the most vivid of my own inner visions, for they were the first objects that I saw after we were left to ourselves, and had turned our whole hearts to Grasmere as a home in which we were to rest. (180)

She is able, however, to turn these 'visions' into W. Wordsworth's recollections, by keeping her journal; she turns his heart to home at Grasmere. Thus, the way she writes about herself, her interior construction, enables W. Wordsworth to produce value for categories that define 'higher consciousness' and 'complete' subject development, and a whole and complete literary development, both of which scholars have been looking for in D. Wordsworth. Her text allows W. Wordsworth to 'gaze' upon her as an 'undeveloped' and 'natural' subject; conversely, her text also allows W. Wordsworth to transform the beggar woman into a figure of pathos who could not 'become.' Thus, what D. Wordsworth articulates and what she does not articulate is a clue to how her philanthropic vocation—her special duty to improve man and mankind—produces her relation to the relations of production in both a material sense (W. Wordsworth's poetic production which financially supports their home) and an ideological sense (D. Wordsworth's construction of a interior feminine subjectivity through writing her journal). She is the individual who is 'evermore about to be.'

The Ideology of Improvement

Let us look, then, to the acts, events, and duties she does articulate. As Kurt Heinzelman has observed, the *Grasmere Journal* has a 'georgic vision' (54).[20] That 'georgic vision' is manifested in the daily domestic activities that Dorothy Wordsworth, primarily, and William, secondarily, engage in. Heinzelman notes that William Wordsworth locates qualities such as manners, simplicity, candor and comfort and focuses them into 'household laws' which emphasize 'individual work and the cultural value of vocation' (55). Thus, 'domestic activity' becomes the 'infrastructure of support for creativity' (55). Both domestic activity and poetic, or at least discursive, production are linked—domesticity and literacy—within the 'georgic vision' of the *Grasmere Journal*. While Heinzelman recounts how 'Dorothy' was cast by Wordsworth in the role of 'improver' of the '(male) personality,' I would like to focus on how D. Wordsworth constructs herself as the 'improver' of *her* home and family, discourse, and the lower orders by their depiction in the journal. These three constituent elements which compose the basis of bourgeois femininity are, in D. Wordsworth's terms, the paths of usefulness. Therefore, the *Grasmere Journal* serves us with a record of how the ideology of improvement constructs a feminine subjectivity, and reproduces that subjectivity for William, his family, and eventually a reading public.

Not surprisingly, household duties, discursive production, and philanthropic work are also the three categories of activity cataloged in the *Grasmere Journal*. The ideology of improvement is thus the central structuring mechanism for the journal. Raymond Williams has explained the socioeconomic lineage of 'improvement' which overlaps 'making a profit' from the cultivation of land with regard to agrarian capitalism, a definition specifically used in the eighteenth century, and the more general usage from the seventeenth century onwards of 'making something better' (*Keywords* 161). The overlapping definition is important in the journal because, when at Grasmere, the Wordsworths' are extended leaseholders for the first time, and thus had a vested interest in 'improving' their property, employing a servant to help with the duties of the household, and making themselves a social part of the community.[21] Because of their 'improvement' of the land, transforming it into cultivated 'property,'[22] their home at Grasmere achieves a particular value to the Wordsworths, through laborious activities like gardening, landscaping, weeding: 'hoed the first row of peas, weeded, etc., etc., sat hard to mending till evening' (38); 'W. cut down the winter cherry tree. I sowed french beans and weeded' (46); 'Sauntered a good deal in the garden, bound carpets, mended old clothes [...] dried linen. Molly weeded turnips, John stuck the peas' (40).

These images of property improvement are countered by other images of its cultivation or lack thereof. For example, while W. Wordsworth writes a poem 'descriptive of the sights and sounds we saw and heard,' D. Wordsworth describes contrasting scenes of nature. The first is a description of the 'natural' landscape which includes 'the gentle flowing of the stream, the glittering, lively lake, green fields without a living creature to be seen on them' (133). The second is a description of laborers cultivating former pastureland: 'the people were at work ploughing, harrowing and sowing; lasses spreading dung [...]. We then went on, passed two sisters at work (they first passed us), one with two pitchforks in her hand, the other had a spade. We had some talk with them' (133). While W. Wordsworth focuses on the 'natural,' D. Wordsworth lauds both the 'natural' and 'cultivated' landscapes. Her description is juxtaposed to another 'unnatural' landscape:

> Then we went to the Island [...]. The shrubs have been cut away in some parts of the island. I observed to the boatman that I did not think it improved. He replied: 'We think it is, for one could hardly see the house before'. It seems to me to be, however, no better than it was. They have made no natural glades; it is merely a lawn with a few miserable young trees, standing as if they were half-staved. There are no sheep, no cattle upon these lawns. It is neither one thing or another—

neither *natural*, not wholly cultivated and artificial, which it was before [...]. (155)

Improvement of one's property is an aesthetic concept, one which has to do with taste and execution. Improving one's home must be executed properly and tirelessly; otherwise, the trees will not grow, and the lawn will be inhospitable to even cattle and sheep, let alone people.

Along with the cultivation of property is the cultivation of home life. D. Wordsworth details her domestic activities within the house, again with the intention of improving her family's comfort: mending, laundering, baking, canning, etc. These acts are useful, just as improving the property is, because they provide for the health and welfare of the household. She also lists expenses for the upkeep of the household in keeping with the historical function of the journal as an account book.[23] Preoccupations with health concerns and, relatedly, the exercise of walking—to get food and letters, to make visits to the community—are also chronicled. If the ideology of improvement structures the activity in the journal, then health-related activities become an important tool in confirming when her or William's health is impeded or has improved after a 'headache' or other illness. All these domestic and familial concerns seem 'natural' to us because they construct the 'real' in a particular and familiar way: one that normalizes activities performed by, or at least supervised by, women for the comfort and improvement of family members.

Her day is regulated by an ebb and flow of activities which are, importantly, repetitive. Alan Liu has commented on the repetitiveness of the *Journal* as a kind of 'rhythm' which seeks to 'represent' the 'truly continuous line of human identity' (121). However, the repetition of activity that D. Wordsworth's journal depicts is representative of the 'real' labors which need D. Wordsworth's attention and labor on a continuing basis. The similarity of activity exists because she normalizes and catalogues the necessary tasks that the middling-class woman must repeatedly accomplish. Some of these tasks can be accomplished by herself: self-regulatory exercises such as gardening, gathering vegetables, laundering, mending; others must be done by servants. D. Wordsworth has supervisory control over the activities and events at Grasmere. She is omnipresent in the workings of everyday activities. Though Margaret Homans suggests that D. Wordsworth's neglect of the 'I' is indicative of a 'tendency to omit a central or prominent self in her journals' (73), and sees it primarily as a fragmentation of self-identity, the lack of the 'I' may suggest pervasive supervisory control over the domestic duties as well as control over their descriptions in her journal. Thus, the neglect of the 'I' is not necessarily a 'fragmentation' of self-identity, but the construction of an identity defined by the ever-present domestic duties and her capacity to improve her home. As Mellor states, it 'functions as a point of reference and not as a controlling subject' (160). However, the 'I' of the *Grasmere Journal* is assumed by others, giving D. Wordsworth omnipresence in the domestic sphere, though perhaps not control over it.[24]

The second prominent activity is discourse production and circulation, and this activity takes a variety of different forms. D. Wordsworth chronicles the flow of manuscripts: copying and recopying poems and other writing by W. Wordsworth at various stages of composition and publication; writing and receiving letters from her brothers and a variety of friends, including Catherine Clarkson, S.T. Coleridge, Mary Hutchinson; reading and discussing a variety of different texts from Boswell's *Life of Johnson* to W. Wordsworth's 'The Leech Gatherer;' and, of course, D. Wordsworth's own textual productions, one of which is her journal which she attends to as a necessary household duty. The integration of domestic activity and the production of discourse—her own and W. Wordsworth's—has been a topic of much scholarly discussion. But for our purpose it is essential to see that literacy binds D. Wordsworth's household to the middle-class community the journal represents. Experience is transcribed into one kind of discourse or another, and those discourses are read and sometimes scrutinized. Discourse production and circulation becomes a 'natural' part of the flow of domestic activity. In the Wordsworth household, writing produces more writing: letters produce more letters, reading produces writing, D. Wordsworth's journal entries help W. Wordsworth produce poems, her copying of the poems produce a manuscript for publication, etc. That these various kinds of writings will improve the well-being of the members of the community is the impetus; the household will run more efficiently (it is certainly depicted as the hub of activity), the letters will console and improve D. Wordsworth's dejected spirits (especially when W. Wordsworth is far from home), writing poetry and publishing it will ameliorate the minds of the public. Those who find themselves outside literacy are, consequently, outside the 'natural' flow of feminine domesticity and the middling classes. Those who find themselves outside are the laboring classes and, most notably in the *Grasmere Journal*, the destitute.

The third activity, though little discussed in scholarship, is the constant insertion of short descriptions of the poor and D. Wordsworth's interaction with them. In these entries, more than at any other point in the journal, she comes closest to narrative. She chronicles the problem of debt and poverty in the Grasmere countryside, which W. Wordsworth aestheticizes in the 'The Beggar' and 'Home at Grasmere.' She notes more abstract considerations of class in a few entries, but mostly she narrates her interactions with the poor.[25] In the very first entry, below her 'resolve to write a journal,' she writes 'at Rydale, a woman of the village, stout and well dressed, begged a half-penny; she had said she had never done it before, but these hard times!' (37). A little below this passage, in the same entry, D. Wordsworth tells her first beggar story:

> A young woman begged at the door—she had come from Manchester on Sunday morn. with two shillings and a slip of paper which she supposed a Bank note—it was a cheat. She had buried her husband and three children within a year and a half—all in one grave—burying very dear—paupers all put in one place—20

shillings paid for as much ground as will bury a man—a stone to be put over it or the right will be lost—11/6 each time the ground is opened. (38)

Throughout the *Grasmere Journal*, D. Wordsworth catalogues her interaction with the poor, sometimes with sympathy, other times without, sometimes stating the amount of money or piece of food she gave, sometimes noting she gave nothing, sometimes saying nothing at all. That she takes such care in narrating the penury in the Lake Distinct at all is important. On the one hand, it makes poverty seem a 'natural' part of domestic life, which she has some duty to ameliorate by listening to the poor's stories. These are practical actions on which feeling and moral judgment turns. On the other hand, it articulates the trials or the manipulations of the poor as a contrast to the workings of her home as she depicts it in the rest of the journal. 'Their' stories are *not* 'her' stories. She is able to articulate and distance their infelicitous activities of begging from her own more productive and stable home life. D. Wordsworth's supervision extends from the domestic sphere of domestic endeavor to discourse production about the poor: she circulates goods and money to the poor, who traverse the countryside of the Lake Distinct and village of Grasmere, as an extension of her domestic duty while circulating a text about them in the Wordsworth circle.

Because the flow of these daily activities has no particular hierarchical importance in each entry, they seem preeminently personal—a reflection of the reality they describe. As both Alan Liu and Kurt Heinzelman have noted, this is an effect of the 'autobiographical present' which, of course, lay within the foundations of genre in which she worked.[26] The autobiographical present 'normalizes' this kind of activity by chronicling it; but unlike Liu and Heinzelman, I do not think the activity has any particular 'narrative' to it. That she does not create a narrative, a more formal autobiography, is important. The *Grasmere Journal* exists as a record of strictly middling-class, feminine duties which produces an always-improving domestic sphere, and is not a record of self-revelation, conflict resolution, subjective development or aesthetic contemplation.

Notice how the three activities—domestic accomplishments for personal and home improvements, the prominence of reading and composition to improve the mind, and the hardships of poverty from which D. Wordsworth's farming neighbors suffer—are encapsulated in one entry from the journal:

> [November] 24th [1801], Tuesday. A rainy morning. We all were well except that my head ached a little, and I took my breakfast in bed. I read a little of Chaucer, prepared the goose for dinner, and then we all walked out. I was obliged to return for my fur tippet and spencer, it was so colds[...]. I saw a solitary butter-flower in the wood. I found it not easy to get over the stepping stones. Reached home at dinner time. Sent Peggy Ashburner some goose. She sent me some honey, with a thousand thanks. 'Alas! the gratitude of men has', etc. I went in to set her right about this, and sate a while with her. She talked about Thomas's having sold his land. 'Ay' says she, 'I said many a time he' not come fra London to buy our land, however.' Then she told me with what pains and industry they had made up their

taxes, interest, etc. etc., how they all got up at 5 o'clock in the morning to spin and Thomas carded, and that they had paid off a hundred pounds of the interest [...].We sate by the fire without work for some time, then Mary read a Poem of Daniel upon Learning. After tea Wm. read Spenser, now and then a little aloud to us. We were making his waistcoat. We had a note from Mrs. C., with bad news from poor C.—very ill [...]. (82-83)

In the passage, D. Wordsworth is the very nexus of activity: all familial lines and community ties intersect at her home. D. Wordsworth depicts it as a closed, almost cloistered community: domestic production produces 'some goose' or William's 'waistcoat' which is exchanged in the middling-class domestic economy for the payment of gratitude and love. Home runs on its own 'beloved' impetus: 'I shall be beloved; I want no more' (151). The domestic work accomplished in the journal are the 'labors of love' that Liu mentions, to be contrasted with the manual labor of Peggy and Thomas Ashburner who must wake up at 5 o'clock every morning in order to produce yarn even though Molly, the Wordsworths' servant-girl, mentions that Peggy is 'very ill, but one does not know how long she may last' (83). For the Wordsworths, daily activity is ordered by something constitutively different than that of the Ashburners—not by necessity, but by the idea of improvement: if D. Wordsworth is ill, she can breakfast in bed, reading Chaucer, until she feels well enough to prepare the goose for dinner. By sending the goose to the Ashburner's home, she can help improve Peggy's health, and 'set her right' about the 'gratitude of men.' And William, Dorothy and Mary can participate in the pleasure of reading 'Daniel upon Learning' and Spencer, and learn of Coleridge's poor health through his letters. Rather than having the flow of events dictate her activities as with the Ashburners, she enacts these daily events—the domestic space begins and ends with her control over that space, improving herself and the lives of her family and community around her.

And, most importantly, these daily events and activities are perpetuated by her love: her love of man and 'mankind.' It is not the activity itself that the reader is propelled to contemplate and value, but the value assigned to the activity as a reified 'labor of love' put into place by the regulatory presence of D. Wordsworth. Here, love and improvement, rather than the manual labor and monetary exchange, are linked as the required motivation for labor in the feminized middling-class domestic economy. And the happy home she depicts in the *Grasmere Journal* is, of course, the intended result of her labor. She is therefore an indispensable member of the family; her position is central because domestic labor emanates from her love. Domestic labor is not naturalized, but the labor of love, represented by domesticity and community responsibility, in the journal is naturalized.

To this end, D. Wordsworth continually devalues her responsibility for her texts, her authorial authority and her subjectivity. She is not an 'authorizing subject' of her own discourse; she disowns the property of her text and the self through discourse.[27] The function that we, as post-romantic readers, have assigned to journal writing valorizes the private, artless writer: the 'authentic' self in its bare, 'natural' state. We have assumed that this is the 'pleasure' which D. Wordsworth wanted W. Wordsworth to value in his reading of the journal. And we would be correct; not because it is true, but because she used the journal to categorize what is 'real' (domestic concerns, discursive work, poverty) and what is 'imaginative,' what is proper to a masculine sphere of discourse, and what is proper to a feminine sphere of discourse.[28] The journal stands as a testimony that plays out the kind of usefulness suggested by other women writers, such as Hannah More. Textual responsibility is personalized and addressed to a family member, rather than inserted within a larger public discourse, and affection can be displayed discreetly in duties, i.e. labors of love, performed for the family as well as for the poor. Writing her journal is a way to traverse the public and private spheres at this particular historical moment.

Therefore, D. Wordsworth's choice of genre highlighted her respect for, and implicitly demanded recognition for, her femininity. To be the private 'invisible hand' who writes journals describes an internalization of feminine cultural codes (defined by the activities she chose to represent in her *Grasmere Journal*) and ideas of appropriate literacy. She expresses this concern in a letter written to Mrs. Catherine Clarkson, a friend who urged her to publish what we know as 'George and Sarah Green: A Narrative,' in order to amass a profit to give to the orphaned children of the title characters:

> [...] I cannot have that narrative published. My reasons are entirely disconnected with myself, much as I should detest the idea of setting myself up as an Author. I should not object on that score as, if it had been an invention of my own it might have been published without a name, and nobody would have thought of me. But on account of the family of Greens I cannot consent [...] by publishing the narrative, I should bring the children forward to notice as individuals, and we know not what injurious effects this might have upon them. (*Letters* 353-4)

Her unwillingness to enter the visible industry of literary publication must not be thought of as a question of the subversion of talent or devotion to William, but one of feminine power: she does not need to call attention to herself as an author because she can have more practical influence as a woman whose special duty is to 'help' these children through her ability to write well. She clearly perceives authorship, and the notoriety it brings, to be a display of vulgar productivity, complicit with motivations of profit—a clearly masculine domain in her view, rather than one of middling-class vocation. The story's broader publication might also have brought monetary rewards that would have exceeded the amount necessary to keep the children in their appropriate class. The private circulation of the narrative had already raised a sufficient amount of money to secure the children's modest living conditions and their education at a charity school. D. Wordsworth felt that this should be sufficient reward for the children, and for her.

As this incident illustrates, D. Wordsworth's concern with privacy is more of a concern of transgression: the corruption of the children's social and economic values and the corruption of her sphere of domestic influence. Hovering between the public and private spheres, she used her writing to maintain and ameliorate the hardships of these laboring-class children. Her literary and discursive endeavors are vocational, rather than professional, as well as philanthropic. Like many other women writers at the time, D. Wordsworth would be 'ungendered' and 'unclassed' by the authorship of a widespread publication, corrupting herself by displaying the affectation of literary pursuit. Circulation of a text among a private group of subscribers retains her bourgeois propriety, her domestic desires, while still providing for her desire to help the children. Perhaps we can use this framework to understand the production of the journals as a propitious choice of genre in this light, one which allows her a controlled amount of 'display' and yet engages the public, and one which maintains her femininity and economic dependence.

This discursive incident also illustrates her belief in the responsibility and benevolence of women of the middling class to help the lower classes, but it is D. Wordsworth who *can* speak for them. Without any other way to secure a trust for the children, D. Wordsworth voluntarily writes a narrative on their behalf; their vulgar utterances and lowly experience could be transformed into a proper testament to the worthiness of relief for the children. The object of this narrative is to emotionally inspire those in a different economic position to believe it is ethically appropriate to give money to these children; it is on her authority that they believe in the children's worthiness. In the same way, her journal provides a record book of her charitable sensitivity. These children in particular, but the many stories of beggars and poverty-stricken men and women in the *Grasmere Journal*, attest to D. Wordsworth's 'practical' use of aesthetics as 'a special kind of ethical work.'[29] Her ability to use description, dialect, and poetic idioms in these passages make her texts *seem* like expressive sentiments of a 'natural' poet. But she is, rather, a *journalist* whose appeal is to the 'real' of social conditions whether they are conditions of poverty or domesticity. The value she ascribes to her texts is her ability to articulate what she perceives as 'real' and as the domain of womanhood, i.e. the real social problems of the poor and work of domestic and literary production. Her solution for these representations of the 'real' is the ideology of improvement—the poor will be helped by philanthropy, a home will be improved by domestic labor, and all persons will be bettered by her 'ethic of care.'[30]

The journal signals an effective gendered division of discursive labors for the Wordsworths: while D. Wordsworth's journal catalogues her improvement of 'real' bodily labors, W. Wordsworth labors to improve the 'feelings' of mankind. For her, the refinement of feeling should be left for men, such as W. Wordsworth, to write about. He will complete the gaps created by her text, create poems from her journalistic 'sketches' and write to ameliorate the aesthetic sensitivities of the middling classes. D. Wordsworth's writing is purposely non-poetic: it is designed for useful feeling and not sentimental musings. The *Grasmere Journal* produces an internalization of the ideology of improvement, and the journal's success is measured by our own 'natural' acceptance of this woman's benevolence.

Dorothy, the Beloved Woman

Dorothy Wordsworth's *Grasmere Journal* posits a benevolent feminine identity central to reconceiving what she presumes are 'real' gender and class relations. It depicts these relationships as private, and internalizes the notion of female benevolence, making it seem natural. It constructs a model of femininity designed to enable the happiness and well-being of others to be realized through a woman's labors of love and textual production. The result is that 'Dorothy,' as the 'subject' in her text, as well as in the scholarship on her writing, vanishes within the symbolic network of the nineteenth century, casting her in the role of the ideal feminine companion for William, the ideal benevolent woman for her society. Therefore, the model of 'Dorothy' is a production of D. Wordsworth's journals, and has an effect upon William Wordsworth and his writing. Her success is only visible in the continuity of scholars' responses to the journals and William Wordsworth's representation of 'Dorothy.'

When W. Wordsworth evokes his sister in Book Six of *The Prelude*, he looks upon his figurative Dorothy as treasure:

> The presence, Friend, I mean
> Of that sole Sister, who hath been long
> Thy treasure also, thy true friend and mine,
> Now, after separation desolate
> Restor'd to me, such absence that she seem'd
> A gift first bestow'd.   (VI. 195-203)

He evokes her again in his moment of crisis in Book Twelve as the savior of his sanity:

> Ah! then it was
> That Thou, most precious Friend! about this time
> First known to me, didst lend a living help
> To regulate my Soul, and then it was
> That the beloved Woman in whose sight
> Those days were pass'd, now speaking in a voice
> O sudden admonition, like a brook
> That does but cross a lonely road, and now
> Seen, heard and felt, and caught at every turn,
> Companion never lost through many a league,
> Maintain'd for me a saving intercourse
> With my true self [....] (XII 309-344)

'Dorothy' essentially serves the same function in both of these passages: she is identified as a natural caretaker, rejuvenating his mind and 'regulat[ing]' his soul from the sterile study of the rational sciences and the suffering of political struggle. Her function, as Margaret Homans has described, is to 'restore the poet to a more appreciative and receptive attitude toward nature' which would allow the progression of his imagination and the continued production of his poetry (51). She is cast as a stage in human development that W. Wordsworth has surpassed. Aligned with Nature, Dorothy functions to preserve, or cure, the self and to direct it to its true course: W. Wordsworth's poetic genius.

What joins these two representations of Dorothy is hinted at in the title of Book Eight: 'Retrospect: Love of Nature Leading to Love of Mankind.' For it is a transitional book that describes Dorothy's presence in his life. W. Wordsworth depicts his entrance into the natural world of Grasmere and the love of Dorothy as the resolution to his inner conflict, which results in his own spiritual and mental health. Though he can only be a visitor in that natural and domestic place, the effect of it, which is imbued with Dorothy's love of *this* man, enables him to once again 'love mankind': a restoration of balance unites the contrarieties of rationality and sense, and his true self is restored. Through this reunification of faculties, he is able to produce poetry which in turn will aesthetically reproduce this balance. W. Wordsworth removes Dorothy from all intercourse with society in his poetry, so that he can represent her as a private space to which he can always return.

He thus acknowledges her position as a powerful one—for without her, his personal crisis would continue; but her curative power is subordinate to his poetic power to heal. Her power to heal is neutered, in a sense, by the higher 'mind' of the masculine poet. It is not the way that D. Wordsworth has represented herself to William in her journal?

For the Wordsworths, the 'true' project of poetry appropriates this 'healing power' though aesthetic acts, by creating the Romantic belief that the aesthetic can ameliorate the minds of men, creating a greater society of mankind. As W. Wordsworth's final stanza of *The Prelude* concludes:

> Prophets of Nature, we to them will speak
> A lasting inspiration, sanctified
> By reason and by truth; what we have loved,
> Others will love; and we many teach them how;
> Instruct them how the mind of man becomes
> A thousand times more beautiful than the earth
> On which he dwells, above this Frame of things
> (Which, 'mid all revolutions in the hopes a
> And fears of men, doth still remain unchanged)
> In beauty exalted, as it is itself
> Of substance and of fabric more divine. (XIII 423-445)

Poetry functions to 'teach' the 'mind of man;' it becomes the ameliorating force 'mid all revolutions.' Poetry is a superior realm of articulation within a public sphere of discourse from which domestic women, like Dorothy, are necessarily excluded. But this exclusion is based in part on D. Wordsworth's own articulations of self. Through the logic of the journal, she teaches W. Wordsworth how he should view her—as sympathetic, charitable, and domestic. She constructs her community and her interactions with it in a particular way so that it is distinct from his interactions with her and the greater community that his audience serves. In this way, she maintains her role as supervisor and improver of home and of others, which help her become the beloved and devoted sister we know.

When D. Wordsworth judges her own inarticulation, when we look at the *Grasmere Journal*, we tend to 'judge' it on the basis of what it lacks: form, narrative, and metaphor, etc. We attempt to read it as if it were a 'literary' discourse. Consequently, we find D. Wordsworth's discourse lacking: lacking creativity and subjective development, leading the reader to draw conclusions about the repression or suppression of her imagination and human development. However, the point of D. Wordsworth's journal is to catalog, categorize and order reality in a particular way: according to levels of literacy for genders and for classes. In other words, she defines a 'good' subject for poetry and a 'good' subject for charity, a 'proper' articulation for a middling-class woman, and an 'improper' articulation for laboring-class woman or man. She defines who writes, who can tell stories and, most importantly, how those stories can be told. At the same time, these distinctions produce 'Dorothy Wordsworth' (our cultural product) as 'more than half a poet,' which becomes a characteristically feminine position within the Romantic aesthetic. What she does not, cannot, and chooses not to articulate becomes the *Grasmere Journal*'s central ideological function, and creates the distinctions of gendered literacy and class identity.

Notes

1 I am using the term 'ideology' developed by Louis Althusser in 'Ideology.' This definition posits that ideology represents 'the imaginary relationship of individuals to their real condition of existence' (162). It is important to note that ideologies are not 'born' in apparatuses or in discourse. They are 'born' in a class's 'condition of existence, their practices, their experience of the [class struggle]' (186). Subjective experience is the mechanism through which ideology is not only experienced, but also produced and reproduced: that is, ideology (in general) is a 'structure' required by society in order to understand and 'represent' it. Discourse, in turn, manifests ideolo*gies*, allowing discourse to represent reality through an ideological lens. For a fuller discussion of 'ideology,' see Terry Eagleton *Ideology.*

2 See Nancy Armstrong, *Desire and Domestic Fiction, A Political History of the Novel* (New York: Oxford UP, 1987) 91.

3 Although cumbersome at times, to avoid the condescending standard practice of referring to 'Dorothy' in relation to Wordsworth, I will refer to her as D. Wordsworth and William Wordsworth as W. Wordsworth. Referring to her as 'Dorothy' only highlights the personal discourse that the chapter is attempting to deconstruct.

4 As Linda Colley states: '[...] in Britain the boundaries supposedly separating men and women were, in fact, unstable *and becoming more so*' (25). One of the ways in which women were becoming more publicly active in the course of the eighteenth century is through philanthropic endeavor, in which 'female reformers [presented] themselves as embodiments of virtue and high morality [...]. Invoking woman's superior morality and virtue proved enormously helpful because it converted their *desire* to act into an

overwhelming *duty* to do so (277). See Colley, *Britons: Forging the Nation, 1707-1837* (New Haven: Yale UP, 1992).

5 Felicity Nussbaum in *The Autobiographical Subject* provides a useful framework in which to understand gender within a 'private' autobiographical genre: 'when we write ourselves and our experience, the language we use derives from our own subjectivity, but that subjectivity is constituted in social relations. Eighteenth-century women who represent their subjectivity were, however, caught in mimicking the dominant ideologies of themselves. Their self-fashionings were inevitably bound up in cultural definitions of gender—those assumed, prescribed, and embedded in their consciousness—as well as in their subversive thoughts and acts of resistance to those definitions' (133-134). Nussbaum points to a formation of an interior feminine subjectivity that is portrayed in discourse as authoritative, natural and truthfully self-evident, but once investigated might reveal a social construction of gender drawn from ideologies internalized so that gender identity is thought to be natural and truthfully self-evident. The interiority of a subject, then, is connected with an internalization of particular discursive forms, ideas and perceptions. If that interiority is defined in terms of privacy—individual thoughts, feelings, desires, then the genre of the journal links the interiority of the private self with the public notions that seek to interpellate that interiority.

6 See for examples M.H. Abrams, ed., et al. *Norton Anthology of English Literature*, headnote, vol. 2 (New York: Norton, 1994). Ernest de Selincourt's footnotes throughout his standard edition of *The Journals of Dorothy Wordsworth* comment on where William Wordsworth and S.T. Coleridge drew upon Dorothy Wordsworth's entries for their poems. See footnotes in *The Journals of Dorothy Wordsworth*, vol 1, (London: Macmillian, 1952). See also Pamela Woof, *Dorothy Wordsworth, Writer* (Grasmere: Wordsworth Trust, 1988).

7 See for examples Margaret Homans, *Bearing the Word: Language and Female Experience in Nineteenth Century Women's Writing* (Chicago: U of Chicago P, 1986); Meena Alexander, *Women in Romanticism* (Savage, MD: Barnes & Nobles) 1989; James Holt McGavran, Jr. 'Dorothy Wordsworth's Journals: Putting Herself Down,' *The Private Self, Theory and Practice of Women' Autobiographical Writings*, ed. Shari Benstock (Chapel Hill: U of North Carolina P, 1988).

8 See Alan Liu, 'On the Autobiographical Present: Dorothy Wordsworth's *Grasmere Journals*,' *Criticism* 26. 2 (1984): 115-137.

9 See Margaret Homans, *Women Writers and Poetic Identity, Dorothy Wordsworth, Emily Bronte and Emily Dickinson* (Princeton: Princeton UP, 1980) and Susan Levin, *Dorothy Wordsworth and Romanticism* (New Brunswick, NJ: Rutgers UP, 1987).

10 For a recent feminist version of this 'Romantic' relationship, see Elizabeth Fay, *Becoming Wordsworthian, A Performative Aesthetic* (Amherst: U of Massachusetts P, 1995). Fay argues that William Wordsworth's poetic efforts were the result of a poetic collaboration between William and Dorothy, which enabled William to 'perform' the role of poet, while Dorothy performed the role of poetic chronicler of 'real scenes.' Fay effectively decenters W. Wordsworth as the univocal voice of his poetry, and reinserts a more complicated version of D. Wordsworth that does not reinvoke William's version of Dorothy as his poetic muse or the 'rural maiden,' but rather enables her to contribute her own 'imagination and poetic voice' to William's work, using him to inspire her own. The Wordsworths we know as readers is thus a product of this aesthetic relationship that is 'composed' through writing both poetry and the journals. Though a complex re-reading of the William-Dorothy relationship and its literary production, it still casts the argument in 'Romantic' terms: Dorothy 'sees' the real and thus she is still

'more than half a poet,' while William is 'always evermore about to be' with the help of Dorothy's perceptive vision of the 'real.'

11 See Anita Hemphill McCormick, '"I shall be beloved—I want no more": Dorothy Wordsworth's Rhetoric and the Appeal to Feeling in *The Grasmere Journals' Philological Quarterly* 69. 4 (1990): 471-493.

12 See Lucinda Cole and Richard G. Swartz, '"Why Should I Wish for Words?" Literacy, Articulation, and the Borders of Literary Culture' in *At the Limits of Romanticism: Essays in Culture, Feminism and Materialist Criticism*, eds. Mary A. Favret and Nicola J. Watson (Bloomington: Indiana UP, 1994) 153.

13 See Susan J. Wolfson, 'Individual in Community: Dorothy Wordsworth in Conversation with William' in *Feminism and Romanticism*, ed. Anne K. Mellor (Bloomington: Indiana UP, 1988) 12-13.

14 See Hannah More, *The Complete Works of Hannah More*. vol 1. New York: Harper and Brothers, 1835.

15 It is worth noting here that I compared this particular passage in the journal with William Wordsworth's 'Beggars' to emphasize the difference between the two kinds of writing—one rhetorical and the other aesthetic—that is based on gendered distinctions of discursive value. I do not wish to claim, as Elizabeth Fay has done, that there is collaboration between Dorothy and William which produces both forms of writing, which then creates a complete Romantic 'unity' that cannot be put asunder.

16 See Cole and Swartz 153.

17 McCormick's article suggests that entries about vagrant women 'allowed her to pity her own vulnerability, and simultaneously to impress William with her own virtue and compassion' (483). Susan Levin's book, *Dorothy Wordsworth and Romanticism*, also emphasizes D. Wordsworth's identification with these women and her anxiety about the 'possible disintegration' of her own position in W. Wordsworth's thoughts, affections and home before and after his marriage to Mary Hutchinson. See Levin 21-22.

18 McCormick points out that the designation of William as audience is 'likely to have influenced what she chose to write about and the attitudes she took,' 476.

19 Elizabeth Fay uses an alternate understanding of 'becoming' in the Wordsworthian aesthetic which largely hinges on the notion of 'performativity,' 109-154. I am, however, arguing that Dorothy Wordsworth's 'becoming' is an effect of her discourse which seeks to produce an understanding of the female subject that is in a constant state of 'improvement,' or the improvement of others that comes to be understood as natural. As Clifford Siskin has argued, the desire for 'ongoing revision' of the self is a particularly Romantic phenomenon that structures how we come to know ourselves. See *Historicity*,13.

20 See Kurt Heinzelman, 'The Cult of Domesticity, Dorothy and William Wordsworth at Grasmere' in *Feminism and Romanticism*, ed. Anne K. Mellor (Bloomington: Indiana UP, 1988) 54. Heinzelman's article usefully discusses the model of production as a principal value of the household.

21 Dove Cottage was rented from John Benson of Tail End, see Stephen Gill, *Wordsworth: A Life* (New York: Oxford UP, 1989) 169.

22 On this point, see Pepper 371-373.

23 Historically, the 'journal' and 'diary' are used interchangeably according to Arthur Ponsonby, *English Diaries*, vol 1. (London: Metheun, 1923) 5; Felicity Nussbaum 23-25. Ponsonby also suggests that the journal had a domestic purpose: a household record in which ordinary activities, such as domestic details, food, accounts of marriages and births, travel, health, weather are events that would be commonly found in journals

written before and after D. Wordsworth's, 14-24. He does not, however, suggest that this purpose becomes gendered at a certain point in history.

24 For another opposing view, see Pamela Woof, *Dorothy Wordsworth, Writer* in which Woof states that D. Wordsworth's 'identity is "absorbed" in self-forgetfulness,' 41.

25 D. Wordsworth mentions the divisions between the 'rich' and poor, 40; upper- and middling-class distinctions, 62-63; and the benevolence of the middling-class woman, 99-100.

26 Cole and Swartz note that the conformity to the journal is an internalization of the 'commitment to the spread of literacy' defined in terms of Hannah More's philanthropic projects, with the 'corresponding prohibition against women writing poetry,'153.

27 In 'What is an Author?' Michel Foucault notes that 'the author's name serves to characterize a certain mode of being of discourse: [...] this discourse is not ordinary everyday speech that merely comes and goes, not something that is immediately consumable.' See *Language, Counter-Memory, Practice*, trans. Donald F. Bouchard and Sherry Simon (Ithaca: Cornell UP, 1988) 123. But Dorothy Wordsworth's discourse functions differently, because her particular genre is 'immediate' and 'consumable' by a reader, but not by publication in the usual sense.

28 Hannah More's *Strictures on a Modern System of Female Education*, written only a few years before D. Wordsworth's journal, claims that the aesthetic, particularly the sublime, is the domain of men's writing and the narrative and polite letters are the discursive domain of women. See More 311-417.

29 See Cole and Swartz 154.

30 Anne K. Mellor in *Gender and Romanticism* (New York: Routledge, 1993) uses Carol Gilligan's terms 'ethic of care' which 'insists on the primacy of the family or the community and their attendant practical responsibilities,' 3. It is this concept on which Mellor bases her romantic model of feminine alternity one that is based on 'sympathy and likeness.' But again, that sympathy and likeness is constructed by texts like D. Wordsworth's *Grasmere Journal*.

Conclusion

Philanthropy was a crucial site of societal reformation in the late eighteenth and early nineteenth centuries. As many scholars such as Janet Todd, Dorice Williams Elliott, and Ann Mellor have already observed, philanthropy and reform gave middling-class women a way to exert some social and political power in a patriarchical society. They offered a unique sense of 'usefulness,' as Hannah More would say, to these women. At the same time, however, their usefulness is born within an historical contradiction. While Elliot claims that middling-class women's 'philanthropy did contribute to British culture a new sense of what women of all classes, cultures, and races desired and were capable of attaining' (217), she also acknowledges that some of their achievements were gained at the expense of the laboring classes. It is within this contradiction that the important analyses lie: it is our task to understand how what is desired and what one is capable of attaining comes into being. After all, these desires and capabilities should not be taken as *prima facie*, but as those that are constructed in discourses, like the ones in this study, in their historical moment. It is quite possible that those desires and capabilities, though we might see them as universal were, in origin at least, very historically specific. The power dynamics of this relationship between the privileged and poor, while perhaps imbued with altruistic intentions, cannot escape history.

What I have been calling vocational philanthropy in this study enables us to understand both the constructedness of women's benevolence and women's practical reform, one of which was writing. It enables us to understand philanthropy's historicity, its contradictions, its accomplishments and its failures. Vocational philanthropy is a historically-specific social practice which helped produce a model of middling-class feminine benevolence and, in turn, helped produce a set of discourses designed to privatize the public problem of poverty and harmonize social relations among all classes. To say this, however, does not mean that philanthropy and reform are unequivocally positive; rather, they are complex modes of participation in the public sphere.

More specifically, the texts I have chosen to study are not necessarily unique or original in their endeavors. Many other women writers, Mary Hays, Sarah Trimmer, and Elizabeth Inchbald for example, write novels, tracts, and tales with similar 'pedagogical' purposes. The texts and writers I have chosen to discuss, however, demonstrate that it is a combination of writing across genres which repeatedly 'teaches' the reader (and primarily the female reader) how to read or how to read properly, thereby reenvisioning the act of reading as an act of understanding a rewritten relationship between genders and classes. And that relationship is rewritten by these middling-class women writers who value the power of print to forge harmony within the nation. It is not these women writers who are powerful; rather, the power lies in the combination of middling-class women writers across a political, religious and intellectual spectrum that produces a feminine community who are interested and invested in constructing literature that will be of benefit to mankind. It is with this impetus that these women contribute to the stability of English culture and society.

This power is the primary function of vocational philanthropy: one that enables the transmission of ideologies through the lessons of literature. What this paradigm of vocational philanthropy allows us to do, in the twenty-first century, is to view these texts as *productive* of the value of reading and the practices of literacy. In the last analysis, what is produced is a 'common' notion of 'principles and habits,' as Hannah More put it, of morality that we take as natural.

This notion of feminine production has often been absent from even recent criticism of late eighteenth- and early nineteenth-century women writers. We often see women writers united in a critique of patriarchy or in an effort to promote positive reform of the masses, but we are not as quick to point out the how the effects of that critique or that reform have contributed to the creation of the social and economic system that prevailed in the eighteenth and nineteenth centuries. If women writers were always critiquing and reforming, then their texts only have a negative function. I am interested in what their texts *do*: what is their positive function? What I have argued is that women's discourse has produced, not just critiqued, ideology. The ideologies produced in women writers' discourses helped, for better or worse, to stabilize an unstable economy and revamp the social bonds between genders and classes that were undergoing radical historical change. This is another way, in addition to critique and reform, that we can understand women writers and their writing: the production of the ideologies of benevolence, earnestness and continual improvement that contribute to a revamping of communal identities which are lived differently by different genders and classes. The fact that we so readily accept these ideologies (or neglect to see them as ideologies), that they seem so right to us in the narratives that we read, is a testament to their very transparency in our culture. These women writers and their writing have become a 'vanishing mediator': that is, self-help philanthropy is the condition by which capitalism survived and thrived by 'universalizing' its relevance (Zizek *For They Know* 182).[1] It is these ideologies, so necessary to the notion of self-help philanthropy, that have penetrated our cultural unconscious. Because of this penetration, we no longer need that form of literature, or discourse, to function in that pedagogical manner; its use vanishes and so does its writers. What is left is the content: the work of ideologies in other discourses like the developing novel form to produce subjects who see themselves as benevolent, hard-working, and always improving (or 'evermore about to be'). Using the lens of vocational philanthropy enables us to see didactic and polemical literature, not as an exercise in the excess of morality or an aberration (bad literature), but as an important stage in the mediation of one social/economic system to another.

It also enables us to view women writers of the late eighteenth and early nineteenth centuries as productive social forces. This is also why these women writers were, until recently, 'forgotten' or relegated to the fringes of developing notions of the novel, feminism or literary history. Clifford Siskin has traced this vanishing act of women writers as the Great Forgetting.[2] The important work had been done already: women had been acculturated to read, write and reform; the poor had been acculturated to believe in the efficacy of these practices. These women writers, as subjective and subjectivizing agents, vanish within the new discursive systems they helped to bring about: the flourishing of the novel form in the nineteenth century (as suggested in chapter 4) and six-poet Romanticism (as suggested in chapter 5), for instance. Their writing remains outside Literature, and thus outside literary history as we have come to understand it. These writers and their texts have sutured the gender and class determinants which are their conditions of existence, and by doing so they elide their own history.

It has been my intention to examine the historicity of these texts and to think about how writing becomes an important way that self-help philanthropy is disseminated. While the intersection of philanthropy and writing has begun to be explored, we need new ways to think beyond 'representations' of philanthropy: a reflectionist model that while helpful leaves the work of writing, the work of ideology, largely unexamined. Critique of representations is important work, but so is understanding ideological production. We need a way to think through what writing does, not just what it represents.

Notes

1 See Fredric Jameson, 'The Vanishing Mediator; or, Max Weber as Storyteller,' *Ideologies of Theory*, vol 2 (Minneapolis: U of Minnesota P, 1988). Jameson discusses, as an example, the role of Protestantism in the rise of capitalism. See also Slavoj Zizek's discussion of Jameson's 'vanishing mediator' in *For They Know* 182-188.
2 See Siskin *Work of Writing* 195.

Bibliography

Abrams, M.H. headnote. *Norton Anthology of English Literature.* 7th ed. New York: Norton, 1993. 219-221.

Alexander, Meena. *Women in Romanticism.* Savage, MD: Barnes & Noble, 1989.

Allen, Julia. 'The Uses and Problems of a "Manly" Rhetoric: Mary Wollstonecraft's Adaptation of Hugh Blair's *Lectures* in Her Two *Vindications.' Listening to Their Voices: The Rhetorical Activities of Historical Women.* Ed. Molly Meijer Wertheimer. Columbia, SC: U of South Carolina P, 1997. 320-336.

Althusser, Louis. 'Ideology and Ideological State Apparatuses (Notes towards an Investigation).' *Lenin and Philosophy.* New York: Monthly Review, 1971. 127-186.

Andrew, Donna T. *Philanthropy and Police: London Charity in the Eighteenth Century.* Princeton: Princeton UP, 1989.

Armstrong, Nancy. *Desire and Domestic Fiction: A Political History of the Novel.* New York: Oxford UP, 1987.

Atkinson, Colin B. and Jo Atkinson. 'Maria Edgeworth, Belinda and Women's Rights.' *Eire-Ireland: A Journal of Irish Studies* 19.4 (1984): 94-118.

Barker-Benfield, G.J. *The Culture of Sensibility: Sex and Society in Eighteenth-Century Britain.* Chicago: U of Chicago P, 1992.

Barrell, John. 'Sportive Labour: The Farmworker in Eighteenth-Century Poetry and Painting.' *The English Rural Community: Image and Analysis.* Ed. Brian Short. New York: Cambridge UP, 1992. 105-132.

Bennett, Tony. *Formalism and Marxism.* New York: Metheun, 1979.

Bradley, Ian. *A Call to Seriousness: The Evangelical Impact on the Victorians.* London: Jonathan Cape, 1976.

Briggs, Asa. *A Social History of England.* London: Weidenfield & Nicolson, 1983.

Burke, Edmund. 'Thoughts and Details on Scarcity.' *The Works of the Right Honorable Edmund Burke.* 6th ed. vol 5. Boston: Little Brown, 1880.

Butler, Marilyn. *Maria Edgeworth: A Literary Biography.* Oxford: Oxford UP, 1972.

Clarke, W.K. Lowther. *A History of the S.P.C.K.* London: S.P.C.K., 1959.

Cohen, Murray. *Sensible Words: Linguistic Practice in England 1640-1785.* Baltimore: Johns Hopkins UP, 1977.

Cole, Lucinda and Richard G. Swartz. '"Why Should I Wish for Words?" Literacy, Articulation, and the Borders of Literary Culture.' *At the Limits of Romanticism: Essays in Culture, Feminism and Materialist Criticism.* Eds. Mary A. Favret and Nicola J. Watson. Bloomington: Indiana UP, 1994. 143-169.

Colley, Linda. *Britons: Forging the Nation 1707-1837.* New Haven: Yale UP, 1992.

Colquhoun, Patrick. *A Treatise on Indigence; exhibiting a General View of the National Resources For Productive Labour; with Proposition for Ameliorating the Condition of the Poor, and Improving the Moral Habits and increasing the comforts of the Labouring People, particularly the rising Generation; by regulation of political economy, calculated to prevent poverty from descending into Indigence, to produce sobriety and Industry, to reduce the parochial rates of the Kingdom, and generally promote the Happiness and Security of the Community at Large, by the Diminution of moral and penal offences, and the future prevention of crimes.* London: J. Hatchard, 1806.

Crafts, N.F.R. 'The Industrial Revolution: Economic Growth in Britain, 1700-1860.' *New Directions in Economic and Social History.* Eds. Anne Digby and Charles Feinstein. London: Macmillan, 1988. 64-75.

Cressy, David. 'Levels of Illiteracy in England 1530-1730.' *Literacy and Social Development in the West: A Reader.* Ed. Harvey J. Graff. New York: Cambridge UP, 1981. 105-124.

Davidoff, Leonore and Catherine Hall. *Family Fortunes: Men and Women of the English Middle Class, 1780-1850.* Chicago: U of Chicago P, 1987.

Demers, Patricia. *The World of Hannah More.* Lexington: U of Kentucky P, 1996.

de Bolla, Peter. *The Discourse of the Sublime: Readings in History, Aesthetics and the Subject.* Oxford: Basil Blackwell, 1989.

Douthwaite, Julia. 'Experimental Child-rearing After Rousseau: Maria Edgeworth, *Practical Education* and *Belinda.' Irish Journal of Feminist Studies* 2.2 (1997): 35-56.

Eagleton, Terry. *Heathcliff and the Great Hunger: Studies in Irish Culture.* New York, Verso, 1995.

  Ideology: An Introduction. New York: Verso, 1992.

  The Ideology of the Aesthetic. Cambridge: Basil Blackwell, 1990.

Eden, Frederic Morton. *The State of the Poor: A History of the Labouring Classes in England, with Parochial Reports.* Ed. A.G.L. Rogers. New York: Benjamin Blom, Inc, 1971.

Eden, Robert. *The Harmony of Benevolence, A Sermon Preached in the Cathedral-Church of Worcester, Sept 10, 1755, at the Annual meeting of the three Choirs of Worcester, Gloucester and Hereford.* London: W. Sandby, no date.

Edgeworth, Frances, Ed. *A Memoir of Maria Edgeworth with a Selection from Her Letters.* 3 vols. London: Joseph Masters and Son, 1867.

Edgeworth, Maria. *Belinda.* Ed. Eilean Ni Chuilleanain. Vermont: Everyman, 1993.

  Practical Education. vol. 1. 3rd ed. London: J. Johnson and Co, 1811.

  Tales and Novels. vol. 2. London: Routledge, no date.

Elliott, Dorice Williams. *The Angel Out of the House: Philanthropy and the Gender in Nineteenth-Century England.* Charlottesville: UP of Virginia, 2002.

  '"The Care of the Poor is her Profession": Hannah More and Women's Philanthropic Work.' *Nineteenth-Century Contexts* 19 (1995): 179-204.

Fay, Elizabeth. *Becoming Wordsworthian: A Performative Aesthetic.* Amherst: U of Massachusetts P, 1995.

Feldman, Paula R. and Theresa M. Kelley, Eds. *Romantic Women Writers: Voices and Countervoices.* Hanover, NH: UP of New England, 1995.

Ferris, Ina. *The Achievement of Literary Authority: Gender, History and the Waverley Novels.* Ithaca: Cornell UP, 1991.

Ford, Charles Howard. *Hannah More: A Critical Biography.* New York: Peter Lang, 1996.

Foucault, Michel. *Power/Knowledge: Selected Interviews and Other Writings, 1972-1977.* New York: Pantheon, 1980.

  'What is An Author?' *Language, Counter-Memory, Practice.* Trans. Donald F. Bouchard and Sherry Simon. Ithaca: Cornell UP, 1988.

Gallagher, Catherine. *Nobody's Story: The Vanishing Acts of Women Writers in the Marketplace 1670-1820.* Berkeley: U of California P, 1994.

Girard, Jessica. 'Lady Bountiful: Women of the Landed Classes and Rural Philanthropy.' *Victorian Studies* 30 (1987): 183-210.

Gill, Stephen. *Wordsworth: A Life.* New York: Oxford UP, 1989.

Graff, Harvey J. *The Legacies of Literacy: Continuities and Contradictions in Western*

Culture and Society. Bloomington: Indiana UP, 1987.

Introduction. *Literacy and Social Development in the West: A Reader*. Ed. Harvey J. Graff. London: Cambridge, 1981. 1-13.

Gonda, Caroline. *Reading Daughters Fictions, 1709-1834: Novels and Society from Manley to Edgeworth*. New York: Cambridge UP, 1996.

Guest, Harriet. 'A Double Lustre, Femininity and Sociable Commerce, 1730-1760.' *The Eighteenth Century* 23.4 (1990): 479-501.

Guralnick, Elissa S. 'Radical Politics in Mary Wollstonecraft's *A Vindication of the Rights of Woman*.' *Studies in Burke and His Time* 18 (1977): 155-166.

Gunther-Canada, Wendy. 'The Politics of Sense and Sensibility: Mary Wollstonecraft and Catherine Macauley Graham on Edmund Burke's *Reflections on the Revolution in France*.' Ed. Hilda L. Smith. *Women Writers and the Early Modern British Political Tradition*. New York: Cambridge, 1998. 126-147.

Harden, Elizabeth. *Maria Edgeworth*. Boston: Twayne, 1984.

Hawkes, David. *Ideology*. New York: Routledge, 1995.

Heinzelman, Kurt. 'The Cult of Domesticity, Dorothy and William Wordsworth at Grasmere.' *Feminism and Romanticism*. Ed. Anne K. Mellor. Bloomington: Indiana UP, 1988. 52-78.

Himmelfarb, Gertrude. *The Idea of Poverty: England in the Early Industrial Age*. New York: Knopf, 1984.

Hitchcock, Tim, Peter King and Pamela Sharpe, Eds. *Chronicling Poverty: The Voices and Strategies of the English Poor, 1640-1840*. New York: St. Martin's, 1997.

Hobsbawm, E.J. *The Age of Revolution 1789-1848*. New York: New American Library, 1962.

Homans, Margaret. *Bearing the Word: Language and Female Experience in Nineteenth-Century Women's Writing*. Chicago: The U of Chicago P, 1984.

Hunter, J. Paul. *Before Novels: The Cultural Contexts of Eighteenth-Century English Fiction*. New York: Norton, 1990.

Jameson, Fredric. *The Political Unconscious: Narrative as a Socially Symbolic Act*. Ithaca, Cornell UP, 1981.

'The Vanishing Mediator; or, Max Weber as Storyteller.' *Ideologies of Theory*, vol 2. Minneapolis: U of Minnesota P, 1988.

Janes, Regina M. 'On the Reception of Mary Wollstonecraft's *A Vindication of the Rights of Woman*.' *Journal of the History of Ideas* 39 (1978): 292-298.

Johnson, Claudia. *Equivocal Beings: Politics, Gender, and Sentimentality in the 1790s, Wollstonecraft, Radcliffe, Burney, Austen*. Chicago: U of Chicago P, 1995.

Johnson, Samuel. *Samuel Johnson: Selected Poetry and Prose*. Eds. Frank Brady and W.K. Wimsatt. Berkeley: U of California P, 1977.

Jones, M.G. *The Charity School Movement*. London: Frank Cass, 1964.

Hannah More. New York: Cambridge UP, 1952.

Jordan, W.K. *Philanthropy in England, 1480-1660*. New York: Russell Sage, 1957.

Kaestle, Carl F. '"Between the Scylla of Brutal Ignorance and the Charybdis of Literary Education": Elite Attitudes toward Mass Schooling in Early Industrial England and America.' *Schooling and Society: Studies in the History of Education*. Ed. Lawrence Stone. Baltimore: Johns Hopkins UP, 1976. 177-191.

'The History of Literacy and the History of Readers.' *Perspectives on Literacy*. Eugene R. Kintgen, Barry M. Kroll and Mike Rose, Eds. Carbondale: Southern Illinois UP, 1988. 95-126.

Keen, Paul. *The Crisis of Literature in the 1790s: Print Culture and the Public Sphere*. New York: Cambridge UP, 1999.

Kelly, Gary. 'Class, Gender, Nation, and Empire: Money and Merit in the Writing of the Edgeworths.' *The Wordsworth Circle* 25.2 (1994): 89-93.

    'Revolution, Reaction and the Expropriation of Popular Culture: Hannah More's *Cheap Repository.*' *Man & Nature* 6 (1987): 147-159.

    English Fiction of the Romantic Period 1789-1830. New York: Longman, 1989.

Kernan, Alvin. *Samuel Johnson and the Impact of Print.* Princeton: Princeton UP, 1987.

Kestner, Joseph. *Protest and Reform: The British Social Narrative by Women, 1827-1867.* Madison: U of Wisconsin P, 1985.

Kitch, Malcolm. 'Population Movement and Migration in Pre-Industrial Rural England.' *The English Rural Community: Image and Analysis.* Ed. Brian Short. New York: Cambridge UP, 1992. 62-84.

Klancher, Jon. *The Making of English Reading Audiences, 1790-1832.* Madison: U of Wisconsin P, 1987.

Kovacevic, Ivanka. *Fact Into Fiction.* Leicester: Leicester UP, 1975.

Kowaleski-Wallace, Elizabeth. *Their Fathers' Daughters: Hannah More, Maria Edgeworth and Patriarchal Complicity.* New York: Oxford UP, 1991.

Kramnick, Isaac. *Republicanism and Bourgeois Radicalism, Political Ideology in Late Eighteenth-Century England and America.* Ithaca: Cornell UP, 1990.

Krueger, Christine L. *The Reader's Repentance: Women Preachers, Women Writers, and Nineteenth-Century Social Discourse.* Chicago: The U of Chicago P, 1992.

Lacan, Jacques. *The Seminars of Jacques Lacan, Book II: The Ego in Freud's Theory and in the Technique of Psychoanalysis 1954-1955.* Ed. Jacques-Alain Miller. Trans. Sylvana Tomaselli. New York: Norton, 1988; 1991.

Larson, Magali Sarfatti. *The Rise of Professionalism.* Berkeley: U of California Press, 1977.

Laqueur, Thomas Walter. *Religion and Respectability: Sunday Schools and Working-Class Culture 1780-1850.* New Haven: Yale UP, 1976.

    'Working-Class Demand and the Growth of English Elementary Education, 1750-1850.' *Schooling and Society: Studies in the History of Education.* Ed. Lawrence Stone. Baltimore: Johns Hopkins UP, 1976. 192-205.

Levin, Susan. *Dorothy Wordsworth and Romanticism.* New Brunswick, NJ: Rutgers UP, 1987.

Lightfoot, Marjorie. '"Morals for Those that Like Them": The Satire of Edgeworth's *Belinda,* 1801.' *Eire-Ireland: A Journal of Irish Studies* 29.4 (1994): 117-131.

Liu, Alan. 'On the Autobiographical Present: Dorothy Wordsworth's *Grasmere Journals.*' *Criticism* 26. 2 (1984): 115-137.

MacFadyen, Heather. 'Lady Delacour's Library: Maria Edgeworth's Belinda and Fashionable Reading.' *Nineteenth-Century Literature* 48.4 (1994): 423-439.

Markley, Robert. 'Sentimentality as Performance: Shaftesbury, Sterne, and the Theatrics of Virtue.' *The New Eighteenth Century.* Eds. Felicity Nussbaum and Laura Brown. New York: Metheun, 1987. 210-230.

Marx, Karl. *Capital.* vol 1. Trans. Ben Fowkes. New York: Vintage, 1977.

McCormick, Anita Hemphill. '"I shall be beloved–I want no more": Dorothy Wordsworth's Rhetoric and the Appeal to Feeling in *The Grasmere Journals.*' *Philological Quarterly* 69. 4 (1990): 471-493.

McGavran Jr., James Holt. 'Dorothy Wordsworth's Journals: Putting Herself Down.' *The Private Self: Theory and Practice of Women's Autobiographical Writing.* Ed. Shari Benstock. Chapel Hill: U of North Carolina P, 1988. 230-253.

Mellor, Anne K. 'British Romanticism, Gender, and Three Women Artists.' *The Consumption of Culture, 1600-1800: Image, Object and Text.* Eds. Ann Bermingham and John Brewer. New York: Routledge, 1995. 121-142.

Gender and Romanticism. New York: Routledge, 1993.

Mothers of the Nation: Women's Political Writing in England, 1790-1830. Bloomington: Indiana UP, 2000.

Michals, Teresa. 'Commerce and Character in Maria Edgeworth.' *Nineteenth-Century Literature* 49.1 (1994): 1-20.

Michael, Ian. *The Teaching of English: From the Sixteenth Century to 1870.* New York: Cambridge UP, 1987.

More, Hannah. 'Tales for the Common People: Advertisement.' *The Complete Works of Hannah More.* vol 1. New York: Harper and Brothers, 1835. 190.

'Betty Brown, the St. Giles Orange Girl: with some Account of Mrs. Sponge, the Money-Lender.' *The Complete Works of Hannah More.* vol 1. New York: Harper and Brothers, 1835. 247-250.

'Black Giles, The Poacher.' *The Complete Works of Hannah More.* vol 1. New York: Harper and Brothers, 1835. 251-258.

'Essays on Various Subjects.' *The Complete Works of Hannah More.* vol 1. New York: Harper and Brothers, 1835. 548-561.

'The Shepherd of Salisbury Plain.' *The Complete Works of Hannah More.* vol 1. New York: Harper and Brothers, 1835. 190-200.

'Strictures on a Modern System of Female Education.' *The Complete Works of Hannah More.* vol 1. New York: Harper and Brothers, 1835. 311-417.

Myers, Mitzi. '"A Peculiar Protection": Hannah More and the Cultural Politics of the Blagdon Controversy.' *History, Gender and Eighteenth-Century Literature.* Ed. Beth Fowkes Tobin. Athens, GA: U of Georgia P, 1994. 227-257.

'Hannah More's Tracts for the Times: Social Fiction and Female Ideology.' *Fetter'd or Free? British Women Novelists, 1670-1815.* Eds. Mary Anne Schofield and Ceclia Macheski. Athens, OH: Ohio UP, 1986. 264-284.

'My Art Belongs to Daddy? Thomas Day, Maria Edgeworth, and the Pre-Texts of *Belinda*: Women Writers and Patriarchal Authority.' *Revising Women: Eighteenth-Century 'Women's Fiction' and Social Engagement.* Ed. Paula Backschieder. Baltimore: Johns Hopkins UP, 2000. 104-146.

'Politics From the Outside: Mary Wollstonecraft's First Vindication.' *Studies in Eighteenth-Century Culture* 6 (1977): 113-132.

'"Reform or Ruin": A Revolution in Female Manners.' *A Vindication of the Rights of Woman.* By Mary Wollstonecraft. Ed. Carol Poston. New York: Norton, 1988. 328-343.

'Shot from cannons; or, Maria Edgeworth and the Cultural Production and Consumption of the Late Eighteenth-Century Woman Writer.' *The Consumption of Culture, 1600-1800: Image, Object and Text.* Eds. Ann Bermingham and John Brewer. New York: Routledge, 1995. 193-214.

'"We Must Grant A Romance Writer A Few Impossibilities": "Unnatural Incident" and Narrative Motherhood in Maria Edgeworth's Emilie de Coulanges.' *The Wordsworth Circle* 27.3 (1996): 151-157.

Neuberg, Victor. *Popular Literature: A History and Guide.* New York: Penguin, 1977.

Niell, Anna. 'Civilization and the Rights of Woman: Liberty and Captivity in the Work of Mary Wollstonecraft.' *Women's Writing* 8.1 (2001): 99-117.

Nussbaum, Felicity. *The Autobiographical Subject: Gender and Ideology in Eighteenth-Century England.* Baltimore: Johns Hopkins UP, 1989.

Omasreiter, Ria. 'Maria Edgeworth's Tales: A Contribution to the Science of Happiness.' *The Function of Literature: Essays Presented to Erwin Wolff on His Sixtieth Birthday.* Ed. Ulrich Broich, et al. Tubingen: M. Niemyer, 1984. 195-208.

Owen, David. *English Philanthropy 1660-1960*. Cambridge: Belknap, 1964.

Patterson, Annabel. *Pastoral and Ideology, Virgil to Valery*. Berkeley: U of California P, 1987.

Pearson, Jacqueline. *Women's Reading in Britain, 1750-1835*. New York: Cambridge UP, 1999.

Pedersen, Susan. 'Hannah More Meets Simple Simon: Tracts, Chapbooks, and Popular Culture in Late Eighteenth-Century England.' *Journal of British Studies* 25 (1986): 84-113.

Pepper, W. Thomas. 'The Ideology of Wordsworth's "Michael: A Pastoral Poem"' *Criticism* 4 (1989): 367-382.

Poovey, Mary. 'Aesthetics and Political Economy in the Eighteenth Century: The Place of Gender in the Social Constitution of Knowledge.' *Aesthetics and Ideology*. Ed. George Levine. New Brunswick, NJ: Rutgers UP, 1994. 79-105.

   The Proper Lady and the Woman Writer. Chicago: U of Chicago P, 1984.

Ponsonby, Arthur. *English Diaries*. vol. 1. London: Metheun, 1923.

Poynter, J.R. *Society and Pauperism, English Ideas on Poor Relief, 1795-1834*. London: Routledge & Kegan Paul, 1969.

Price, Richard. *A Discourse on the Love of Our Country*. 1789. *The Vindications*. Eds. D.L. Macdonald and Kathleen Scherf. Peterborough: Broadview, 1997. 355-370.

Prochaska, F.K. *Women and Philanthropy in Nineteenth-Century England*. Oxford: Clarendon, 1980.

Raven, James. *Judging New Wealth: Popular Publishing and Responses to Commerce in England, 1750-1800*. Oxford: Clarendon, 1992.

Richardson, Alan. *Literature, Education, and Romanticism: Reading as Social Practice, 1780-1832*. NY: Cambridge UP, 1994.

Rogers, Betsy. *Cloak of Charity, Studies in Eighteenth-Century Philanthropy*. London: Metheun, 1949.

Rule, John and Roger Wells. 'Crime, Protest and Radicalism.' *Crime, Protest and Popular Politics in Southern England 1740-1850*. Eds. John Rule and Roger Wells. London: Hambledon, 1997. 1-15.

   'Social Crime in the Rural South in the Eighteenth and Early Nineteenth Centuries.' *Crime, Protest and Popular Politics in Southern England 1740-1850*. Eds. John Rule and Roger Wells. London: Hambledon, 1997. 153-168.

   'The Manifold Causes of Rural Crime: Sheep-Stealing in England, c. 1740-1840.' *Crime, Protest and Popular Politics in Southern England 1740-1850*. Eds. John Rule and Roger Wells. London: Hambledon, 1997. 237-253.

Schofield, R.S. 'Dimensions of Illiteracy in England 1750-1850.' *Literacy and Social Development in the West: A Reader*. Ed. Harvey J. Graff. New York: Cambridge UP, 1981. 201-213.

Siskin, Clifford. 'Eighteenth-Century Periodicals and The Romantic Rise of the Novel.' *Studies in the Novel* 26 (1994): 26-42.

   The Historicity of Romantic Discourse. New York: Oxford UP, 1988.

   The Work of Writing: Literature and Social Change in Britain, 1700-1830. Baltimore: Johns Hopkins UP, 1998.

Smith, Adam. *A Theory of Moral Sentiments*. New York: Cambridge UP, 2002.

Smith, Olivia. *The Politics of Language, 1791-1819*. Oxford: Clarendon, 1984.

Spinney, G.H. 'Cheap Repository Tracts: Hazard and Marshall Edition,' *Library* 3 (December 1939): 295-340.

Street, Brian V. *Literacy in Theory and Practice*. New York: Cambridge UP, 1984.

Spufford, Margaret. *Small Books and Pleasant Histories*. London: Metheun, 1981.

Sutherland, Kathryn. 'Hannah More's Counter-Revolutionary Feminism.' *Revolution in Writing: British Literary Responses to the French Revolution*. Ed. Kelvin Everest. Philadelphia: Open UP, 1991. 27-63.

    'Writings on Education and Conduct: Arguments for Female Improvement.' *Women and Literature in Britain, 1700-1800*. Ed. Vivian Jones. New York: Cambridge UP, 2000. 25-45.

Taylor, John Tinnon. *Early Opposition to the English Novel: The Popular Reaction from 1760-1830*. New York: King's Crown, 1943.

Tobin, Beth Fowkes. *Superintending the Poor: Charitable Ladies & Paternal Landlords in British Fiction, 1770-1860*. New Haven: Yale UP, 1993.

Todd, Janet. *Sensibility: An Introduction*. New York: Methuen, 1986.

    The Sign of Angellica: Women Writing and Fiction, 1660-1800. New York: Columbia UP, 1989.

Tompkins, J.M.S. *The Popular Novel in England*. (Lincoln: U of Nebraska P, 1961).

Turner, Cheryl. *Living By the Pen: Women Writers in the Eighteenth Century*. New York: Routledge, 1992.

Turner, M.E. 'Parliamentary Enclosures: Gains and Costs.' *New Directions in Economic and Social History*. Eds. Anne Digby and Charles Feinstein. London: Macmillan, 1988. 22-34.

Valenze, Deborah. *The First Industrial Woman*. New York: Oxford UP, 1995.

Wakefield, Priscilla. *Reflections on the Present Condition of the Female Sex*. 1798. New York: Garland, 1974.

Wells, Roger. 'The Development of the English Rural Proletariat and Social Protest, 1700-1850.' *Class, Conflict and Protest in the English Countryside, 1700-1880*. Eds. Mick Reed and Roger Wells. Savage, MD: Frank Cass, 1990. 29-51.

    Wretched Faces. New York: St. Martin's Press, 1988.

    'The Revolt of the South West, 1800-1: A Study in English Popular Protest.' *Crime, Protest and Popular Politics in Southern England, 1740-1850*. Eds. John Rule and Roger Wells. London: Hambledon, 1997. 17-51.

    'Social Protest, Class, Conflict and Consciousness, in the English Countryside 1700-1880.' *Class, Conflict and Protest in the English Countryside, 1700-1880*. Eds. Mick Reed and Roger Wells. Savage, MD: Frank Cass, 1990. 121-214.

Williams, Raymond. *Keywords*. New York: Oxford UP, 1983.

    The Country and the City. New York: Oxford UP, 1973.

Wilson, Carol Shiner and Joel Haefner, Eds. *Re-visioning Romanticism: British Women Writers, 1176-1837*. Philadephia: U of Pennsylvania P, 1994.

Wolfson, Susan J. 'Individual in Community: Dorothy Wordsworth in Conversation with William.' *Feminism and Romanticism*. Ed. Anne K. Mellor. Bloomington: Indiana UP, 1988. 139-166.

Wollstonecraft, Mary. *A Vindication of the Rights of Men*. Eds. D.L. Macdonald and Kathleen Scherf. Peterborough: Broadview, 1997.

    A Vindication of the Rights of Woman. Ed. Carol Poston. New York: Norton, 1988.

    Letters Written During a Short Residence in Sweden, Norway and Denmark. Eds. Janet Todd and Marilyn Butler. vol. 6. New York: NY UP, 1989.

    The Female Reader. Eds. Janet Todd and Marilyn Butler. vol. 4. New York: NY UP, 1989.

Woof, Pamela. *Dorothy Wordsworth, Writer*. Grasmere: The Wordsworth Trust, 1988.

Wordsworth, Dorothy and William Wordsworth. *The Letters of William and Dorothy Wordsworth 1806-1811*. Eds. Ernest de Selincourt and Mary Moorman. vol 2. Oxford: Clarendon, 1969.

Wordsworth, Dorothy. *George and Sarah Green: A Narrative*. Ed. Ernest de Selincourt. Oxford: Folcroft, 1969.

    The Journals of Dorothy Wordsworth. vol 1. Ed. Ernest de Selincourt. London: Macmillan, 1952.

Wordsworth, William. *The Oxford Authors: William Wordsworth*. Ed. Stephen Gill. New York: Oxford UP, 1984.

Work, James A. Introduction. *Tristram Shandy*. By Lawrence Sterne. Indianapolis: Odyssey, 1940.

Wrigley, E.A. 'Population Growth: England, 1680-1820.' *New Directions in Economic and Social History*. Eds. Anne Digby and Charles Feinstein. London: Macmillan, 1989. 105-116.

Zaw, Susan Khin. 'The Reasonable Heart: Mary Wollstonecraft's View of the Relation Between Reason and Feeling in Morality, Moral Psychology, and Moral Development.' *Hypatia* 13.1 (Winter 1999): 78-117.

Zizek, Slavoj. *For they know not what they do: Enjoyment as a Political Factor*. New York: Verso, 1991.

    The Sublime Object of Ideology. New York: Verso, 1989.

Index